Wills of
𝕮𝖍𝖊𝖘𝖙𝖊𝖗 𝕮𝖔𝖚𝖓𝖙𝖞
Pennsylvania

1766-1778

Based on the Work of
Jacob Martin

HERITAGE BOOKS
2007

HERITAGE BOOKS
AN IMPRINT OF HERITAGE BOOKS, INC.

Books, CDs, and more—Worldwide

For our listing of thousands of titles see our website
at
www.HeritageBooks.com

Published 2007 by
HERITAGE BOOKS, INC.
Publishing Division
65 East Main Street
Westminster, Maryland 21157-5026

Copyright © 1995 F. Edward Wright

All rights reserved. No part of this book may be reproduced or transmitted in any form or by any means, electronic or mechanical, including photocopying, recording or by any information storage and retrieval system without written permission from the author, except for the inclusion of brief quotations in a review.

International Standard Book Number: 978-1-58549-309-0

INTRODUCTION

The wills of Chester County were first abstracted by Jacob Martin of Marshallton, Pennsylvania and indexed by the indefatigable Gilbert Cope.

The abstracts done by Jacob Martin appear to be accurate and complete. Some minor corrections have been added. Recently it was noted by the Chester County Historical Society that the abstract of the will of James Whitaker was in error in that Martin had incorrectly given Whitaker's son's name as Edward Clayton which during mid 1700s would have suggested that Edward was a son-in-law and husband to daughter Ann Clayton. An examination of the original will showed Edward Whitaker to be son of James Whitaker while daughter Ann Clayton is mentioned as having a husband, but unnamed. This error occurs in our earlier volume for the period, 1713 through 1748. This volume was also checked against the original volume with only a few corrections noted. Nevertheless, the reader is cautioned that the original should be examined whenever possible. All the wills covered by this volume are available on microfilm through Family History Centers (LDS).

The first date given is normally the date that the will was written; subsequent dates are usually dates on which witnesses appeared to attest to the validity of the will or the date the court proved the will. Dates are frequently given numerically in the following order: month, day and year. Prior to 1752, March 25th (Feast of the Annunciation) was the first day of the new year by traditional acceptance of the ecclesiastical calendar. Later as the Gregorian calendar was being accepted the double dates were used from January 1st until March 25th.

Basic information on the records of administration was included in Martin's work along with data gathered by him from deeds and other court records, all of which has been included here. Information on administrations can be especially helpful when no will exists (died intestate). Martin uses the phrase, "Adm. to ---" to indicate the name of the administrator/administratrix to whom the administration was assigned. The first name appearing in each entry, will or administration, is always the name of the deceased.

F. Edward Wright
Westminster, Maryland 1994

EAVENSON, NATHANIEL. Thornbury. Oct. 12, 1766. Adm. to Elizabeth Eavenson and Moses Palmer.

O'FARRAN, MICHAEL. West Fallowfield. Oct. 13, 1766. Adm. to William Noble.

MOORE, JOB. Uwchlan. Oct. 13, 1766. Adm. to Joseph Rhoads.

MORRISON, ALEXANDER. New London.
Jan. 11, 1759. Oct. 12, 1766.
Provides for wife. To sons Ephraim, Alexr., Joseph, Hugh and James, all real and personal estate paying legacies. To daughter Jean Morrison £60 at 18. To daughter Mary Gray 40 shillings.
Executors: Wife Jean and Ephraim.
Wit: William McMichen, Margret McMichen, Jas. McMichen.

CARSON, SAMUEL. Londongrove.
Aug. 28, 1766. Oct. 16, 1766.
To Margaret wife of David Byers 2 shillings. To daughter Elizabeth McCarter wife of Abraham 2 shillings. To daughter Mary wife of Walter Carson 2 shillings. To daughter Rebecca Carson 2 shillings. To daughter Jane wife of Saml. Corry 2 shillings. To sons William and Walter and daughter Hannah Carson 2 shillings each. To daughter Agnes Carson 2 shillings. To son Francis £140 it being a just debt due for services done, also Executor. All remainder of estate to wife Sarah.
Wit: Morris Thomas, David Wiley, Nathl. Wallas.

FRIER, JAMES. Londonderry.
Oct. 12, 1766. Oct. 20, 1766.
To wife Jean 1/3 of all est. during life. To son Robert £130. To son in law Andrew Bear and daughter Jean Bear £5. To son James £70. To son in law Abel Hodgson £50. To servant boy John Owens £7 at expiration of his time.
Executor: Son in law Abel Hodgson.
Wit: James Law, Moses Corry.

LAWRENCE, RICHARD. Lower Chichester. Oct. 20, 1766. Adm. to Isaac Lawrence.

MC LOGHLIN, PHILIP. Chester. Oct. 29, 1766. Adm. to Branson Vanleer.

HOBSON, FRANCIS. New Garden.
June 24, 1758. Oct. 27, 1766.
Provides for wife Martha. To son Joseph plantation whereon I now live in New Garden subject to his mother's life interest. To daughter Martha £50. To daughter Mary Boyes £5 besides what she and her husband Robert hath already got. To sons Francis and John 10 shillings each.
Executors: Wife and son Joseph.
Wit: Thomas Hutton, Stephen McFarson, Nehemiah Hutton.

JOHN, SAMUEL. Uwchlan.
--, 1761. Oct. 31, 1766.
To son Samuel £20. To daughter Mary Griffith £5. To daughter Margaret wife of James John £5. To daughter Eleanor wife of Wm. Downing £10. To daughter Rebecca wife of Stephen Philips £10. Provides for wife Margaret. To son Daniel plantation whereon I now live cont. 130 acres, also Executor. "Note that Saml. John's daughter Mary Griffith above mentioned is now the wife of John Griffith."
Wit: James Packer, Thomas Martin, Geo. Phipps.

TAYLOR, GEORGE. Springfield.
11/15/1765. Nov. 1, 1766.
To wife Sarah £300 and all household goods. To sister Hannah wife of Nathan Thompson and her 2 children Esther and Margaret £30. To sister in law Margaret Palmer £5. To Springfield Meeting £5 toward enclosing their burying ground. Executors to sell plantation in Springfield containing 117 acres. Remainder of estate to child if one should be born to his wife, otherwise to sister Hannah.
Executors: Friends Lewis Davis, Wm. Lewis.
Wit: Wm. Fell, Joel Willis, John Taylor.
(Wife Sarah married Philip Lynch.)

FORD, PHILIP. Chester.
Oct. 23, 1766. Nov. 3, 1766.
Executors to sell tract of land on Tinicum Island bought of Thomas Taylor dec'd. and lotts of land conveyed to me by Joseph Taylor. Proceed div. as follows: To wife Margaret 1/3, also 1/2 personal estate. All remainder of estate real and personal to 5 children, viz.: William, Ann, Benjamin, Jane and Philip, to be equally divided as they attain the age of 21. John Morton guardian for children.
Executors: Wife Margaret and John Morton, Esq.
Wit: Benjamin Ford, John Taylor, H. H. Graham.

SMITH, JOHN. Little Britain, Lancaster Co.
4/20/1762. Nov. 15, 1766.
To wife Dorothy £200. To daughter Lydia Allen £5. To son John £10 having given him and his sister their portion heretofore. To 3 daughters Ann Webster, Ruth Gregg and Sarah Webb £100 each. To son Thomas all remainder of estate.
Executors: Son in law Wm. Webster.
Trustees: Friends Geo. Churchman, Jr., Joshua Brown.
Wit: Isaac Williams, Richard Stedman, Michael King.

MOORE, ELIZABETH. West Nantmeal.
Apr. 11, 1764. Nov. 6, 1766.
To second son Moses £10. To youngest son John all household goods. To granddaughter Elizabeth Meek £3. To son Daniel £4 and to his son Wm. £3 and to his daughter Elizabeth £3. To daughter Sarah 5 shillings. To daughter Ann 5 shillings. To son John cow and calf. To daughter in law Jane Moore ewe and lamb.
Executor: Son John.
Wit: David Long, Mary Laverty.

CALDWELL, MARGARET. Aston.
Feb. 24, 1759. Nov. 8, 1766.
To daughter Jane Moore 10 shillings. To grandson Wm. Moore £10 at 21. To grandson Robert Moore £15 at 21. To the other 3 children of daughter Jane Moore £20 to divided at 21. To daughter Elizabeth Buyers, bed and to the 4 children of said daughter £30 to be divided as follows: to John £10, to Robert £15 and to the other 2 £6 each to be put in the hands of their father Saml. Byers. All remainder to daughter Margaret Buyers.
Executors: Friends Hugh Linn, John Fairlamb. Letters to Wm. and Margaret Byers, Executors named being deceased.

YARNALL, MARY. Wife of Isaac. Edgmont.
Oct. 25, 1766. Nov. 8, 1766.
To eldest son James Yarnall £5 at 21. To son Benjamin large Bible. To daughter Abigail case of drawers. Remainder to 3 youngest children, viz.: John, Benj. and Abigail.
Executors: Friends Abel Green, Thomas Bishop.
Wit: Cadwallader Evans, Danl. Calvert, Margaret Mattson.

JONES, THOMAS. Tredyffrin. Nov. 8, 1766. Adm. to Hannah Jones and Sampson Davis.

HIBBERD, JOHN. Willistown. Nov. 11, 1766. Adm. to Phinehas, John and Samuel Hibberd.

MARIS, REBECCA. Springfield. Nov. 18, 1766. Adm. to Jesse Maris.

JONES, WILLIAM. East Bradford. Nov. 25, 1766. Adm. to John Jones.

RICHARDS, LYDIA. Aston. Nov. 26, 1766. Adm. to Jonathan Richards.

NEWLIN, NATHANIEL. Concord.
5/25/1766. Nov 14, 1766.
Provides for wife Esther. To daughter Edith wife of Saml. Schofield £5. To daughter Jane wife of Isaac Pyle £4. To daughter Mary Dickinson £19. To son Nathaniel part of my plantation in Concord containing 116 acres, also the plantation adj. purchased of my Uncle John Newlin containing 100 acres paying the legacies to my 5 daughters. To son Cyrus part of plantation in Concord containing 161 acres at 21 years of age, paying to daughter Tobitha £50. To daughters Abigail and Rebecca £50 each at 21. To son Thomas part of my plantation in Concord containing 124 acres at 21.
Executors: Wife Esther and son Nathaniel.
Wit: Wm. Seal, John Palmer, Joseph Peirce.

RHOADS, JOHN. Marple.
Dec. 24, 1761. Nov. 26, 1766.
To mother Elizabeth Rhoads all estate during life and her decease to my brothers and sisters: Joseph, Isaac, Elizabeth and Mary Rhoads.
Executor: Mother Elizabeth Rhoads.
Wit: Seth Pancoast, Henry Lawrence, Jr., Jas. Rhoads.

LINEDIGER, NICHOLAS. Lower Chichester. Nov. 17, 1766. Adm. to John Marshall.

OWEN, EDWARD. Tredyffrin. Nov. 28, 1766. Adm. to David Jenkins and Jas. Evans.

REA, GEORGE. Goshen. Dec. 13, 1766. Adm. to Joseph Rea.

CUNNINGHAM, JOHN. East Nottingham. Dec. 19, 1766. Adm. to Jane Cunningham.

OTLEY, JAMES. Goshen. Dec. 22, 1766. Adm. to Anne Otley.

WILLSON, ROBERT. Concord. Dec. 25, 1766. Adm. to Rees Peters.

SMEDLEY, GEORGE. Middletown. 2/7/1766. Dec. 8, 1766.
To son James plantation in Upper Providence containing 98 acres paying to son Thomas £50. To son Ambrose plantation where I now dwell in Middletown containing 198 acres paying to son Thomas £50 and providing during life for wife Mary. To son Thomas a piece of land in Middletown on the South side of great road, also 1/2 of my lott of ground in Philadelphia, also £100. To daughter Sarah Moore 1/2 of above mentioned lott in Philadelphia. To sons Joshua, William and Caleb and daughter Jane Larkin 2/6, each having heretofore advanced them. To cousin Sarah Yarnall £5 when of age. Remainder to wife Mary, also with son Ambrose Executors.
Wit: Geo. Miller, Phebe Miller, Veronica Nuphrin.

RING, NATHANIEL. West Marlborough. Nov. 29, 1766. Dec. 20, 1766.
To wife Elizabeth 1/3 of all estate absolutely. To wife's granddaughter Margaret Rankin £50 at 18. To wife's son Archibald McNeal £20. To son Benjamin Ring £10. All remainder of estate real or personal to daughter Hannah wife of Thomas Gibson. Executors to sell tract of land in East Fallowfield, also tract in West Marlborough bought of David Reynolds, also tract in Kennet and New Castle Co. purchased of John McFarson.
Executors: Wife Elizabeth and kinsman John Hannum.
Wit: Aaron Baker, Wm. Harlan, Geo. Passmore.
Letters to Elizabeth the other renouncing.

MORRISON, JAMES. Weaver. Concord. Dec. 3, 1766. Jan. 30, 1767.
Provides for wife. To sons Nathaniel and Robert and daughter Agnes 5 shillings each. To son Joseph plantation whereon I now dwell subject to wife's life interest and maintenance of daughter Esther and paying to children, Agnes, Mary, James, Elizabeth, Jane, John and Priscilla 1/2 the value of said plantation, "also the loom he weaves on." To daughter Mary, son James, daughter Elizabeth, daughter Jane, son John and daughter Priscilla 5 shillings each.
Executors: Wife Mary and son Joseph.
Wit: Nathaniel Newlin, John Reynolds, Daniel Green.

EVANS, JOHN. Vincent. Jan. 12, 1767. Adm. to James Evans.

BYERS, JOHN. East Caln.
May 31, 1766. Feb. 7, 1767.
To sons Samuel and William £20 each. To daughter Ann Creely £80 to be paid her as she stands in need of it. To daughter Elizabeth Byers £75 and to her 3 children by her first husband, viz., David, John and Mary Byers, £25 each. To daughter Florence Clark £40. To daughter Mary McFarlan £80. To the children of son Joseph deceased, viz., to John, Saml., Joseph and Margaret Byers £50 each. To grandson John son of Saml. Byers riding mare and saddle. To granddaughter Jane Clark colt. To wife Florence all remainder of estate, to wife Florence to dispose of as she sees fit. Mentions granddaughter Margaret Elliot.
Executors: Friend Thos. Pimm and son in law John Clark.
Wit: David Stewart, Alex. Stewart, Archibald Stewart.

HOWELL, MARGARET. Thornbury.
Oct. 30, 1766. Feb. 25, 1767.
To sons Robert and John 1 shilling sterling each. To son Thomas and daughter Mary wife of Patrick Muller all remainder of estate.
Executor: Son Thomas.
Wit: John Hickman, John Cheyney, Cal. Peirce, Jr.

EVENWINE, ALVERTUS. Coventry. Feb. 26, 1767. Adm. to John Evenwine.

BOUND, JOHN. Vincent. Feb. 25, 1767. Adm. to John Conway.

FILSON, WILLIAM. Frederick Co., Md. Mar. 17, 1768. Adm. to John and Jane Filson. Copy of Maryland letters. Recorded Aug. 28, 1769.

PENNELL, JAMES. Middletown.
Dec. 22, 1763. Mar 6, 1767.
Provides for wife Jemima. To son Timothy 1/2 part of plantation purchased of Stephen Ogden when he is 21. To son Jonathan the other 1/2 of ditto. at 21. To son William messuage where I now dwell containing 105 acres at 21 he paying to son James £50. To son Jonathan £20. To son Nathan £50 and to son Timothy £50 as they reach the age of 21. To son James tract of land in Middletown containing about 109 acres at 21. To son Nathan tract of land in Middletown containing about 111 acres at 21. To daughter Hannah Talbot 20 shillings. To daughter Edith £100 and to daughters Ruth and Rebecca £100 each. To granddaughters Mary Talbot £5. To son Thomas, messuage and 2 lots in Chester wherein my mother Mary Pennell now lives, at the decease of said mother. Codicil names Geo. Miller, Executor, John Fairlamb being deceased.
Executors: Friends John Fairlamb and John Minshall.
Wit: Geo. Miller, Robt. and Wm. Pennell.
Letters to Minshall and Miller.

HUTCHISON, JAMES. New London.
Apr. 16, 1766. Mar. 16, 1767.
To son James plantation whereon I now live. To son Joseph

plantation in Londonderry and £20. To son David bond of £8 due me from John Orr. To son Samuel £10. To son Robert and daughter Agnes £2 each.
Executor: Son David.
Wit: John Fultorm, Thomas Minor.

MOORE, MOSES. Lower Chichester. Apr. 3, 1767. Adm. to Mary Moore.

HENDRICKSEN, ISRAEL. Ridley. Apr. 15, 1767. Adm. to Susanna and John Hendricksen.

BULLAR, RICHARD. Newlin. Apr. 20, 1767. Adm. to Jane and John Bullar.

PARKE, JONATHAN. East Bradford. Apr. 25, 1767. Adm. to Deborah Parke and Saml. Coope.

FEAGAN, CHARLES. Newtown. May 14, 1767. Adm. to Sarah Feagan.

LEWIS, SAMUEL. Newtown. May 16, 1767. Adm. to John Stull.

CAHOON, JOHN. East Caln. May 16, 1767. Adm. to Phillis Cahoon.

BROWN, JEREMIAH. West Nottingham.
12/21/1762. Mar. 20, 1767.
Provides for wife Mary. To heirs of son Jeremiah deceased 5 shillings having heretofore given my real estate to him by deed of 5/14/1749 on payment of £100 at my decease which I dispose of as follows. To daughter Patience Hadley £20. To son Joshua £20. To son Isaac £40. To wife Mary £20, also executor.
Wit: Rebecca Trimble, Geo. Churchman, Jr., Jno. Churchman.

CHALFANT, ROBERT. Birmingham.
Mar. 3, 1767. Apr. 6, 1767.
To wife Martha income of real estate during life. To 2 daughters Mary Shields and Ruth Frame messuage I now live on to be divided. To son Robert 5 shillings being already advanced. To son Thomas 1/2 of tract of land whereon he now lives. Executors to sell land that was formerly called *Coopers*. To granddaughter Martha Barnet £5. To granddaughter Jane Frame cow. To daughter Elizabeth Barnet £2 a year during life. Remainder to wife.
Executors: Friends Nathan Frame and Robert Green, Jr.
Wit: Nathl. Ring, Benja. Ring, Robert Green.

BOYD, WILLIAM. Oxford.
Apr. 14, 1767. May 20, 1767.
Executors to sell tract of land in Londongrove now in tenure of George Lockey. Provides for wife Jane including plantation where I now dwell until son James comes of age. To son James 2/3 of said plantation at 21 paying legacies. To each of my other children, viz., Hannah, Mary, John, William and Jane Boyd £50 as they come of age.
Executors: Geo. Currey, Esq. and James Evans. Letters to Correy,

the other renouncing.
Wit: David Drew, David Fleming, Robt. Correy.

BOYD, JANE. Relict of Wm. Oxford.
Apr. 25, 1767. May 20, 1767.
To son James Boyd that 1/3 of real estate left me by my husband, at 21 paying to the other children, viz., Hannah, Mary, John, Wm. and Jane Boyd £5 each as they arrive at 21.
Executors: Geo. Correy, Esq. and Jas. Evans. Letters to Geo. Correy.
Wit: David Fleming, David Drew.

CALDWELL, ROBERT. Marple.
Apr. 12, 1767. May 22, 1767.
To my children, William, John, Mary, Martha, Robert, Sarah and Alexander £1 each. All rest of estate to wife Sarah.
Executors: Wife Sarah and son-in-law David Cather.
Wit: John Cochran, James Maris. Letters to Sarah, the other refusing.

ANDERSON, SAMUEL. West Nottingham.
Dec. 19, 1766. May 25, 1767.
Provides for wife Agnes including negroes Dinah and Syrus during life and then to son John. To son John £75. To son James mare. To son Henry 1/2 of plantation at wife's decease. To 2 daughters Rose Jameson and Sarah Glasgow 5 shillings each.
Executors: Wife and son John.
Trustees: Wm. Allen and Robt. Finley.
Wit: Wm. Allen, Francis Boyd, Wm. Johnson.

WILSON, ALEXANDER. Londonderry.
Feb. 21, 1767. May 27, 1767.
Provides for wife Mary. To each of my children, Robert, Elizabeth and Sarah 1 shilling sterling. To daughter Jean 40 shillings at 18. Remainder of estate to sons James and John to be equally divided at 21.
Executors: Wife Mary and friend Wm. Montgomery. Letters to Mary, the other renouncing.
Wit: Wm. Montgomery, Robert Graham.

FLEMING, JAMES. East Caln.
Apr. 27, 1767. May 27, 1767.
Provides for wife Ann. To son Joseph plantation in East Caln containing 100 acres, he paying £388 in annual payments. To son William £25. To son Henry £20. To son Joseph £20. To daughter Sarah Davinson £25. To daughter Susanna Robb £25. To daughter Mary Hart [not given]. To daughter Ann Fleming £25. To daughter Margaret Fleming £100. To grandson James Fleming, son of John deceased £20. To Ann McBeth £5. To Susanna, widow of son Jas. Fleming deceased £5. Plantation I now live on to sons Henry and Joseph at wife's decease, they paying to their sister Mary Hart £40.
Executors: Sons Henry and Joseph.
Wit: John Fleming, Alexander Fleming, Thos. Pimm.

BEARAT, JAMES.
Apr. 17, 1767. May 1, 1767.
Children Mary, James and William to have equal shares of estate.
Son James to be bound to Jas. Kirkpatrick to learn trade of shoemaker.
Executors: Robt. and Thos. Ker. Letters to Robert.
Wit: William Marsh, Andrew Kirkpatrick.

ALEXANDER, SUSANNA. London, Britain. June 8, 1767. Adm. to Abraham Emmitt.

THOMAS, DAVID. West Nantmeal. June 12, 1767. Adm. to Saml. Muckleduff.

BELL, MARY. Vincent.
Jan 20, 1767. June 1, 1767.
To daughter Elizabeth new spinning wheel. To sons William and Edward Bell all lands tenements, also executors.
Wit: David Thomas, James Evans, Erasmus Lloyd.

HOOPES, STEPHEN. Yeoman. Westtown.
3/21/1767. June 4, 1767.
To son Isaiah that part of my plantation whereon I now live lying on the west side of road from great valley to Chester paying to his brother Ezekiel £30. To son Ezekiel Hoopes that part of my land lying on east side of said road, subject to provision for wife Elizabeth. To daughters Margaret and Hannah Hoopes £40 each. To granddaughter Martha Thompson 20 shillings at 18. All remainder to 3 daughters, Elizabeth John, Margaret and Hannah Hoopes.
Executors: Wife Elizabeth and brother Thomas Hoopes.
Wit: John Hoopes, Jr., Amos Hoopes, David Hoopes.

FLEMING, HENRY. East Caln.
June 6, 1767. June 17, 1767.
To only son John Fleming plantation I now live upon. To only daughter Alice Fleming lot of land bequeathed by my father, Jas. Fleming, after the decease of my mother. All my wife's apparel to be kept for her except a damask gown to my sister-in-law Sarah Babb and a black gown to Rose Vernon. Remainder to be equally divided when children come of age. Mentions brothers Joseph and Wm.
Executor: Cousin John Fleming.
Wit: Jos. Bishop, Jr., Alexander Fleming.

BUTCHER, MARY. East Nottingham.
10/3/1766. June 29, 1767.
All personal estate to be equally divided among my 5 sisters, viz., Margaret Collet, Susanna Passmore, Rachel Oldham, Hannah Butcher and Sarah Day. All my title to 3/4 of a tract of land formerly belonging to my father Zachary Butcher in East Nottingham to be sold and divided among 5 sisters above named.
Executrix: Sister Hannah Butcher.
Wit: David Brown, John Mears, John Cornthwait.

PHILLIPS, THOMAS. Darby.
July 6, 1767. Aug. 3, 1767.

To wife plantation I now live on during life, after her death to
sons Griffith and Thomas they paying to daughter Sarah £200 and
£100 to daughter Elizabeth. To daughter Anne all the land Jonathan
Evans rents of me or 30 acres, 2 of meadow adjoining. To sons
Griffith and Thomas £60 each. To daughter Ann £60. To daughter
Sarah £40. To sister Rebecca £10. To cousin Wm. Jenkins £5.
Executors to sell fulling mill in Darby when Wm. Davis makes a deed
according to our articles.
Executors: Wife Elizabeth, Lewis Davis and Wm. Lawrance.
Wit: Isaac Davis, Wm. Davis, Jr., James Davis.

WORRALL, PETER. Ridley.
7/10/1767. Aug. 5, 1767.
To brother Thomas best velvet breeches. To cousin Phebe wife of
Wm. Worrall silver shoe buckles. To brothers Joshua and Benjamin
remainder of wearing apparel. All remainder of estate to brothers
Jonathan and Thomas and sisters Hannah Nuzum and Esther Worrall,
except walnut chest to Saml., son of Richard Crosby.
Executors: Cousin Wm. Worrall and brother Thomas.
Wit: Richard Crosby, Elisha Worrall.

HAIR, JAMES. West Bradford. Aug. 10, 1767. Adm. to Lydia Hair.

MC GLISTER, JOHN. Londonderry. Aug. 15, 1767. Adm. to Wm.
McGlister. (Two sets of papers, only one record of letters
granted.)

KIRK, WILLIAM. East Nottingham in Province of Pennsylvania or so
reputed.
May 18, 1767. Aug. 26, 1767.
To wife Mary plantation I now live on in East and West Nottingham
until son Wm. is 21. Also profits of plantation bought of Jas.
Dogherty in West Nottingham until said son is 21. To oldest son
Joseph £80 and carpenter tools. To second son Abner my fulling and
saw mills at 23, also land belonging thereunto. To 3rd son Wm.
plantation bought of Jas. Dogherty in West Nottingham containing
100 acres at 21. To fourth son Nathaniel £80 at 21. Remainder to
3 younger children, viz., Ezekiel, Jacob and Elisha Kirk.
Executrix: Wife Mary.
Wit: Timo. Kirk, Edward Ramsey, Elisha Hughes.

VERNON, MOSES. North Providence.
7/18/1767. Sept. 1, 1767.
Provides for wife Abigail. To son Nathan tract of land containing
120 acres. To son Elias tract of land adjoining above containing
60 acres, he paying £20 to my daughter Abigail wife of Frederick
Engle. To daughter Mary Vernon tract of land containing about 11
acres, also £60. To son Moses remainder of land whereon I now
dwell containing about 62 acres. To son Edward part of tract
formerly Jos. Vernon's (the whole containing about 132 acres)
containing about 61 acres. To son Gideon remainder of above tract
about 71 acres, also £40 at 21. To daughter Abigail Engle £60.
Mentions brother Aaron Vernon.
Executors: Son-in-law Frederick Engle and son Nathan.
Wit: John Sharpless, Job Ridgway, Wm. Swaffer.

BARNARD, RICHARD. Newlin. Sept. 8, 1767. Adm. to Jeremiah Barnard.

FLING, DAVID. East Bradford. Sept. 12, 1767. Adm. to Abigail Fling.

FORREST, MATTHEW. Upper Providence. Sept. 19, 1767. Adm. to Joseph Worrall.

HUEY, GENNET. Westtown.
Sept. 5, 1767. Oct. 1, 1767.
To son James Huey my riding horse and to his wife Mary wearing apparel. To daughter Mary Enterkin remainder of wearing apparel. To grandson James Enterkin £50 at 21. To granddaughter Rachel Enterkin bed and bedding at 18. To granddaughter Eleanor Huey ditto at 18. All remainder to be sold and money divided among grandchildren; William Huey to have a double share. Eleanor, Mary and Jane Huey; George, Mary, Jane and Saml. Enterkin to have shares alike as they come of age.
Executors: Isaac Haines, Jr. and Thomas Taylor.
Wit: Wm. Johnston, Wm. Hawley, Alice Johnston.

BLACK, NEWTON. New Garden.
Sept. 4, 1767. Oct. 1, 1767.
All estate equally divided between son William and wife Sarah Black. Moses Rowan of New Garden to be guardian of son Wm.
Executors: Wife Sarah and Jas. Rowen.
Wit: Morris Thomas, Saml. Miller, Hannah Black.

MARIS, AARON. West Marlborough. Oct. 1, 1767. Adm. to John Maris.

MC KEAD, JOHN. Darby. Oct. 1, 1767. Adm. to William Garrett.

LOWNES, BENANUEL. Springfield. Oct. 8, 1767. Adm. to Alice Lownes.

GUY, SAMUEL. Oxford. Oct. 9, 1767. Adm. to Isabella Guy.

JOHN, DAVID. Vincent. Oct. 23, 1767. Adm. to Margaret and James John.

MC KEE, JOSEPH. Weaver. West Nantmeal.
Apr. 24, 1767. Oct. 6, 1767.
All estate to father if alive, otherwise to be equally divided between my 2 brothers John and Robert.
Executor: James Hair.
Wit: John McGoun, James Lusk.

MOORE, WILLIAM. Marple.
Sept. 12, 1767. Oct. 13, 1767.
To brother Philip Moore my share of plantation in Marple lately belonging to father Charles Moore deceased. To 3 sisters Hannah Godfrey, Margaret and Rachel Moore 40 shillings each. All remainder to mother Elizabeth Moore.

Executors: Mother and Henry Lawrence.
Wit: Griffith Davis, James Maris.

NICKOLS, JOHN. Kennett.
Sept. 10, 1767. Oct. 17, 1767.
To wife Ann £100 and all household goods she brought with her. To daughter Hannah household goods. To sons Thomas and James 20 shillings each. To grandchildren Robert and Phebe Clendennin 50 shillings each. Remainder divided between son Jacob and daughters Charity, Ann and Hannah.
Executors: Brother Saml. Nickols and son Geo. Sharp.
Wit: John Eves, Michael Gregg, Thomas Sharp.

ASGIL, WILLIAM. [Place not given.]
Sept. 16, 1767. Oct. 26, 1767.
Appoints friend Alice Lownes to measure and value certain work done and collect balance due and use the same as she thinks proper, also Executrix.
Wit: Jas. Lownes, Joseph Gibbons, Jr.

O'HEER. Laborer. New Garden.
Oct. 5, 1767. Oct. 27, 1767.
Estate to be equally divided between brother Neil O'heer, sister Sarah Sands and her son Patrick Sands.
Executors: Moses Montgomery and Jas. Orr. Letters to Montgomery, the other renouncing.
Wit: Lawrence Woods, John Hanlin, James Murphy.

ELLIOTT, ENOCH. Darby.
8/13/1767. Oct. 30, 1767.
Provides for wife Martha. To son John all my plantation westward of Darby Creek commonly called *Smith's Fields* reserving a house and 2 acres for a settlement for my old negro Primus during his life, also 2/3 of my island in the Delaware called *Little Tenicum*. To son Benjamin the plantation where he now dwells during life and then to his children. To son Peter plantation where I now dwell excepting my new house and 30 acres of land with reserve to his brothers. Also remainder 1/3 of *Tenicum*. To 2 granddaughters Martha and Elizabeth Hanbest £50 each at 21 with reserve to their brother Peter. To son Christopher new house and 30 acres as reserved above, a piece of marsh at Kingsess. Tract of land in Easttown whereon Geo. Turner now dwells, to kinsman Israel Moore when he is 27. Rents until that time to his 3 sisters, Mary, Elizabeth and Ruth. To grandson Peter Hanbest messuage where his father Robert now lives at 21. To brother Peter my 1/2 interest in 100 acres of unlocated land. £50 to go toward building a wall around the graveyard and at brother Peter's where some of our family have been interred. Personal property divided among sons including 8 negroes besides old Primus who is to be free.
Executors: Brother Peter, son Christopher, and friend Benjamin Lobb, Sr.
Wit: Jacob Webber, Isaac Lloyd, John Lenderman.

DAVIS, WILLIAM. Darby.
7/23/1767. Nov. 10, 1767.
Provides for wife. To son William all lands in Darby, 1/2 of tract of land described paying to son James £50 and use of the shop he now works in. To son Isaac the other 1/2 of above mentioned land, he paying to daughter Hannah £15. To son Jesse 22 acres of land and buildings where John Cerns now lives, he paying to my daughter Elizabeth Moore £15. To son Asa all remainder of my lands paying to daughter Hannah £25.
Executors: Wife Elizabeth, sons Isaac and Wm. Letters to sons, wife renouncing. Cousin Lewis Davis to be assistant.

MILLER, WILLIAM. At present of Kennett, late of New Garden.
8/28/1767. Nov 14, 1767.
To daughter Mary wife of James Miller 1/4 of all estate real and personal. To granddaughter Ruth Miller, daughter of Jas. and Mary, bed &c. Executors to sell all estate and proceeds equally divided between daughter Mary aforesaid, daughter Hannah wife of Wm. Whitesides, daughter Margaret wife of Jonathan Hanson and my granddaughter Ruth.
Executors: Nephews Jesse of Kennet and Saml. Miller of New Garden.
Wit: Lydia Miller, David Hayes, T. Woodward.

JACKSON, PAUL. Chester. Nov. 20, 1767. Adm. to Jane Jackson.

RING, BENJAMIN. "Being by accident sorely wounded." Birmingham.
12/8/1767. Nov. 14, 1767.
To son Nathaniel plantation where I now dwell containing about 70 acres, also plantation purchased of Robt. Chalfant containing about 67 acres. Provides for wife Susanna. To daughter Elizabeth Chandler remainder of personal estate.
Executor: Son Nathl.
Wit: John Thatcher, Thos. Gibson, Benja. Ring, Jr.

BURGESS, GERVASE. [Place not given.]
Sept. 18, 1766. Nov. 17, 1767.
To wife Elizabeth £30. To son John messuage &c. in Chester Twp. To daughters Elizabeth and Ann Burgess all remainder of estate to amount of £400, anything over that sum to son John. To cousin Saml. Shaw Jr. of Chester 10 pistoles.
Executor: Cousin Saml. Shaw Sr., in case of his death his son John.
Wit: Wm. Elliott, Thomas Horsfall.

PASSMORE, JOSEPH. Blacksmith. Newberry Twp., York Co.
4/16/1767. Nov. 25, 1767.
Provides for wife Elizabeth. To 2 sons Joseph and Abraham 1/2 of remainder of estate at 21. Remainder to 3 daughters Phebe, Lydia and Elizabeth at 18. Provides for a child with which wife is now pregnant.
Executors: Brothers-in-law Geo. Martin and Joseph Hayes. Letters to Hayes, the other renouncing.
Wit: James Dilworth, Charles Dilworth, Jos. Pierce.

LOUGHRIDGE, JOHN. East Nottingham. Nov. 26, 1767. Adm. to John Morrison and John Galbreath.

DOUGHERTY, JAMES. [Place not given.]
June 24, 1766. Nov. 25, 1767.
Provides for wife Margaret. To son Samuel best coat and waistcoat. To daughter Mary Ferguson 7.6. To daughter Janet Davidson 2 ewes and lambs. Son John to be put to a trade "against the first of Jan in the 18th year of his age" and to have £25 when free. To daughter Martha £25. To son James 2/3 of all estate at 21 and remainder at death of wife.
Executors: Wife and Jas. Glasgow.
Guardians: Jonathan Hartshorn and Jas. Maxwell.
Wit: John Beard, Archd. Henderson, Wm. Glasgow.

FINNEY, THOMAS. New London.
June 21, 1766. Nov. 25, 1767.
Provides for wife Mary. To son Robert £3 and all wearing apparel. After death of wife real estate divided into 3 parts between son Robert's children and daughters Ann and Dorothea Finney.
Executrix: Wife Mary and friend Patrick Ewing, assistant.
Wit: David Hunter, John Finney, John Lane.

PHILLIPS, THOMAS. Darby.
Nov. 22, 1767. Dec. 9, 1767.
To brother Griffith a bond of £100 I hold against him and all wearing apparel. To friend John Trapnall £10. Remainder to be equally divided between my mother, brother Griffith and sisters Elizabeth, Ann and Sarah.
Executor: John Trapnall.
Wit: Hans Boon, Israel Morton.

HAMPTON, BENJAMIN. Willistown. Dec. 14, 1767. Adm. to Rachel Hampton.

REYNOLDS, FRANCIS. Chichester. Jan 6, 1768. Adm. to Saml. Reynolds.

HAVILAND, ARTHUR. Westtown. Jan 9, 1768. Adm. to James Heany.

PARKS, SAMUEL. Springfield. Jan 19, 1768. Adm. to Richard Parks.

BROWN, DANIEL. Yeoman. Upper Chichester.
Jan. 19, 1767. Dec. 12, 1767.
To wife Susanna all real estate in Upper Chichester or elsewhere during life. At her decease to my 2 daughters Susanna wife of Nathan Newlin and Hannah wife of James Rigby. To sons Joseph and Nathaniel 5 shillings each having done sufficient for them. To granddaughter Rachel wife of John Dutton 5 shillings.
Executor: Friend Edward Linvill.
Wit: Christopher Dingee, Solomon Brown, Jacob Dingee.

NETHERMARK, CHRISTIAN. Island of Tinecum. Ridley Twp.
Sept. 15, 1764. Dec. 15, 1767.
To grandson Luke Frederick six acres of land in Calcon Hook given

me by my father. To granddaughter Christiana Frederick furniture &c. To granddaughter Sarah, daughter of son Mathias deceased, bed &c. Remainder of person[al] estate to 3 grandsons George, Luke and John, sons of daughter Elizabeth and Lawrence Frederick. To daughter Rebecca Taylor £10. To son Luke £5. To granddaughter Christiana Taylor £5.
Executors: Son in law Lawrence Frederick and brother in law Danl. Culin. Letters to Frederick, the other renouncing.
Wit: John Morton, Margaret Buntin.

COOPER, ROBERT. Sadsbury.
Jan 12, 1768. Feb. 3, 1768.
Provides for wife Margaret. To son James 1 shilling sterling. To son Robert £110. To daughter Margaret Cooper £50. To son William plantation in West Caln paying to his brother Robert £100 and to his sister Margaret £50. To son John plantation I now live on and all movables paying to his brother Robert £10.
Executors: Sons Wm. and John.
Wit: William Moore, James Boyd.

WHISTLER, MICHAEL. Pikeland.
Sept. 29, 1766. Feb. 8, 1768.
To wife Lenora the benefit of all estate during widowhood, at her death 2/3 to son Michael and 1/3 to daughter Sophia Whistler. After following legacies are paid, viz. To son John Wolf Whistler 7.6. To son Casper 7.6 and to daughter Barbara 7.6. To daughter Susana 7.6. Son Michael to be put to a trade at 15.
Executors: Michael King and David John. Letters to John, the other renouncing.
Wit: Casper Bierbower, Michael Rhodes, Hans Adams.

SMITH, JOHN. West Nantmeal.
Jan 26, 1768. Feb. 11, 1768.
To son Joseph all my right title, &c. to tract of land in East Nottingham containing 200 acres purchased of Mary Porter. To son James tract of land in East Nottingham containing 260 whereon I formerly lived and negro boy Tom. To daughter Margaret Robinson £100. To son William plantation in West Nantmeal whereon I now dwell and all remainder of personal estate. The heirs of John Whigam former husband of my wife Hannah to have £80 of my estate. Son Wm. to erect a stone over wife Hannah's grave.
Executors: Sons James and Wm.
Wit: Joseph Gray, Matthew Robertson, Robt. Brown.

WALKER, DAVID. East Caln. Feb. 18, 1768. Adm. to John Walker.

ANDERSON, JOHN. Kennett. Feb. 24, 1768. Adm. to James Anderson.

MARTIN, MATTHIAS. Charlestown.
Feb. 12, 1768. Feb. 23, 1768.
To wife Eleanor 60 acres off the S.W. end of plantation absolutely and rents of all remainder of estate until son David is 21 for schooling and maintaining children. To son David all remainder of my lands in Charlestown containing 140 acres at 21 paying to daughter Dinah £60. Friend John Griffith and kinsman Griffith

Jones guardians for my children.
Executrix: Wife Eleanor.
Wit: John Griffith, Sr., Joel Martin, David John.

MARSHALL, ABRAHAM. West Bradford.
4/12/1760. Feb. 24, 1768.
Provides for wife Mary. To son Isaac £10. To son James £5. To daughter Hannah Gibbons £5. To son-in-law Wm. Woodward £50 to divide among his children as he sees cause. To oldest son Saml.'s daughter 5 shillings. To son John's widow 5 shillings. To son Abram's widow 5 shillings. Remainder to wife.
Executors: Sons Humphrey and James.
Wit: Richard Baker, Joel Baily, Faithfull Stuart.

COLLINS, MARY. Goshen.
1/10/1768. Feb. 24, 1768.
To only son Elisha all real estate and all personal estate not otherwise disposed of, for the bringing up and educating said son till he is 21. To mother and two sisters Ann and Charity all wearing apparell.
Executor: Uncle Thomas Mercer.
Wit: John Hoopes, Nathaniel Moore, Joseph Pierce.

CULBERTSON, JOHN. East Caln.
Aug. 26, 1767. Dec. 10, 1767.
Provides for wife Abigail. To step-children Margaret, John and Jean Whitehill £5 to be divided when they arrive to maturity. To son Saml. £25. To daughter Elizabeth Culbertson mare and furniture. To son Benjamin £20 at 21. All lands in East Caln to be sold and remainder of personal and proceeds equally divided between my 6 children, viz., Andrew, James, John, Samuel, Elizabeth and Benjamin Culbertson. Son Benj. to be put to a trade.
Executors: Son Andrew and Abigail [his] wife. Letters to Andrew, the other renouncing.
Wit: John Carmichael, Wm. Long.

VANEMAN, ISAAC. Naamans Creek, New Castle Co.
Feb. 20, 1762. Mar. 8, 1768.
To sister Mary Harding 1/2 of all estate and to her son John Harding the remaining 1/2 of ditto at 21. If above mentioned John Harding should die (being yet an infant) the whole estate to sister Mary.
Executors: Sister Mary Harding and Abraham Robinson.
[no wit. mentioned.]

GILKEY, WALTER. Sadsbury.
Feb. 18, 1768. Mar. 11, 1768.
To son Samuel £8. To son William £20. To daughter Margaret £6. To daughter Mary £30. To Rev. Adam Boyd £2. Provides for wife Leah. To son Jonathan plantation whereon he now lives, also plantation John Jones formerly lived on. Remainder to grandson Walter Gilkey at 21.
Executors: Son Jonathan and Robt. Cowan.
Wit: Saml. Martin, Wm. Glendining.

NEWLIN, NICHOLAS. [Nathaniel marked through and Nicholas added.]
Concord. Mar. 14, 1768. Adm. to Anne Newlin and Micajah Speakman.

JORDAN, JOHN. Oxford. Mar. 29, 1768. Adm. to Rachel Jordan.

TAYLOR, JANE. Marple.
---- 1765. Mar. 25, 1768.
To friends Thos. Minshall and Seth Pancoast £150 in trust for use of daughter Sarah Woolley. To daughter Rachel Reese £50. To granddaughter Ann Woolley £10. To granddaughter Jane Woolley £10. To grandson John Woolley £30. To granddaughter Mary Morris £20 at 18. To granddaughter Jane Morris £20 at 18. To grandson Robert Morris £20 at 21. To granddaughter Phebe Morris £20 at 18. To granddaughter Hannah Morris £20 at 18. To son-in-law John Morris 1/2 acre of land adj. lott already conveyed to him, also all remainder of estate and Executor.
Wit: Jas. Heacock, John Lewis.

HOWELL, JACOB. Chester Borough.
--- 1766. Mar. 31, 1768.
All lands and tenements in Chester and Chichester Twps. to 4 sons, Joseph, Samuel, Isaac and Joshua each of them paying £4 yearly to son Jacob during his life. To son Isaac 6 acres, part of my 20 acre lot. To son Joseph 6 acres of ditto, also a lott in borough of Chester. To 2 grandchildren Sarah and John, children of son John, my 3 lotts known by the name of the L lot, also to said grandchildren £25. To granddaughter Deborah Howell £10. To granddaughter Sarah Jones £100 at 24 with reserve to her father Charles Jones and granddaughter Abigail Howell. To grandson Jacob Howell, son of Saml., lot in Chester. To grandson Joseph do. To granddaughter Sarah, daughter of son Joseph, silver ware and to Abigail, Anne, Deborah and Katherine, daughters of ditto silver ware.
Executors: Sons Jos., Saml. and Joshua.
Wit: John Eyre, Isaac Eyre, Isaac Taylor.

AXLINE, CHRISTOPHER. Pikeland. Apr. 1, 1768. Adm. to Catharine and Adam Axline.

POWELL, DAVID. East Fallowfield. Apr. 6, 1768, David died Mar. 16. Adm. to Elizabeth Powell. (She is said to have been Elizabeth Chalfant and to have m. 2nd John Bentley. She d. Jun. 7, 1814 in 93rd yr.)

WOODBURN, JOHN. Pikeland. Apr. 6, 1768. Adm. to John Francis.

BEST, JOHN. West Nottingham. Apr. 9, 1768. Adm. to John Blackburn.

EVANS, WILLIAM. Cordwinder. Willistown.
Mar. 24, 1768. Apr. 4, 1768.
To brother Jonathan Evans £10. To sister Mary, wife of Ezekiel Bowen £5. To Levi Bowen and his wife Ann, my sister, all remainder of estate real or personal.
Executor: Levi Bowen.

Wit: Rowland Ellis, Enoch Lewis, Danl. Cornog.

BILHA, Negro. Westtown.
Feb. 18, 1768. Apr. 18, 1768.
To Deborah, daughter of John Darlington, silver shoe buckles. To Elizabeth, daughter of John Darlington, my other green grazatt apron and my other pair of silk mittens. To brother Negro Jack £5. To Sarah, wife of Jos. Hunt's negro Jacob, household goods. To cousin Jacob the said negro £30 now in hands of Abm. Darlington Sr. and all remainder of estate.
Executors: Wm. Hunt and Peter Osborne. Letters to Hunt, the other refusing.
Wit: John Hunt, Edward Dougherty, Thos. Taylor.

COCHRAN, JAMES. West Fallowfield.
Mar. 10, 1768. Codicil Apr. 12, 1768. Apr. 21, 1768.
To 2 uncles David and Stephen Cochran all real and personal estate in trust to divide as they see fit between my brother Stephen and sister Jane Cochran.
Executors: Brother Stephen and sister Jane.
Codicil gives to sister Ann Roan 5 shillings and to Isbel Cochran, daughter of brother Robert, 5 shillings. To brothers George and John 5 shillings each.
Wit: Jos. Gardner, Jos. Wilson, John Boyd.
Letters to Stephen and Jane Cochran.

JONES, JOSEPH. Middletown. May 16, 1768. Adm. to Thomas Walter.

MEANES, EDWARD. [Place not given.]
Sept. 21, 1767. Apr. 26, 1768.
All estate after debts are paid to wife Catrine, also with Wm. Patton, Executors. Letters c.t.a. to Dennis Dougherty, the Executors named declining to act.
Wit: Joseph Nisbitt, Thomas Patten, Wm. Patten.

KIRKPATRICK, HUGH. West Nottingham.
Mar. 19, 1766. May 18, 1768.
To son John all estate real and personal. To son David £5. To sons Hugh and William, daughters Margaret Clinging, Hannah Barkly, Elizabeth Nisbet and Mary McConnell 20 shillings each, they having had their portion already.
Executor: Son John.
Wit: Robt. Givans, James Petterson.

HEMPHILL, ALEXANDER. Goshen.
4/15/1768. May 28, 1768.
To son-in-law John Fox 5 shillings. To grandson James Fox £10 when of age. To granddaughter Hannah Fox £10 when of age. All remainder to 2 sons James and Joseph Hemphill.
Executors: Son James and friend Thomas Wills. Letters to James, the other refusing.
Wit: Geo. Ashbridge, Jr., Samuel Waln, Robt. Rushton.

THOMAS, THEOPHILUS. Vincent.
Apr. 9, 1768. June 1, 1768.

Provides for wife Catherine. To son-in-law Humphrey Bell the use
of land on which he now lives in Vincent and manor of Callowhill,
containing 108 acres during life of his wife, my daughter, and at
her death to their children. To grandson Wm. Bell the land where
I now live containing 59 1/2 acres, on my wife's decease. To
daughter Mary Watkin £40. To son John Thomas £20 and all Welch
books &c. To grandson John Bell £4. To granddaughter Ann Thomas
£10 at 18. To Rev. Mr. John Griffith in Charlestown £3.
Executors: Son John and grandson Wm. Bell.
Wit: Wm. Evans, Wm. West, David John.

HANNINS, JOHN. West Bradford. Jun. 1, 1768. Adm. Rachel Hannins.

FISHER, CHRISTIAN. West Braddford. Jun. 13, 1768. Adm. Magdalen
Fisher and Jacob Yoder.

GARDNER, JOHN. West Nantmeal. Jun. 17, 1768. Adm. Rachel Gardner.
To widow Rachel and children: Samuel, Rebecca and Sarah. Rebecca m.
James Crawford. Mary m. John Gardner.

GLASSFORD, HENRY. London, Britain. Jun. 21, 1768. Adm. Elizabeth
Glassford.

GRANTHAM, CHARLES. Ridley.
Feb. 14, 1768. Aug. 6, 1768.
Provides for wife Lydia. To son Jacob plantation and 2 pieces of
land purchased of John Broom, also house and lot bought of John
Knowles in Southwark, also £100. To daughter Margaret, wife of
Thos. Thompson, tenement and lot of ground in Southark until John
Grantham, son of my son George deceased, comes of age. Also her
full share of the landed estate of her mother Catherine, my former
wife. To grandsons Charles and George, sons of Geo. deceased,
plantation on which my son Geo. lived, also meadow in Darby when of
full age paying to their brother John £50 each. Also to granddaughter Lydia their sister £50 at 21. To son William plantation
on which I now dwell in Darby, 2 tracts of meadow and 8 acres of
woodland and all remainder of estate at 21. Reserved to grandson
Chas. Thompson paying to grandsons Thos. and Nathan Thompson £50
each. Also mentions grandson Isaac Thompson.
Executors: John Morton, Esq., and son Wm.
Wit: Wm. Edwards, Alexander Tate, Margaret Vaneman.

MARSHALL, MARY. Darby.
June 29, 1768. Aug. 16, 1768.
To sister Sarah Hatten £5. To sister Hannah Sheuton £5. To sister
Johanna's 3 children, viz., Sarah, Margaret and John £5 to be
divided. To sister-in-law Margaret Marshall saddle. To cousin
Hannah Hays whip. To sister Susanna Marshall table cloth. To 4
sisters Hannah Sheuton, Rachel Hays, Martha Johnson and Susanna
Marshall all wearing apparel giving what they think proper to
sister-in-law Mary Marshall.
Executors: Brother John and sister Susanna.
Wit: John Sellers, Nathan Sellers.

HAINES, ISAAC. Goshen.
7/6/1766. Aug. 16, 1768.
Provides for wife Catherine. To son Isaac 20 shillings having given him a plantation in Goshen. To son Ellis plantation containing 146 1/4 acres, also 20 shillings. To son Josiah remainder of plantation where I now live containing 133 acres. To daughter Sarah Haines case of drawers. To grandsons Isaac Yarnall and Hugh Derbrow 10 shillings at 21. All remainder of personal estate to wife and 3 daughters Hannah Eachus, Mary Martin and Lydia Williams.
Executors: Son Isaac and friend Geo. Ashbridge, Jr.
Wit: Thomas Hoopes, Jr., Thomas Scholfield, Isaac Haines the 3rd.

HOPKINS, WILLIAM. Oxford.
June 30, 1768. Aug. 18, 1768.
Provides for wife Sarah. To daughter Mary £50. To daughter Sarah £50. To daughter Ruth £50. To son Ezekiel £50 providing he comes to live with his mother and sisters, otherwise but £30. To brother Matthew wearing apparel.
Executors: Robert Smith of Oxford and daughter Mary. Letters to Mary Hopkins, the other renouncing.
Wit: Saml. McNeal, Jas. Dysant, Wm. Ross.

STARR, ALEXANDER, Londongrove, Aug. 31, 1768. Adm. to David Harlan.

SHARP, THOMAS. New Garden. Sept. 3, 1768. Adm. to Rachel Sharp.

GARDNER, JOHN. West Nantmeal. Sept. 10, 1768. Adm. to James Crawford, Rebecca Crawford and Jas. Hair.

MILLER, WILLIAM. New Garden.
7/28/1768. Codicil 7/31/1768. Sept. 5, 1768.
To son William all real estate in Chester and New Castle Cos., also personal estate to amount of £300. Confirms will of deceased wife Ann devising certain lots of land in Philadelphia. To daughter Mary, wife of Joshua Pusey, goods to amount of £205. To daughter Ann Miller goods to amount of £1050. To son-in-law Ellis Lewis 20 shillings. To granddaughter Mary Lewis £500 at 18. My cousin John Miller is indebted to me on mortgage out of which I give to Ann, daughter of Samuel Hill £14, for her support as Friends of New Garden Meeting think fit.
Executor: Son Wm.
Codicil gives to 4 grandchildren, viz., Wm., Joshua, Ann and Mary Pusey £20 each.

Wit: Wm. Jackson, John Curle, Isaac Jackson.

TREGO, WILLIAM. Goshen.
Aug. 1, 1768. Sept. 16, 1768.
Provides for wife Margaret. To each of my grandchildren now living 1 shilling each. To Wm. McPherson and Phineas Eachus 1 shilling each. To sons Joseph and William 5 shillings each. Remainder of personal estate to my daughters, Elizabeth and Mary Malin, Sarah Eachus and Ann Hunt. The share of Sarah to be at the disposal of

my Executors and not subject to any demand of her husband. To son
Benjamin after decease of wife plantation whereon I now dwell in
Goshen containing 100 acres paying £70 to 3 daughters, Elizabeth,
Mary and Ann.
Executors: Son Joseph Trego of Nantmeal and Geo. Ashbridge, Jr.
Wit: Wm. Bane, Thomas Scholfield, Aaron Hoopes.

LEWIS, ABRAHAM.   Darby.   Oct. 22, 1768.   Adm. to Anthony and
Abraham Lewis.

NETHERMARK, LUKE.   Tinicum Island.
July 18, 1766.   Sept. 27, 1768.
Provides for wife Margaret. To cousin Luke Frederick after my
wife's decease all remainder of my lands unsold wherever they may
be at 21, with reserve to his brother George first and to cousin
John Frederick second. To wife's sister's daughter Ann Walker £50
at 18 with reserve to children of sister Elizabeth Frederick, viz.,
George, John and Christiana. £10 to the congregation at Wicacoe to
be by them applied to the use of St. James Church in Kingsessing.
Executors: Wife Margaret, Philip Ford, Esq. and John Morton.
Letters to Margaret and Morton, Ford being deceased.
Wit: Jacob Fritz, John Justason.

ADAMS, JAMES.   East Nottingham.
Sept. 15, 1766.   Nov. 7, 1768.
To wife Frank Adams 1/2 of all estate real and personal. To son
Jonathan the remaining 1/2 of estate. To son Samuel 40 shillings.
To daughter Margaret Adam 40 shillings. To daughter Jean Adam 40
shillings.
Executors: Wife Frank, son Jonathan and Joseph Vance. Letters to
wife and son.
Wit: David Moore, Hugh Adam.

MATHER, JOHN.   Chester Borough.
May 28, 1768.   Nov. 19, 1768.
To son-in-law Charles Thomson and wife Ruth, my daughter, brick
messuage and lot in Chester where Valentine Weaver now dwells, also
3 other lots all now in possession of said Weaver during their
lives and then to their children with reserve to granddaughter Mary
Jackson. Also to said daughter Ruth £300. To daughter Jane, widow
of Paul Jackson, brick messuage where I now dwell and 4 lotts
belonging. Son Joseph plantation known by name of Ridley on Ridley
Creek, he releasing any claim he may have on any other of my real
estate in right of his mother Mary Mather deceased. To grandson
John Mather Jackson stone messuage now in tenure of Francis
Richardson in Chester, also £100. To grandson Charles Jackson
£100. To nephew John Mather, son of brother Thomas [Francis
crossed out and Thomas added] £10 and all wearing apparel. To
nephew James and his sisters Jane, Mary, Elizabeth and Sarah
Mather, children of brother Thomas, £10 each. All remainder to
daughter Jane Jackson.
Executors: Son-in-law Chas. Thomson and daughters Ruth and Jane.
Letters to Jane Jackson, the others refusing.
Wit: James Mather, Edward Russell, David Jackson.

KERR, JOSEPH. West Nantmeal.
Oct. 12, 1768. Nov. 22, 1768.
Provides for wife Margaret. To daughter Elizabeth £10. To daughters Margaret and Martha £10. To son James £100. To sons Joseph and David all real estate to be divided paying above legacy to James. Remainder to wife.
Executors: Sons Jas., Jos. and David.
Wit: Wm. Sheerer, Robt. Robinson.

MOORE, MOSES. Lower Chichester. Nov. 24, 1768. Adm. to James Moore.

MOORE, MARY. Lower Chichester. Nov. 24, 1768. Adm. to James Moore.

STRODE, CALEB. East Bradford. Nov. 28, 1768. Adm. to Richard Strode and Jos. Peirce.

WOODWARD, AMOS. East Bradford. Nov. 28, 1768. Adm. to John Woodward.

THOMAS, TAMER. Willistown. Dec. 3, 1768. Adm. to Joseph Thomas.

EVANS, CADWALLADER. Yeoman and tanner. Edgmont.
11/16/1768. Dec. 7, 1768.
Provides for wife Anna. To son Pennell £10. To 3 grandchildren by my son Pennell, viz., Cadwallader, Sarah and Ann Evans, remainder of tract of land bought of Executors of Job Harvey deceased in Berks Co. To son-in-law Rowland Parry £10 and to my daughter Hannah his wife £150 (the interest during life only). To son-in-law Jonathan Morris £50. To son Robert Evans £100. To daughter Ann, wife of Joshua Cowpland £150. To Middletown Meeting £5. To son Thomas tract of land in Edgmont whereon I now dwell willed me by my father-in-law Jos. Pennell, also tract adj. containing about 30 acres. To wife Ann 2 lotts of land bought of Jacob Yarnall.
Executors: Wife and son Thomas.
Wit: Nehemiah Baker, Danl. Bromall, Danl. Calvert.

PUGH, JONATHAN. Uwchlan.
Mar. 27, 1768. Dec. 1 and 12, 1768.
To son David plantation in Uwchlan containing 150 acres and all remainder of estate not otherwise devised. To son Samuel all my property now in his possession and all he may owe me at my decease. To son Jonathan £30. To daughter Mary £30. To daughter Sarah £30. To Hannah wife of son David bed and bedding. To each of my grandchildren now born 20 shillings when 21.
Executor: Son David.
Wit: Wm. Hanna, John Jacobs, Jr.

MC FARLAND, GEORGE. Vincent. Dec. 15, 1768. Adm. to Elizabeth McFarland and John McFarland.

PENNELL, MARY. Widow. Chester Borough.
7/23/1765. Dec. 17, 1768.
To daughter Hannah Ellis household goods. To Hannah Tolbert

wearing apparel. To son Wm. and his wife knives and forks. To granddaughter Elizabeth Pennell 50 shillings and dishes at 18. To daughter Ann Worrall wearing apparel. To granddaughter Mary Edge furniture. To granddaughter Ann Edge ditto. To granddaughter Edith Pennell ditto. To granddaughter Rebecca Pennell silver spoon. To Ruth Pennell ditto. To grandson Jacob Halcombe £7. To daughter Hannah Ellis £6.
Executors: Friend and kinsman John Sharpless.
Wit: John Eyre, Rebecca Eyre.

BOYD, ADAM. Sadsbury.
Feb. 12, 1768. Dec. 21, 1768.
Provides for wife Jane. To son Andrew my plantation in Sadsbury with stock &c.,paying legacies. To daughters Mary, Hannah and Elizabeth £60 each. To son Samuel all remainder of my books provided he enter the ministerial office, otherwise to be divided. To daughters Margaret Tate, Janet McMordie and Agnes Smith 5 shillings each. To sons Thomas, John and Adam 5 shillings each. To son Samuel £5.
Executors: Sons Thomas and Andrew.
Overseers: Rev. Sampson Smith and John Miller, Esq.
Wit: Wm. Armstrong, Alex. Rogers, John Sharp.

RUDULPH, JOHN. Darby. Dec. 26, 1768. Adm. to Mary Rudulph and Jesse Bonsall.

SHIELDS, JAMES. Newlin. Jan 11, 1769. Adm. to Mary and Robert Shields.

ROUTH, FRANCIS. Chichester.
Sept. 30, 1767. Dec. 30, 1768.
To grandson Isaac Carter 5 shillings. To granddaughters Lydia Carter and Mary Palmer £10 each at 18 or marriage. Half of remainder to son Francis and the other 1/2 to son John Routh and daughter Ann Dutton to be equally divided. Daughter Ann's legacy to be paid to the Overseers of Chichester Meeting to be managed and kept for her use.
Executor: Son Francis.
Wit: Hannah Johnson, Jno. Power.

DAWSON, THOMAS. Cordwainer. West Caln.
July 11, 1748. Jan 6, 1769.
To wife Mary and son Abraham all real estate during her widowhood, afterward to son Abraham. To son Richard 5 shillings. To son Isaac £20 in 1750 and £15 in 1752. To daughter Ann £10. To daughter Fortunata £10. "Having dun unto the rest of my chil[dren] (2) that are not mentioned here, I give to each of them one shilling."
Executors: Wife Mary and son Abraham. Letters to Mary, the other being deceased.
Wit: Thos. Dawson, Jr., Margaret Dawson, Wm. McKnight.

BRANNEN, JOHN. Upper Darby.
Feb. 11, 1766. Jan 9, 1769.
Provides for wife Grace. To son Benjamin all land in Darby. To

daughter Margaret, wife of Ephraim Armstrong, £20. To daughter Mary £150. To grandson John Armstrong £20 at 21 with rev. to his brother Joseph. All remainder to son Benjamin.
Executors: James Ewing and son Benjamin.
Wit: Wm. McClelan, John Brooks.

TELFORD, JOSEPH. Sadsbury.
Feb. 6, 1754. Jan 10, 1769.
To wife Mary all estate during life including warrant right of a tract of land now in my possession in Fallowfield. To Joseph son of Danl. Henderson of Sadsbury the said land on death of wife. To Mary Scott now dwelling with me £3. Also a book for Danl. Campbell.
Executors: Brother-in-law Daniel Henderson and wife Mary. Letters to Henderson, the other being absent.
Wit: Jas. Boyd, Matthew Henderson.

JOHNSTON, HUMPHREY. Chester Twp.
Dec. 11, 1768. Jan 26, 1768.
Plantation in Bethel to be sold. Plantation I now live upon to be kept for support of wife and children until youngest comes of age and then to be sold and proceeds equally divided among children.
Executors: Wife Mary and brother David Johnson.
Wit: Hugh Linn, William Dennen.

GRUBB, SAMUEL. Kennett.
1/19/1768. Jan 30, 1769.
Provides for wife Lydia. To son Isaac 160 acres part of the plantation whereon we formerly lived in Brandywine Hundred, the est end[ing] thereof paying £50 to my Executors. Refers to his brother John having 60 acres left him during life by his father "and then to fall into my Estate." To son Samuel, all my plantation in Kennett whereon I now dwell purchased of Jos. Harlan and John Clark ,at 21, paying £50 to my Estate. Son-in-law Thos. Robinson to have two lotts in Wilmington purchased of Esther Bishop. Remainder of land to be sold. Makes provision for a child expected to be call John if a male or Hannah if female. Remainder divided between daughters Jemima Robinson, Prudence, Mary, Rachel, Rebecca, Charity, Sarah and Lydia Grubb as they come of age.
Executors: Wife Lydia and brother-in-law Richard Baker of West Bradford.
Wit: Adam Redd, Moses Mendenhall, Thos. Gibson.

SHARPLESS, JOSEPH. Middletown. Feb. 25, 1769. Adm. to Mary and Jos. Sharpless.

MEARS, SAMUEL. New London. Feb. 17, 1769. Adm. to Martha Crawford and Robt. Allison.

MC CADDEN, HENRY. Londonderry. Feb. 28, 1769. Adm. to Elizabeth McCadden and Thos. White.

ELLIOTT, PETER. Darby. Feb. 18, 1769. Adm. to Christopher Elliott.

TAYLOR, ISAAC. Thornbury. Mar. 27, 1769. Adm. to Thomas and Jacob Taylor. (£500. Susannah the widow renounces on same date.
Wit: James Taylor, Joshua Marshall. Inventory by Caleb Peirce Jr. and Samuel Mendenhall 3/30/1769 not summed up.)

MC CLEAN, ALEXANDER. East Caln. Mar. 2, 1769. Adm. to Wm. McClean.

WOMSLEY, JONATHAN. Darby.
Feb. 2, 1769. Feb. 18, 1769.
Non. Cupative will "gave all that he had to his mother (meaning Sarah Waldren) saying it was all little enough for her trouble she had with him." Letters to Sarah Waldren.
Wit: Wm. Glover, Philip Heiser, John Mitchell, Sr.

SHIRLEY, THOMAS. East Caln.
Jan 7, 1769. Feb. 24, 1769.
To daughters Margaret Kincede and Sarah Lafferty, son Thomas, daughter Agnes Cole 5 shillings each. All remainder to wife Agnes, also Executrix.
Wit: William McClain, William McFarlan.

WILLSON, THOMAS. Newlinton.
4/11/1768. Mar. 11, 1769.
To Jane wife of John Patterson £12. To son Charles out of what he is now indebted to me £62. To son Robert £30. To daughter Mary wife of John Clark £30. To son Thomas £19 and gun. To daughter Elizabeth wife of Saml. Alexander £22. To son Caleb, out of what he is now indebted to me, 5 shillings. To daughter Phebe wife of Chas. Graham £12. To Esther wife of Wm. Hanna, Jr. £22. To daughter Agigail wife of John Hanna £22. To son Elijah £62.
Executors: Sons Charles and Thomas.
Wit: T. Woodward, Wm. Wickersham, Jr., Peter Wickersham.

YARNALL, MARY. Edgmont.
6/4/1768. Mar. 14, 1769.
To son David £20. To children of son Abraham Yarnall deceased, viz., Rachel, Abner, Mary, Uriah, Ezekiel, Samuel and Elizabeth £20 to be diivided. To daughter Jane Griffith £20. To grandson Philip Bolsel 20 shillings. To grandson Philip son of David Yarnall 40 shillings. Remainder to 4 daughters, Jane, Elizabeth, Estherd and Mary.
Executors: Brother-in-law Nathan Yarnall and daughter Elizabeth Yarnall.
Wit: John Smedley, William Williamson.

WILLIAMS, SAMUEL. Chichester.
Mar. 4, 1769. Mar. 17, 1769.
All estate real and personal to wife Elizabeth, also Executrix.

WOODWARD, NAYL. East Marlborough.
3/9/1769. Mar. 25, 1769.
To wife Lydia £100, 2 horses and 2 cows. To sons Eli and Caleb plantation whereon I now dwell in East Marlborough to be divided by the great road that passes through it, also £8 each. Executors to

sell land in Birmingham and all remainder of estate to 5 daughters, viz., Hannah, Phebe, Sarah, Lydia and Ann Woodward, share and share alike. Uncle Richard Woodward to have the house and 3 acres of land where he now dwells until son Eli is 21.
Executors: Wife Lydia and friend John Webster.
Wit: Mordecai Hayes, Joseph Williams.

HADLEY, PHEBE. Widow. West Bradford.
9/2/1767. Mar. 27, 1769.
To the heir of my late husband Simon Hadley 5 shillings. To daughter Phebe wife of John Wall all wearing apparel. To son Nathaniel all his indebtedness to me. To son Peter and son-in-law John Wall what they now owe me. £30 to be equally divided between all my children now living and son-in-law Saml. Osborn and granddaughter Frances Buffington, "it being for building a house on my land." All remainder to son John, also Executor, he keeping and burying me.
Wit: Richard Buffington, John Snow, Robert Buffington.

DAWSON, MARY. Widow of Thomas. West Caln.
Feb. 4, 1769. Mar. 27, 1769.
To Rev. Thomas Barton £12 and to son Thomas £8 for use of Church of St. John at Pequa and £10 for support of the poor of West Caln. To son Isaac £20 for schooling of his children. To granddaughter Rachel Park £10. To daughter Ann Berwick £10. To granddaughter Mary wife of Wm. Mallis £10. To granddaughter Mary Montgomery, now Hughes, £7. To grandson Jacob Dawson £7. To grandson Thos. Dawson 5 shillings. To daughter Fortune 5 shillings. To Mary and Sarah, daughters to son David Dawson deceased, 5 shillings each. To son Thomas £200 and to his daughter Mary £10 and to his wife Margaret my cooking glass. To grandson David Dawson who was prisoner in France £5. All remainder to son Thomas, also Executor.
Wit: Francis Alexander, John Fleming.

LOBB, BENJAMIN. Darby. Apr. 18, 1769. Adm. to Isaac and Benj. Lobb.

GEST, JAMES. Concord. Apr. 14, 1769. Adm. to Joseph Gest.

CLARK, THOMAS. West Caln.
July 4, 1767. Apr. 12, 1769.
Provides for wife Ann. To son David Clark £50. To grandchildren Thos. Gibbs, Thos. Fullerton, Thos. Clark, Thos. Park and Elizabeth Gibbs £10 each. If son Joseph shall educate his son Thomas for a minister of the Gospel, I give my said grandson £40 more for his learning, otherwise to any other son whom he may so educate. To granddaughter Ann Clark £50 if she live to have need of it. To son Joseph 5 shillings having lately given him £100. Remainder equally divided among children Mary Gibbs, John Clark, Ann Fullerton, Rachel Kennedy, Rebecca Park, Susanna Young and Margaret Kerr. Portions of Mary Gibbs and Rachel Kennedy to be in trust for their use. Mentions son-in-law Humphrey Fullerton.
Executors: Sons John and Joseph and James Thompson. Letters to Jos. Clark and Jos. Thompson.
Wit: Robt. Whitehill, John Miller, Wm. Crawford.

COCHRAN, JACOB. West Nantmeal.
Mar. 20, 1769. Apr. 13, 1769.
Provides for wife Mary. To son James the holding he now enjoys during the term specified in Article between him and me. To son Jacob the improvement whereon he now lives and 7 acres of plow land adj. To son William 2 yr. old colt. All remainder sold and equally divided between children, viz., James, Jacob, William, Josiah, Andrew, David, John and Mary Cochran. Son James and daughter Mary to have £20 each additional and son John £20 less than the others. To sister-in-law Margaret Gregory £5.
Executors: Wife Mary and sons James and Jacob.
Wit: Robert Brown, Abel Griffith, Joseph Gray.

WILCOX, JAMES. Upper Providence. May 19, 1769. Adm. to Purdence and Mark Wilcox.

ROMAN, MARY. Chester. Mary 31, 1769. Adm. to Isaac Roman.

ELLIS, EDWARD. Darby. May 10, 1769. Adm. to Jas. McClees and Wm. Garrett.

WILLSON, JAMES. London Britain.
Mar. 22, 1769. Apr. 14, 1769.
Provides for wife Anne. All remainder of estate real and personal to son Henry at 21 with reserve. To brother Thos. Wilson, paying to my sister Jane Wilson £10 and to sister Lettice Wilson £10 and to brother Saml. Wilson £5. James Kennedy to be Guardian of son Henry.
Executors: Wife and Ephraim Morrison. Letters to Anne Wilson, the other being absent.
Wit: John Fleming, Neill Morrison, Morris Thomas.

MORTON, TOBIAS. Taylor. Darby.
Mar. 31, 1769. May 1, 1769.
To sons Israel and Mark my house and lot in Darby to maintain their mother and divided at her death. Also all lands in Manitony except 100 acres to daughter Rebecca.
Executors: Sons Israel and Mark.
Wit: Amos Moore, Elizabeth Moore.

GARRETT, JOHN. Cordwinder. West Whiteland.
4/21/1769. May 4, 1769.
Provides for wife Hannah. Oldest son Benjamin to be bound out until he is 16 and then put to a trade. Also mentions youngest son Elisha and daughters Anne and Hannah Garret.
Executors: Father-in-law Paul Bond and wife Hannah.
Wit: Jacob Leamy, Esther Garrett, John Bowen.

ELLIOTT, WILLIAM. West Nantmeal.
Dec. 20, 1768. May 19, 1769.
Provides for wife Mary. To son Samuel my plantation subject to wife's life interest, also mare and colt. To daughter Agnes horse &c. Mentions 3 bonds coming due from John Rosbrough which is divided between wife, sons Thomas and Saml. and daughters Agnes and Jean. To grandson Wm. Willey £4. To grandson John Willey £4 &c.

£2 to daughter Jean's children. To son John 5 shillings. To son by the law James Miller 1 shilling. Executors to make title to land to John Rosebrough when his payments are completed.
Executors: Wife and sons Thomas and Saml. Letters to Thos. and Saml.
Wit: Wm. Brown, John Millison, Thomas Elliot.

HANLEY, JOHN. Chester Borough.
May 12, 1769. May 24, 1769.
Executors to sell tract of land in Twp. of Chester purchased of John Lownes, commonly called *Mount Millick*. To wife Eleanor and her heirs, stone messuage wherein I now dwell and lots belonging. To kinsman John Hogan brick messuage now in possession of Peter Steel. To cousin Mary Gorman 1/2 of certain lot of ground now in possession of Peter Steel. To Hannah Gorman the other 1/2 of said lot. All remainder to wife Eleanor.
Executors: Wife, kinsman John Hogan and Henry H. Graham. Letters to wife and Hogan, the other renouncing.
Wit: George Craig, Elisha Price.

EDMISTON, WILLIAM. Oxford.
Mar. 22, 1769. May 31, 1769.
Provides for wife Mary. To oldest son James £6. To David Edmiston £5. To James Tanner £5 on condition that he pay the £5 that Wm. Edmiston is bound for him. To daughter Jean Edmiston 40 shillings. To daughter Elizabeth Edmiston £5. To granddaughter Rachel Edmiston £3, cow and calf when of age. To grandson Abraham Edmiston calf and 2 sheep. To sons Moses and William all real and personal estate paying legacies.
Executors: Son Moses and brother-in-law John Templeton. Letters to Moses, the others renouncing.
Wit: James Poak, William Poak.

BONSALL, ENOCH. Darby.
12/12/1767. May 31, 1769.
To son Enoch 50 acres of land bought of Jos. Bonsall where he now dwells in Darby, also 2 acres of meadow in Kingress. To son Joseph 50 acres on the north easterly part of plantation where I now dwell. To son Joshua plantation where he now dwells bought of Stephen Paschall containing 118 acres paying to daughter Sarah £100 and house room while unmarried. To son Jonathan all remainder of land where we now dwell in Darby containing about 100 acres paying to daughter Hannah £100 and maintenance while unmarried. To son Benjamin £20. To son David £150. To son Joseph £100 of the amount he stands indebted to me. To the son and daughter of son Isaac deceased £15 each at 21. Remainder equally divided.
Executors: Sons Benjamin, Enoch and Joseph.
Wit: Jacob Webber, Joseph Pearson, Isaac Pearson.

LEWIS, ABRAHAM. Upper Darby.
5/17/1768. June 2, 1769.
To son Abraham that part of my land bought of my brother Saml. Lewis containing 150 acres in Upper Darby paying £20. To son Anthony remainder of land bought of brother Samuel containing 100

acres in Haverford reserving 6 acres bequeathed to daughter Esther. To daughter Esther Lewis 6 acres as reserved above including house where Elisha Taylor now lives while she remains unmarried. To daughter Mary, wife of Henry Trimble £5. To the children of deceased daughter Elizabeth Warner £2 each. To grandson Lewis Trimble £3. To "my old servant girl" Hannah Griffith cow. Executors to sell all share in mill on Darby Creek. All remainder to son Anthony and daughter Esther.
Executors: Sons Abraham and Anthony Lewis.
Will not signed. Tried June 2, 1769 and letters granted to Abraham and Anthony Lewis.

WILLIAMS, DAVID. London Britain.
Oct. 25, 1767. Codicil May 16, 1769. June 9, 1769.
To daughter Lettice Williams £30. To daughter Margaret wife of James Reed £17.10. Provides for wife Margaret. To son John remainder of personal property having made over the plantation to him by deed some years ago, also Executor. Codicil gives to son-in-law Jas. Reed £12.10 borrowed of me in addition to legacy to wife.
Wit: Morris Thomas, Charles Black, David Rogers.

SALMON, ROBERT. East Nottingham. June 26, 1769. Adm. to Hugh Thomson.

WOODWARD, JOHN. West Bradford. July 7, 1769. Adm. to Sarah Woodward and Richd. Barnard.

DREWITT, JOHN. Lower Chichester. July 25, 1769. Adm. to Mary Drewitt.

SINGLETON, JOHN. White Clay Creek Hundred, New Castle Co. Mar. 11, 1770. Mar. 26, 1770.
Provides for wife Elizabeth. To nephew John McDowell that plantation on which his father Wm. McDowell lives containing about 200 acres, also all books, surveying instruments, maps and charts &c. To niece Phebe McDowell £100. All remainder equally divided between John and Phebe McDowell, their mother Jane McDowell, and her 3 other daughters, Cathrine, Ann and Jane. All debts and rents that brother Thomas Singleton stands charged with to be forgiven him. Wearing apparel to brother Thos. and brother-in-law Wm. McDowell. To nephew John McDowell my silver hilted sword. My wife, her son Thomas, daughters Nancy and Jane Thompson, my 3 sisters Jane McDowell, Sarah McDowell and Catharine Lunn, also my sister Sarah's daughter Catherine, my brother Thomas, brother-in-law Wm. McDowell, each to have a suit of mourning apparel. Debt owing from brothers-in-law Wm. and Joshua McDowell to be forgiven them.
Executors: Wife Elizabeth, Dr. Robert Bines and brother-in-law Thos. Lunn. Letters to wife and Thos. Lunn, the other renouncing.
Wit: Saml. Platt, Jno. McClean, Wm. Golden.
** Dr. John McDowell of New London was son of Alexander McDowell, who died intestate. See diary June 20, 1875.

SLAUGHTER, JACOB. Laborer. Willistown.
July 23, 1769. Aug. 5, 1769.
To son Philip £5 having advanced him very considerable. To grandson Jacob Slaughter that now lives with me £5 at 21. To wife Mary all remainder of estate.
Executors: Wife and friends John Gronow and David Davis, both of Tredyffrin. Letters to wife Mary, the others renouncing.
Wit: Lewis Gronow, Thomas Davis, Philip Housekeeper.

WILLSON, MARY. Vincent.
Dec. 12, 1767. Aug. 18, 1769.
To eldest son Thomas Wilson messuage in Vincent and household goods paying to son John £100 at 21 and to daughter Jane £40 at 21 and to daughter Sarah £40 at 21. I give to daughter Elizaqbeth £5. To daughter Ann 50 shillings. To daughter Jane furniture including plates marked M.M. To daughter Mary, bed &c. and to daughter Sarah household goods.
Executors: Son Thomas and John Mathers of Radnor.
Wit: John Melchior, John Mathers, Jr.

DILWORTH, JAMES. Birmingham.
Aug. 10, 1769. Aug. 29, 1769.
Provides for wife Lydia including use of plantation devised to son Wm. at 21 subject to such right as my Uncle Charles Turner may have in the same. To son Charles mansion house and piece of land, he paying out of the same £230, to wit; to daughter Sarah £100, to daughter Mary £100, to son George £30 at 21. To sons Joseph and William remainder of land purchased of Wm. Dean, Richard Dilworth and Thos. Wood in Birmingham containing about 288 acres to be divided. Son Wm. to have the part on which the house stands where my Uncle Chas. Turner now lives. Son Joseph paying to daughter Lydia £100 and to daughter Hannah £50 at 18. Son Wm. to have his land at 21 and pay to daughter Hannah £50 at 21 and to daughter Letitia £100 at 21. To son James all my land south of the great road leading to Birmingham Meeting at 21. To son Caleb remainder of land purchased of Wm. and Titus Bennett at 21 paying to son George £200. To son George house and lott in Wilmington bought of John Chamberlin at 21.
Executors: Wife Lydia and sons Charles and Joseph.
Wit: Levi Massey, David Brinton, Jos. Pierce.

WILLIAMS, HUGH. Vincent. Aug. 30, 1769. Adm. to Robt. and Alex. Williams.

SHARPLESS, JOHN. North Providence. Sept. 9, 1769. Adm. to Thomas Swayne.

WOODWARD, WILLIAM. West Bradford.
7/30/1769. Aug. 29, 1769.
Provides for wife Hannah. To son Abraham £70. To daughter Hannah Woodward £40 and furniture. To son James £10. To daughter Mary Mendenhall £10. To step-daughter Betty Lewis £10. To son John plantation whereon I now dwell. Remainder divided between 4 sons and 2 daughters, viz., James, Abraham, William, John, Mary and

Hannah.
Executors: Wife Hannah and son Wm.
Wit: George Carter, Jas. Marshall, Jas. Woodward.

HOPE, AMOS. Kennett.
8/27/1769. Sept. 12, 1769.
Provides for wife Anne. To 2 daughters Mary and Elizabeth all real estate except tenement and 5 perches purchased of my brother John Hope which I give to Wm. Reath during his life as tenants in common, at 21, with reserve to Thomas son of brother Thomas Hope. Authorizes Executrix to convey tract of land sold unto Joshua Peirce in Kennett containing about 170 acres.
Executrix: Wife Anne.
Wit: Abrm. Marshall, Jos. Pierce, Wm. Harvey.

WAIT, MOSES. East Caln. Oct. 2, 1769. Adm. to James Marshall.

MC FETTRIDGE, DANIEL. East Fallowfield. Oct. 3, 1769. Adm. to Matthew McFettridge.

VERNON, NATHAN. Aston. Oct. 4, 1769. Adm. to Edward Vernon.

DILWORTH, RICHARD. East Whiteland. Oct. 7, 1769. Adm. to Susanna Dilworth.

HARLAN, EBENEZER. Londongrove.
2/28/1769. Sept. 23, 1769.
To brother Solomon 10 shillings. To sisters Betty and Ann 10 shillings each. To Joseph Harlan son of brother Solomon 10 shillings. To sister Hannah all remainder of personal estate. Gives his claim and interest in a tract of land in Concord devised by his Grandfather Henry Oburn to his 2 daughters Hannah and Susanna. To his brother Henry, also Executor.
Wit: Saml. Morton, Thomas Morton, Isaac Jackson.

CHANDLER, MARY. Widow. Birmingham.
March 21, 1769. Oct. 2, 1769.
To nephew Mankin James £4. To nephew Philip James £4. To Elizabeth wife of Isaac Chandler £8. To cousin Mary wife of John Robinson £8. To Ruth wife of John Champion £8. To Catherine wife of John Cann 10 shillings. To Richard brother of aforesaid Catherine Cann and son of Jos. James 10 shillings. To Ruth daughter of Thos. Buffington £5 at 18. Remainder to Thos. Buffington of Newlinton, also Executor.
Wit: Jas. Trimble, John Taylor, Wm. Cooper.

KNOWER, CHRISTOPHER. East Nantmeal.
July 5, 1766. Oct. 11, 1769.
Provides for wife Elizabeth. To son John plantation I now live on with mill at 21. To second son Christopher plantation on which Jacob Murry dwells on east side of French Creek containing 160 acres at 21. To daughters Barbara, Margaret, Catherine and Elizabeth £100 to be paid by 2 sons.
Executors: Friends Michael Severd and Daniel High. Letters to Michael Cypher, the other renouncing.

Wit: Robert Richey, Borick Beckholt, Mathias Lora.

HOOPES, JOSHUA. Westtown. Oct. 14, 1769. Adm. to Hannah Hoopes.

CULBERTSON, JANE. Kennett.
Sept. 17, 1769. Oct. 12, 1769.
To daughter Sarah Culbertson 46 acres of land now in my possession paying to grandson John Culbertson £10, also all personal estate. Executors to sell all remainder of real estate. To Rev. Jos. Smith £5. Remainder equally divided between daughters Jane, Mary and Marthew. To grandchildren, viz., David, Samuel and Nancy Porter 1 shilling each.
Executor: John McKim.
Wit: Robt. Brown, Jno. Hancock, Jno. McMickin.

SULLIVAN, DENNIS. Kennett.
Sept. 5, 1769. Oct. 19, 1769.
To wife Mary all estate until youngest child arrives at 18, then to be divided wife 1/3 and remainder equally divided among children who are not named.
Executrix: Wife Mary.
Wit: John Hancock, John Brown, John Eves.

PUGH, JAMES. Uwchlan.
11/25/1768. Oct. 21, 1769.
To son David Pugh £5. To daughter Mary wife of Thomas Delrumple £5. To daughter Margaret wife of James McClay £5. To daughter Anna wife of David Jenkin £5. To daughter Jemima wife of Patrick McCarty 20 shillings. To daughter Kezia Pugh £5. All remainder to wife Jemima Pugh, also Executrix.
Wit: Joseph Phillip, Cadwallader Jones, Benjamin Davies.

PHIPPS, JOSEPH JR. East Caln. Oct. 23, 1769. Adm. to Margaret Phipps.

SANDERSON, RICHARD. Concord.
Apr. 3, 1769. Oct. 21, 1769.
To nephew Richard Goff of Sherburn in Yorkshire and to Thomas Clayton of Milford in said shire, (my nephews), all my plantation in Concord whereon I now dwell containing about 210 acres excepting 30 acres hereafter devised. To nephew John Grame son of sister Mary £5. To Richard son of Richard Barker late of Stanford in Northamptonshire £30. To Joshua North, my cousin, £10 and to his wife Susanna £10. To Rev. George Craig of Chester £5. To my trusty and faithful mulatto man James Cherry £20, also during his life my log house where John Sullan now lives and 30 acres of land adjoining. Executors to set him free by manumission. Remainder to be divided between children of 3 sisters except above named, Richard Goff, Thos. Clayton and John Grame.
Executors: Rev. Geo. Craig and cousin Richd. North.
Wit: Benj. Kellam, Wm. Burnett, John Burnett, Jr.

SEAL, WILLIAM. Birmingham.
10/5/1769. Oct. 30, 1769.
Provides for wife Rachel. Real estate to be sold in 3 years to be

equally divided among 9 children, viz., Hannah wife of Peter Baker, Joseph, William, Caleb, Benjamin, Thomas, Rachel, Abraham and Joshua, by my brother Caleb and brothers-in-law Thomas Temple and Abraham Darlington.
Executors: Brother Caleb and friend James Bennett.
Wit: Abraham Darlington, Jr., Wm. McFatrich.

JOHNSON, ABRAHAM. Darby. Oct. 31, 1769. Adm. to Martha Johnson and Benja. Bonsall.

COBOURN, DAVID. Chester. Nov. 8, 1769. Adm. to Mary Cobourn.

PARRY, HANNAH (alias EVANS). Nov. 13, 1769. Adm. to Rowland Parry (her husband, daughter of [Alex]ander Evans).

YARNALL, MOSES. Willistown.
10/10/1768. Oct. 30, 1769.
To son Enoch plantation whereon I now live subject to wife Dows Yarnall's life interest. To wife Dows all personal estate except £50 which I give to daughter Rebecca Yarnall. To son David £10. To daughter Hannah Griffith. To daughter Rebecca Yarnall £20. To daughter Phebe Richards £10.
Executors: Wife Dows and son Enoch and son-in-law Wm. Griffith. Letters to Enoch Yarnall and Wm. Griffith, the other renouncing.
Wit: Isaac Massey, Phebe Massey, Levi Massey.

HALL, JOSEPH.
Feb. 16, 1765. Nov. 10, 1769.
All estate to wife Elizabeth and children Margaret, John, Hannah, Mary, Joseph, Steward, Elizabeth and Andrew Hall.
Executors: Wm. Hall and sons John and Joseph. Letters to John Hall, Wm. Hall being absent and Joseph being a minor under 12 years.
Wit: Hugh Stewart, Walter Hall, Thos. Willson.

MARLING, MARGERY. New London.
Aug. 20, 1769. Nov. 28, 1769.
To sister Sarah wife of James Stones 5 shillings, to Agnes Ferrior bed and bedding, to Agnes wife of Robert Crawford 5 shillings, to Elizabeth wife of Wm. McWhorter 5 shillings. John Robinson with whom I have lived this 20 years to have remainder if any, also Executor.
Wit: Cathrin Shmiser, Mary Gubby, John Scott.

JONES, JOSEPH. Pikeland. Dec. 2, 1769. Adm. to Thomas Lightfoot.

BROWN, MARY. Widow of Jeremiah. West Nottingham.
11/9/1769. Nov. 30, 1769.
To step-grandson Stephen son of Isaac Brown £20 being the payment coming to me from Esther Brown, at interest until he is 21. Best wearing apparel to be sent to my 3 sisters Elizabeth, Abigail and Catherine in Ireland. To cousin Elizabeth Thornton now living in Carolina £20. To Mary wife of Henry Reynolds case of drawers which was her mother's. To Sarah daughter of Isaac Brown riding mare and saddle. To Mary Lockland, my maid, bed at 18. All remainder to

Elisha, Mary, Jeremiah and Saml., children of Joshua Brown, and
George, Jeremiah, Isaac and Elisha, children of Isaac Brown.
Executors: Elisha son of Joshua and Jeremiah son of Isaac Brown.
Wit: John Butterfield, Rachel Johnson.

BUCHANAN, WILLIAM. West Nottingham.
Aug. 2, 1769. Codicil Nov. 25, 1769. Dec. 7, 1769.
Provides for wife Elizabeth. To son William £20. To son George
£10. To daughter Martha in Carolina £5. Executors to confirm to
Matthew Turner, my wife's son, when of age. Title to a certain
tract of land mentioned in a conveyance already made to him. To
son Walter plantation on which I now dwell at 21. Remainder to
wife and her 3 children born to me, viz., Walter, Ann and Elizabeth.
Executors: Wife and John McMillan. Letters to wife Elizabeth, the
other renouncing.
Codicil revokes legacy of plantation to Walter and orders it sold
and proceeds divided between wife and 3 children above named.
Wit: John Carmichael, Jas. Ochiltree.

HENRY, SAMUEL. Middletown. Dec. 12, 1769. Adm. to John
Cunningham.

HENDERSON, DANIEL. Sadsbury. Dec. 12, 1769. Adm. to Isabella
and Jos. Henderson.

BAYLIFFE, EDWARD. Newlin. Dec. 30, 1769. Adm. to Thomas
Bayliffe.

PEIRCE, HENRY. Concord.
Jan 21, 1769. Dec. 16, 1769.
Provides for wife Mary. To son Henry all my tract of land in
Concord at 21 paying to his brother William £50, also silverware.
Executors: Wife Mary and brother John Peirce.
Wit: Charles Perkins, Wm. Peirce, Jas. Johnson.

MILLER, WILLIAM. Middletown.
Dec. 10, 1769. Jan 15, 1770.
Provides for wife Jean. To daughter Elizabeth Love 5 shillings.
To daughter Martha Lindsay 5 shillings. To son William £20. To
daughter Mary Vernon 5 shillings. To daughter Jean Miller £5.
To son John £5. To daughter Isabel Miller £5. To daughter
Rebecca Miller £5. To son Brice Miller £20 at 21. To son Robert
remainder of estate real and personal.
Executors: Wife Jean and son Robert.
Wit: James McClelan, Saml. Trimble.

JOHNSON, DAVID. Lower Chichester.
Dec. 25, 1769. Jan. 16, 1770.
Provides for wife Hannah. To son Benjamin all my tract of land
in Chichester purchased of John Fairlamb, Esq., lately in tenure
of my brother Thomas Johnson containing about 54 acres, also 4
acres of Marsh Meadow. To son David at 21 messuage and tract of
land wherein I now dwell purchased of John Rowan containing about

60 acres, the above 4 acres excepted. All remainder of estate to 3 daughters, viz., Hannah, Rachel and Sarah at 18 or married.
Executrix: Wife Hannah.
Wit: Wm. Kerlin, Benjamin Ford, Joseph Marshall.

ASTON, WILLIAM. West Nantmeal. Jan 19, 1770. Adm. to Margaret Aston.

SCOTT, ABRAHAM. West Bradford. Jan 24, 1770. Adm. to John Dowdle.

POWELL, SUSANNA. Marple. Feby. 22, 1770. Adm. to Benjamin Powell.

THOMSON, JOHN. West Nantmeal. Feb. 28, 1770. Adm. to Elizabeth Thomson and Jas. Moore.

DAVIS, JOHN. Darby.
12/15/1769. Feb. 2, 1770.
To brother Lewis Davis plantation whereon I now dwell in Darby subject to his mother's life interest paying at her death £400. To sister Hannah Smith £50 in trust during her husband's life. To cousins Thos. Levis, Nathan Davis, and Benjamin Davis £10. To Pennsylvania Hospital £50. All remainder to mother and 4 sister[s] Rebecca, Ann, Mary and Sarah. Brother Lewis Davis and brothers-in-law John Levis and Wm. Parker.
Wit: Joshua Thomson, John Hibberd, Isaac Pearson.

STEWART, DAVID. New London.
June 24, 1769. Feb. 28, 1770.
To wife Sarah 1/3 of estate during life and at her death to son John and child expected to be born with reserve to John, Robert and Jane Stewart now living in Ireland.
Executors: John Fleming and John Scott.
Wit: Saml. Kennedy, Andrew Scott.

WALKER, JERMAN. Tredyffrin.
Jan 13, 1770. Mar. 2, 1770.
Provides for the maintenance of children, Thos. J., Lydia, Mary and Sarah during childhood with his sister Mary. To son Thomas Jerman Walker plantation where on I now dwell in Tredyffrin, formerly known as Thomas Jerman's Plantation, at 21. Remainder to 3 daughters.
Executors: Cousin Joseph Walker and friend Joshua Evans.
Wit: John Rowland, John Williams, James Davis.

LINFIELD, MARGARET. Londongrove.
Feb. 21, 1770. Mar. 2, 1770.
To sister Eleanor Barclay £20 and to her husband, John Barclay, 1 (2) shilling and to their children £20 to be divided. To Saml. Brown in Northampton Co. £10 and to his son Robt. £20. To Wm. McFaggon of Northampton Co. £20. To neighbor John Williamson £15 and to his wife Jane £5. To Mary wife of Jas. Harbison £10. To Mary wife of David Wiley £10. To Geo. Miles now of Va. as I am informed £20. To neighbor Jas. Moss £10. To neighbor Jos. Cook £10. To Wm. son of neighbor Jona. Lindley £10 at 21. To Francis

son of cousin John Bullock £10 at 21. To Jane Maxwell spinster £5. To Elizabeth Montgomery spinster of Londongrove £7. To Caleb Vance £5. To Overseers of Poor of Londongrove £5. Servant man Jacob Jackson to be free at my decease and paid £15 at 21. To John and Arthur Sewal of Ireland 1 shilling each.
Executors: Wm. Miller and Jas. Harbison. Letters to Miller.
Wit: Jona. Lindley, Saml. Miller, David Harbison.

HAVARD, JOHN. Tredyffrin. Mar. 20, 1770. Adm. to John Jacobs, Jr. and Saml. Havard.

GLENN, JOHN. Londonderry. Mar. 20, 1770. Adm. to Gilbert Buchannon.

TAYLOR, JOHN. Chester. Apr. 6, 1770. Adm. to Thomas Pedrick and Davis Bevan.

ROGERS, ROBERT. Middletown. Apr. 20, 1770. Adm. to Joseph Talbot, Jr.

HANNA, JOHN. West Nantmeal.
Mar. 7, 1770. Mar. 14, 1770.
Provides for wife Jane. To first born son John 5 shillings. To son William 5 shillings. To son James all real estate, viz., 216 acres in West Nantmeal. To son Robert £30. To daughter Agnes Culbertson £30. To daughter Elizabeth McCool £30. To daughter Margaret Galt £5. Remainder to son James, also Executor.
Wit: John McGoun, George Irwin.

CRABB, WILLIAM. Chichester.
Mar. 12, 1770. Apr. 21, 1770.
To sister Mary and her 5 children, to brother Benjamin's 3 children, Sarah, Mary and William, to sister, Sarah's 3 children Susanna, Sarah and Benjamin and to my granddaughter Margaret Johnston one guinea each. All remainder real or personal to wife Mary, also Executrix.
Wit: Richard Riley, Wm. Moulder.

JAMES, JOSEPH. Willistown.
Jan 6, 1770. May 12, 1770.
To grandson Joseph James all my land in Newtown where John Hambleton now dwelleth. Provides for wife Elizabeth. To 3 grandsons Saml., Wm. and Jesse James and their sister Hannah James £5 each at 21. To grandson Joseph Hoopes £5 at 21. To grandson John son of Jona. Ashbridge £10 at 21 and to daughter Sarah Ashbridge £5. All remainder of estate to daughter Mary Treviller and children of daughter Ann Yarnall to be divided.
Executor: Friend Joshua Evans, Geo. Ashbridge, Assistant.
Wit: Andrew Buchanan, Thos. Smedley, Lewis Gronow.

MILHOUSE, THOMAS. Pikeland.
2/25/1765. May 9, 1775.
To 3 eldest sons John, James and Thomas 5 shillings each they having received their share. Provides for wife Sarah. To son Robert and to daughter Sarah, wife of Thompson Parker, 1/3 of my

estate [each] {missing 1/3} son Bates. To son William, the remaining 1/3 of my estate.
Executrix: Wife Sarah. Letters c.t.a. to Wm. Millhouse, Executrix named renouncing.
Wit: Saml. Lightfoot, Wm. Lightfoot, Jr., Susanna Lightfoot.

FLETCHER, ELIZABETH. Darby.
Dec. 14, 1769. May 19, 1769.
To Mary wife of Richard Collier wearing apparel. To Dinah daughter of Abraham Lobb of Trenton remainder of clothes and furniture. Remainder real and personal to Diana Lobb and John Morton to be equally divided.
Executor: Isaac Lobb of Darby.
Wit: John Hibberd, Hannah Crozer.

NETSILLIS, ARTHUR. Darby.
Nov. 17, 1755. May 25, 1770.
Provides for wife Mary. To daughter Rachel Netsillis £20, furniture and "one of her choice of my negro children," her negro child to be raised and maintained out of my estate until the negro child is 16 years of age. To son Mathias all real and personal estate paying legacies.
Executors: Son Mathias and Wm. Donaldson of Darby. Letters to Mathias Netsillis, the other being deceased.
Wit: John Abm. Lidenus, John Justis, Luke Nidermark.

FLETCHER, JOHN. Londonderry. June 11, 1770. Adm. to Wm. Fletcher.

JOHNSTON, WILLIAM. Goshen.
Feb. 3, 1770. May 29, 1770.
Provides for wife Jane. To sons William, John and Joseph Johnston all real and personal estate subject to wife's life interest. To son James £20. To sons Samuel and Henry £20 each. To son David £50 at 22. To daughter Margaret £10. To daughter Jane £10.
Executors: Wife Jane and son Wm.
Wit: Isaac Haines, Francis Young, Thos. Taylor.

TAYLOR, JEREMIAH. Shoemaker. Kennett.
Mar. 9, 1754. June 1, 1770.
"Having a mind to go a voyage to sea," out of my estate and legacy my grandfather Jos. Taylor gave me, I bequeath -- To brother Joseph £100. To cousin Isaac Taylor £20. To cousin Benjamin Taylor £20. To cousin Elizabeth Taylor £10. To cousin Hannah Taylor £5. To cousin Anne Taylor £5. (children of Benj. and Sarah Taylor). To Mother £10. Remainder to cousins Isaac and Benj.
Executor: Uncle Benj. Taylor.
Wit: Edward Dawes, Wm. Shipley, Jr., Jonathan Rumford.

NOLLART, GEORGE. Baker. East Whiteland.
May 11, 1768. June 12, 1770.
All estate to wife Elizabeth during life and whatever shall remain at her decease to be equally divided among children, viz., Margaret Isinminger, Margaret Elizabeth Peters, Elizabeth Stone, Philip and Catherine Tothre. Share of daughter Margaret Elizabeth Peters to

be put into the hands of the Executor of the estate of her first husband Andrew Hay, late of Germantown, for use of her children by the said Andrew Hay. Mentions granddaughter Elizabeth Hay.
Executrix: Wife Elizabeth.
Wit: John Templeton, Jacob Ernest, Henry Atherton.

CROSBY, RICHARD. Ridley. June 27, 1770. Adm. to Wm. Worrall.

ALFORD, ELIZABETH. Kennett. June 27, 1770. Adm. to Alice Alford.

SHEERER, WILLIAM. West Nantmeal. June 29, 1770. Adm. to Mary Sheerer.

DAVIS, JOHN. East Bradford. July 25, 1770. Adm. to Mary Davis.

CARTER, JOHN. East Bradford. Aug. 15, 1770. Adm. to Hannah Carter.

EDDY, JOSEPH. Vincent. Apr. 18, 1770. Adm. to Mary and Wm. Eddy.

CLARK, JOHN. Kennett.
Aug. 23, 1769. June 12, 1770.
Provides for wife Mary. Remainder 2/3 of estate to be divided among children John, Elizabeth and William. Son Wm. to have £40 additional to raise and school him.
Executors: Wife Mary and son John.
Wit: Rebecca Thomson, William Pyle, Robt. Bratten.
** Elizabeth appears to have married Wm. Elliott. See Orphans Court 28 Dec. 1785.

MARTIN, ROGER. Charlestown.
June 1, 1770. July 7, 1770.
To St. Peters Church in Tredyffrin £10. To friend Roger Little £30. To nephew Roger, son of brother John Martin, £20. To my kinswoman Hannah, daughter of John Conoway, £5 at 19. To wife Jane all remainder of estate real and personal absolutely if she remains a widow, otherwise to be sold and 2/3 to Roger Little and children of brother John Martin.
Executrix: Wife Jane.
Guardians and Assistants: Brother-in-law Jas. Anderson and Robt. Ralston.
Wit: Valentine Fuss, John David, David John.

POWELL, JAMES. Marple.
Oct. 15, 1769. Aug. 11, 1770.
To nephew Benjamin Powell plantation whereon I now dwell, also all personal estate, he paying debts and legacies. To brother John's 2 children Mary and John £5 each when of age. To sister-in-law Susanna Powell £2. To nephew Saml. Powell £5 at 21.
Executors: Nephew Benj. Powell and friend John Morris.
Wit: Henry Lawrence, William Quin, Jas. Maris.

THOMAS, OLIVER. Chester. Aug. 17, 1770. Adm. to Sarah Thomas.

CLOUD, JOSEPH. Concord.
Aug. 11, 1770. Aug. 25, 1770.
To Wm. Vernon son of sister Ann plantation whereon I now live bounded by lands of Wm. Peters, John Skeen and others supposed to contain 130 acres, also stock, he paying to Mary, daughter of Joseph Kerlin of Virginia, £100, but if Wm. Vernon should marry the said Mary Kerlin then he shall pay £50 to his brother Jonathan. To sister Ann Vernon £6 per year during life. To niece Elizabeth Forrester £40. To Ann Bishop daughter of sister Mary Kerlin £20. To Joseph Kerlin of Va. £5. To Ann Dix, daughter of sister Ann Vernon £10. To Lydia Worrall, daughter of ditto. £30. To Frederick Engle son of sister Ann Vernon £100. To Ann daughter of John Kerlin of Whiteland £10. To Mary daughter of Frederick Engle aforesaid £10. To Joseph Engle son ditto. £10 when of age. To Joseph Whipple grandson of Elizabeth Forrester of New York £5 at 21. To Priscilla daughter of Mordecai Cloud £10. To Elizabeth wife of Saml. Vernon of Middletown £10. To John son of Joseph Kerlin of Va. £25 and to his sister Mary Kerlin riding mare. To Peter, Leah, James and Joseph, children of Jos. Kerlin £20 each. To John and Joshua Baldwin bed and furniture.
Executors: Cousins Mordecai Cloud and Frederick Engle.
Wit: Moses Palmer, John Palmer, Jas. Johnson.

GRAVES, JACOB. Uwchlan. Aug. 29, 1770. Adm. to Isaac Lewis.

YEARSLEY, THOMAS. Westtown. Aug. 29, 1770. Adm. to Joshua Smith and Thos. Mercer.

MILLS, JOHN. East Nottingham. Aug. 30, 1770. Adm. to John Lawson.

BALLA, ALEXANDER. Charlestown. Aug. 30, 1770. Adm. to Hannah Balla.

GARRETT, JOSEPH. Goshen.
5/1/1769. Aug. 30, 1770.
Provides for wife not named. To son James tract of land purchased of Robt. Williams. To son Jonathan that tract of land bought of Stephen Becks with a part of that I now live on, 24 acres, altogether 140 acres. To son Joseph plantation whereon I now live in Goshen except as above, paying to son Abram £100, also £300 out of my personal estate. To daughter Sarah White £50. To daughter Jane Haines £100. To grandson Jos. Eldridge £25 at 21.
Executors: Sons James and Joseph.
Wit: John Griffith, John Jacobs.

BENNETT, MARY. Relict of Jas. Aston.
Aug. 18, 1770. Sept. 11, 1770.
To son John Hill of Middletown 10 shillings. To daughter Margaret wife of Morris Matson £30. To daughter Mary wife of George Peirce £20. To my other daughter Christian wife of George Brinton £20. To 3 grandchildren Wm., James and John, sons of my son Alexander Hill deceased £30 at 21. Remainder to son Peter Hill of Middletown, also Executor.
Wit: John Burnet, James Lindsay.

MC LEAN, DANIEL.
Dec. 10, 1768. Sept. 18, 1769.
Provides for wife Isabella. To sons Patrick, James and John £10 each. To the children of my daughter Mary deceased who was wife to Jas. Calhoon 5 shillings each. To daughter Agnes wife of George Robb £1 and to her son Daniel £5 and to her daughter Jean 50 shillings and to her daughter Sarah Robb 50 shillings. To daughter Margaret wife of Matthew Thomson £10. To daughter Jean wife of John Glen £10 and to her oldest child Mary £25. To Jean Bailley daughter of my wife Isabella by her first husband cow and 2 sheep and to Elizabeth daughter ditto. cow &c. Mentions a legacy of about £60 received of estate of a certain Danl. McLene deceased which he leaves to his 3 sons.
Executors: Son John and John Scott of New London. Letters to John McLean, the other being absent.
Wit: Robert Boggs, Jno. Ramsay, John Campbell.

MAXWELL, WILLIAM. Marple. Sept. 20, 1770. Adm. to Jas. Rhoads and Nathl. Holland.

BOWEN, THOMAS. East Whiteland.
Aug. 25, 1770. Oct. 1, 1770.
Provides for wife Hester. Real estate to be sold when son Stephen is 21 and remainder divided amongst my children, viz., Mary, Stephen, Jonathan, Hester, Owen, Thomas, Linard and the child of which my wife is now pregnant. Children to be taught "to Reed, Right and Syfer as far as the rule of three" and sons "bound out to som genteel traid." Mentions his brother Jos. Bowen.
Executors: Wife Hester and cousin Joshua Evans and friend Saml. Davis. Letters to Hester, the others renouncing.
Wit: Josa. Humphreys, Abednego Jones, Richd. Richeson.

GRUBB, HANNAH. Widow. Wilmington.
9/20/1768. Oct. 1, 1770.
To son Benjamin Marshall £30 being already in his hands. To daughter Ann wife of Francis Hickman £5 and to the said Francis 5 shillings. To daughter Martha wife of Wm. Levis £5. To daughter Hannah wife of John Way £5. To daughter Mary wife of Caleb James £5. Wearing apparel and furniture to above 4 daughters. Remainder to son John Marshall, also Executor.
Wit: Vincent Pilkington, Rebecca Pilkington, Robt. Mendenhall.

HASTINGS, JAMES. West Bradford. Oct. 1, 1770. Adm. to James Trimble.

MC DOWELL, JOSHUA. London Britain. Oct. 31, 1770. Adm. to Sarah McDowell.

ABRAHAM, JAMES. East Nantmeal. Nov. 1, 1770. Adm. to Noah Abraham.

BARNARD, THOMAS. Chichester. Dec. 19, 1770. [No further information.]

GREGG, JOSEPH. Kennett.
July 26, 1770. Oct. 4, 1770.
Provides for wife Hannah. To 3 sons, Benjamin, Enoch and Isaac all real estate, that is to son Benj. 1/2 my plantation containing 200 acres to be taken off the end where he now lives. To son Isaac the other 1/2 of same. To son Enoch tract of land he now lives on in New Garden purchased of Geo. Sharp. To son Solomon all personal estate. To son-in-law John Bason 5 shillings.
Executors: 2 sons Benj. and Enoch.
Wit: Michael Gregg, Geo. Sharp, John Pyle, Jr.

LEMON, PHEBE. Willistown.
Nov. 27, 1770. Dec. 19, 1770.
To daughter Phebe Stuard £6 and household goods. To daughter Elizabeth wife of Jacob Melin remainder of wearing apparel. To grandchildren Wm. and Mary Melin all remainder of estate when they come of age.
Executor: Jacob Melin.
Wit: Levi Bowen, James Sill.

FRAME, NATHAN. Birmingham. Dec. 20, 1770. Adm. to Ruth Frame.

ROBINSON, ELEANOR. Jan 12, 1771. Adm. to Robert Robinson.

CLAYTON, ANN. Widow. West Bradford.
12/6/1770. Dec. 22, 1770.
To daughter Sarah Thornbury feather bed I now lie on. All remainder to be sold and divided between 4 daughters Hannah, Sarah, Ann and Susannah after paying 5 shillings each to sons John, Joshua and William, excepting my warming pan to daughter Susanna's child called Ann.
Executors: Son John and son-in-law Jonathan Buffington. Letters to Jona. Buffington.
Wit: Thos. Wickersham, Isaac Harvey, Jr., James Kenney.

OLIVER, JOHN. Chester.
Dec. 13, 1770. Dec. 24, 1770.
Gives 6 shillings to be equally divided among all children. To wife Mary all remainder of estate, also Executrix.
Wit: Rowland Burke, David Ogden.

GEST, PHEBE. Widow. Concord.
Dec. 27, 1770. Jan 22, 1771.
To son Joseph Gest plantation in Concord whereon I now live containing 150 acres paying to his sister Lydia £50. To son Enoch Gest plantation in Concord containing 200 acres commonly known by name of George Leas' place paying to his sister Sarah £50 at 18. To daughter Lydia case of drawers. To daughter Sarah furniture. To son Joseph all remainder.
Executors: Sons Joseph and Enoch. Letters to Joseph, the other being under 17 years of age.
Wit: Thomas Evan, John Parry, Jno. Hannum.

SMITH, JOSEPH. West Nantmeal. Feb. 25, 1771. Adm. to Margaret Smith.

JOHNSTON, ELIZABETH. [Place not given.]
Sept. 3, 1759. Feb. 6, 1771.
To sons Francis and Uphray 5 shillings each. To son David £2. To daughter Elizabeth Lamplay, clothing. To daughter Ann Ford ditto. Remainder to daughter Rachel.
Executors: Son David and daughter Rachel. Letters to Rachel, the other being deceased.
Wit: John Milsom, John Richards, Hugh Linn.

TREGO, ANN. Upper Providence.
11/29/1765. Feb. 26, 1771.
To daughter Mary Worrall wearing apparel. All remainder in trust for use of said daughter during life and at her death to her daughter Abigail Worrall with reserve to sister Susanna Whittaker.
Executors: Friends Gideon Malin and Peter Taylor.
Wit: George Miller, John Heacock.

YEARSLEY, HANNAH. Westtown.
Sept. 20, 1770. Feb. 26, 1771.
To daughter Lydia wife of Joshua Smith and daughters Sarah, Ann, Hannah and Patience Yearsley wearing apparel. To daughter Mary Yearsley 40 shillings which my son John left me. Remainder to sons Robert, Isaac, Thomas and Nathan and daughters Lydia, Sarah, Ann, Hannah, Patience and Mary Yearsley to be divided when sons are 21 and daughters 18.
Executor: Brother Thomas Mercer.
Wit: Jacob Sharpless, Richard Thornbury, Thos. Taylor.

HUNT, JOSEPH. Westtown. Feb. 28, 1771. Adm. to William Hunt.

BUCHANAN, GILBERT. West Nottingham.
Oct. 10, 1770. Mar. 14, 1771.
Provides for wife Mary. To eldest son Walter 5 shillings. To eldest daughter Sarah 5 shillings. To daughter Agnes a cow. To daughter Margaret 5 shillings and heifer. Remainder to daughters Agnes and Janet, also Executrixs.
Overseers: Son Walter and Wm. McLaughlin.
Wit: John McLaughlin, Hugh Murrin, Jas. McLaughlin.

HUNT, REBECCA. Widow. Wilmington.
10/1/1770. Mar. 16, 1771.
To daughter Hannah wife of Edward Bonsall £30. To granddaughter Rebecca Gleave £30. To granddaughter Elizabeth Gleave £30 at 18. To grandson James, son of Mary Gleave, £10 at 21. To daughter Elizabeth Howell all wearing apparel and to her daughter Ruth Howel [1] my clock and to her daughter Mary Kendal furniture.
Executors: Son John Hunt and Edward Bonsal.
Wit: Nathan Wood, Jas. Kightley, Elizabeth Kightley.

THATCHER, EDITH. Widow. Concord.
2/14/1771. Mar. 19, 1771.
To son William Thatcher riding chair, &c. To sons Jonathan, Samuel and Stephen 20 shillings each. To daughter Hannah wife of Joshua Haines £5. To daugher Sarah wife of Daniel Bailiff £10. To daughter Ann wife of Thomas Canby £10. To daughter Phebe Hyett

£10. To daughter Mary Thatcher £30 and her uncle Emanuel Grubb to have care of her. To granddaughters Edith Canby and Edith Thatcher £5 each. Remainder to son Thomas, also Executor.
Wit: Robt. Chamberlin, Ann Chamberlin, Jos. Pierce.

PEIRSOLL, JEREMIAH. West Nantmeal. Mar. 19, 1771. Adm. to Bathsheba Peirsoll.

HOBSON, JOSEPH. Londongrove. Mar. 25, 1771. Adm. to Joseph Hobson.

FULTON, SAMUEL. Oxford. Mar. 25, 1771. Adm. to William Ewing.

WALKER, WILLIAM. Vincent. Mar. 26, 1771. Adm. to Hugh Strickland.

CORSGRAVE, MARY. East Marlborough. Mar. 26, 1771. Adm. to Catharine Johnson.

CHARLTON, THOMAS. Londonderry.
Mar. 21, 1770. Mar. 26, 1771.
Provides for wife Elizabeth. To son Thomas 1/2 remainder of real and personal estate. To 2 daughters Elizabeth and Isabella Amy Charlton the remainder 1/2 of estate.
Executors: Wife Elizabeth, brother Henry and Edward Crooks.
Wit: Michael Roan, Neill Brown, Joseph Caldwell.

CLELAND, SAMUEL. Londonderry.
Dec. 10, 1770. Mar. 27, 1771.
All estate to be sold and proceeds for support of wife Mary and two children, Benjamin and Sarah during her widowhood. At death or marriage 2/3 to Benjamin and 1/3 to Sarah.
Executors: Wife Mary, father-in-law Saml. Bettey and Thos. Strawbridge.
Wit: Wm. Kerr, James Law.

LEPER, ANDREW.
Apr. 9, 1771. Apr. 15, 1771.
Provides for wife Elizabeth. To 3 daughters Margaret Porter, Mary Ramsey and Isabel Maxwell £100 each. If my son James "who hath been long absent doth not return," I give him 5 shillings.
Executors: Sons[in law] Wm. Ramsey and Jas. Maxwell.
Wit: Jos. Coulson, James Scott, John Johnson, David Smith.

MORRIS, THOMAS. Whiteland.
Feb. 20, 1756. Apr. 23, 1771.
To daughter Ester £10. To daughter Ann 20 shillings. To daughter Margaret £20. To grandson Benjamin Jenkin £2.10. To granddaughter Elizabeth Jenkin £2.10. To son Joseph Morris all real and personal estate except above legacies, also Executor.
Wit: Wm. Beale, Mary Beale, David Jenkin.

NOLLART, GEORGE. East Whiteland. Apr. 22, 1771. [No further information.]

MARTIN, GEORGE. West Bradford.
3/5/1771. Apr. 27, 1771.
To wife Martha all estate for support of children until daughter Sarah is 21, then to be divided. To wife 1/3 and remainder divided equally between my 6 children, viz., Sarah, Ruth, Lydia, Thomas, George and Abraham.
Executors: Wife Martha and brother Jos. Martin.
Wit: Jos. Woodward, Jas. Woodward, Jas. Marshall.

ROADS, PETER. Vincent.
Jan 22, 1771. Apr. 29, 1771.
Provides for wife Mary. To oldest son John Roads all plantation containing 270 acres in Vincent paying £300 to my executors. To son Henry tract of land where son John now lives containing 75 acres when he is 21. Younger children referred to, but not named.
Executors: Son John and Henry Acor.
Wit: Peter Miller, Conrod Shunk.

PENNOCK, JOSEPH. West Marlborough.
10/28/1770. May 2, 1771.
Mentions having already given sons Samuel, William, Nathaniel and Joseph and daughter Elizabeth tracts of land. To daughter Elizabeth Tatnall (Matnall, M crossed out and T. added) £20 and each of her 4 children Mary, Joseph, Elizabeth and Sarah £10. To daughter Sarah Marshall £50 to be paid by son Nathaniel and £100 additional. To son Levis plantation whereon I now dwell in West Marlborough containing 700 acres paying to daughter Sarah £50. To grandsons Joseph and Samuel, sons of son Saml. deceased, what money may be due me from their father's estate. Remainder to sons Nathaniel, Joseph and Levis and sons of son Wm. deceased, viz., Wm. Caleb, Saml. and Joshua.
Executors: Sons Nathaniel and Levis.
Wit: George Passmore, John Passmore, Jos. Davis.

JENKIN, JOHN. East Nantmeal.
June 10, 1765. May 6, 1771.
To sons Evan, David, Benjamin and daughters Mary Thomas and Sarah Hines 7 shillings each. All remainder to wife Catherine, also Executrix.
Wit: Hannah Loyd, Thomas Loyd.

CLOYD, JAMES.
Apr. 12, 1769. Codicil Mar. 14, 1771. May 7, 1771.
To son James my plantation in Charlestown where I now dwell containing 110 acres, also stock subject to life interest of wife Margaret. To 2 daughters Rebecca and Elizabeth Cloyd remaining 2/3 of personal estate. Estate in East Whiteland to be sold and proceeds divided. To daughter Rebecca £55 when of age. To daughter Elizabeth £60 when of age. To son David 1 shilling having already advanced him. All remainder to daughters Mary, Sarah, Margaret, Jane, Rebecca and Elizabeth.
Executors: John Jacobs and Richard Richison.
Wit: Benjamin Bond, John Adams, Zepheniah Davies.

GILLESPIE, WILLIAM. New London. May 29, 1771. Adm. to John Gillespie.

BOND, PAUL. Whiteland.
3/19/1764. May 11, 1771.
Provides for wife Hannah. To daughter Hannah Garrett 7 shillings [?] 6. To daughter-in-law Mary Bond 5 shillings. To granddaughter Ann Bond £5 at 18. To son Joseph all my lands, also residuary legatee and Executor with wife Hannah.
Wit: Thomas Lewis, Lewis Williams, Miriam Williams.

PALMER, JOHN. Concord.
Mar. 14, 1758. May 16, 1771.
To son John my plantation in Concord containing 175 acres subject to wife Martha's life interest. To son Moses 20 shillings. To daughter Elizabeth Eavenson 20 shillings. To daughter Martha Chamberlin 20 shillings. Remainder to wife Martha.
Executors: Wife and son John. Letters to John, the other renouncing.
Wit: John Milson, Wm. Walter, Jno. Hannum.

JENKIN, JOHN. Uwchlan.
June 18, 1770. May 30, 1771.
To sons John, Jeremiah, Amos, David, Jehu and 3 daughters, Margaret widow of Evan John, Ann wife of Wm. Davis and Mary widow of Isaac Lewis, an equal share of all my estate real and personal.
Executors: Isaac Lewis and Noble Butler, Sr.
Wit: Stephen Phillips, David Phillips, Danl. Phillips.

CARLETON, SARAH. Kennett.
12/22/1770. June 3, 1771.
To kinsman Thomas Carleton, Jr. and Lydia Carleton furniture and household goods. To kinswoman Susanna Harlan £15 and wearing apparel and to her children Hannah and Sarah £5 each. to kinsman Thos. Carleton's children £5 at 21, viz., Hannah, Dinah, Martha, Mark and Samuel. To sister Mary Mills, if living, wearing apparel.
Executors: Brother Thos. Carleton and kinsman Thos. Carleton, Jr.
Wit: John Lamborn, Saml. Heald, Thos. James.

SHAW, EDWARD. Ridley. June 3, 1771. Adm. to John Bryan.

ROWAN, MICHAEL. Londonderry. June 17, 1771. Adm. to (widow) Agnes and James Rowan. Left children, James, Jane, David, Mary, Agnes, Sarah, Samuel, Mary Ann and Dorcas 160 acres in Londonderry.

HETHERINTON, HENRY. West Fallowfield. July 18, 1771. Adm. to John Hetherinton.

MILLER, DOROTHY. Upper Providence.
5/27/1771. June 11, 1771.
To Susanna daughter of sister Sarah Coats all wearing apparel. To Sarah daughter to brother George Miller silverware. Remainder for use of brother Henry Miller.
Executors: Thos. Bishop and John Minshall.
Wit: Mary Grubb, John Minshall.

GRUBB, HENRY.   Middletown.
July 3, 1770.   Aug. 28, 1771.
To cousin Curtis Grubb of Lancaster Co. £90 and to his son Peter £10. To cousin Peter Grubb of Lancaster Co. plantation where I now dwell in Middletown containing about 253 acres and all other real estate.
Executor: Cousin Peter Grubb.
Wit: John Ross (Phila.), Geo. North, Jr. (Phila.), James Lukens.

BLACK JOSEPH.   Edgmont.
Aug. 18, 1769.   July 20, 1771.
Provides for wife Anne. To 2 daughters Anne and Mary £30 each at 18. To son Joseph plantation in Edgmont purchased of Thos. Bishop when he is 21. To son Samuel plantation in Edgmont purchased of Richard Sill at 21. To son William 5 shillings. All remainder to 5 children Joseph, Samuel, Anne, Margaret and Mary when of age.
Executors: Wife Anne and friend James Hemphill. Letters to wife, the other renouncing.
Wit: H. H. Graham, Jno. Pedrick, Edwd. Bettle.

CLAYTON, ADAM.   Chichester.   July 22, 1771.   Adm. to Hannah Clayton.

COX, JOHN.   Chester.   July 23, 1771.   Adm. to Mary Cox and John Lewis.

BARTRAM, JAMES.   Marple.
4/23/1771.   Aug. 5, 1771.
Provides for wife Elizabeth. To granddaughter Elizabeth wife of Isaac Maris plantation whereon I now dwell in Marple containing about 242 acres, allowing to my granddaughters Eliza and Sarah Howell house room until marriage. To granddaughter Eliza Howell my messuage and lotts in Wilmington at 21 or marriage, also £100. To granddaughter Sarah Howell plantation and 2 tracts of land in Marple containing together 200 acres, also £50 at 21 or marriage. To kinsman James Bartram son of brother John £5. Remainder to wife.
Executors: Lewis Davis and James Rhoads.
Wit: Seth Pancoast, Elisha Worrall, Isaac Pearson.

RALSTON, JOHN.   Vincent.
July 29, 1771.   Aug. 26, 1771.
To sister Margaret Fitzsimons 10 shillings. To brother Robert Ralston 20 shillings and to his wife Elizabeth £30. To Rev. William Currey 40 shillings. Remainder to John and James Ralston my brother's sons.
Executors: Brother Robert and neighbor Aaron Watkin.
Wit: John Fitzsummons, Joseph Cox, Edw. Bell.

HANLEY, JOHN.   Londonderry.   Aug. 22, 1771.   Adm. to John Wickersham.

RICHEY, ALEXANDER.   Oxford.   Aug. 31, 1771.   Adm. to John and Geo. Richey.

JONES, RICHARD. Now of Thornburry.
Feb. 8, 1769. Aug. 28, 1771.
To son Rees Jones all wearing apparel. To daughter Deborah wife of John Cheyney furniture. To daughter Rebecca wife of Wm. Rettew ditto. Divides remainder among children Rees Jones, Ann Goodwin, Rebecca Rettew, Deborah Cheyney and children of deceased son Nehemiah, viz., Robert and Rebecca Jones.
Executor: Son in law John Cheyney.
Wit: Thos. Cheyney, Thos. Mercer, Thos. Howell.

MASHMAN, JOHN. West Nottingham.
7/7/1771. Aug. 29, 1771.
Provides for wife Phebe. Plantation whereon I now live to be sold when youngest son James is 10 years old and money equally divided among my 5 children, viz., Joseph, John, Esther, Margaret and James.
Executrix: Wife Phebe.
Wit: Wm. Haines, Saml. Reynolds, Job Haines.

COOPER, ADAM. Oxford.
Feb. 4, 1771. Aug. 31, 1771.
To wife Mary £40. To brother Jas. Cooper my books. To son James my jockey coat. To son Adam all wearing apparel. To son Hugh £5. To daughter Mary cow and calf. Executors to sell all real estate and divide among children, viz., John, Thomas, James, Adam, Alexander, Hugh, Mary, Margret Jane, Finval and the child my wife is now pregnant with.
Executors: James Cooper and John Stuart.
Wit: Jas. Henry, John Murray, Jos. McConnell.

WILLIAMSON, THOMAS. Thornbury. Sept. 16, 1771. Adm. to Geo. Eavenson and Thos. Bishop.

RICHEY, ANDREW. Oxford.
Feb. 5, 1771. Aug. 31, 1771.
Provides for wife Mary. To son John the land on which he now lives which is to be 100 acres. To daughter Susanna £30. To son William the land he now lives on which is to be 100 acres during life, at his decease to his son Andrew. To son George plantation whereon I now live which is 166 acres.
Executors: Sons John and George.
Wit: Jas. Cooper, Jas. Henry, Robert Smith.

CHAMBERLIN, ISAAC. Aston.
8/8/1771. Sept. 3, 1771.
To wife Elizabeth messuage of 41 acres in Aston. To brother Wm. Chamberlin, brother John and sister Mary wife of Andrew McCoy 20 shillings each. All remainder to wife Elizabeth, also Executrix.
Wit: Jos. Chamberlin, Saml. Sharpless, Danl. Sharpless.

WHITE, MARGARET. Widow of Thomas. Oxford.
Aug. 17, 1759. Sept. 17, 1771.
To son Thomas £3. To son Robert £3. To granddaughter Margaret McCaddon who hath lived with me £10 and wearing apparel. To son Henry McCaddon what little money he owed me. Remainder to son

Mathew, also Executor.
Wit: Henry McCadden, John Fleming.

FIKE, CHRISTIAN. East Whiteland.
Aug. 27, 1771. Sept. 20, 1771.
To 2 sons John and Christian Fike all my plantation in East Whiteland whereon I now live containing 160 acres, also my interest in a late purchase made of Executors of James Cloyd deceased. Provides for wife Barbara. To daughters Ann, Barbara, Mary, Margaret and Cathrin £50 each. Remainder to sons John, Christian and Jacob and 5 daughters above named.
Executor: Son John.
Wit: Adam Rickenberger, John Zug, John Showalter.

MILLER, JOHN. New London. Sept. 20, 1771. Adm. to Ann Miller.

THOMAS, MARY. Widow. Charlestown.
Sept. 19, 1771. Sept. 30, 1771.
To son William balance due me from my deceased husband's estate and negro man Dick. To son Benjamin negro lad and his bond of £50 due to me. To grandson Wm. son of Benj. Thomas the plantation whereon I now dwell containing 100 acres at 18. To granddaughter Mary Thomas case of drawers and silver watch. To granddaughters Ann and Rebecca Thomas clothing. To daughter Sarah Martin negro wench called Hegor. Remainder to son Benjamin and daughter Sarah Martin. Bond of James Martin for £50 to be delivered up to him.
Executors: Richard Richison and John Jacobs.
Wit: Jonathan Wells, Hezekiah Davies, Nicholas Foose.

MC HARG, JOHN. Sadsbury.
Aug. 30, 1771. Oct. 4, 1771.
To brother George McHary all my estate.
Executor: Alexander Simral.
Wit: Alexander McPherson, James Simrall.

MC PHERSON, JANE. Sadsbury.
Oct. 24, 1768. Oct. 4, 1771.
To grandson John and granddaughter Jane McPherson £5 each. To son Robert McPherson's 2 daughters Cathrin and Jane £5 each. To son Robert £30. To neefue [nephew] Jean White £25 and household goods. To son Alexander all remainder of estate.
Executors: Alex. and Robt.
Wit: James Blelock, William Blelock.

MAXFIELD, JOHN. Sadsbury. Oct. 11, 1771. Adm. to Margaret Maxfield.

JOHNSON, HENRY. Lower Chichester. Oct. 17, 1771. Adm. to John Flower.

ALEXANDER, WILLIAM. Darby. Oct. 18, 1771. Adm. to Margaret Alexander.

REECE, DANIEL. Easttown. Oct. 19, 1771. Adm. to Sarah Reece.

WHARRY, JAMES. East Nottingham.
July 19, 1771. Oct. 17, 1771.
Provides for wife Ann. To daughters Mary and Ann £80 each.
Remainder of estate to be divided between sons James and David when
James comes of age which will be in 1777.
Executrix: Wife Ann.
Wit: Danl. Brown, Robert Thompson.

PENNELL, HANNAH. Marple.
Jan 4, 1771. Oct. 19, 1771.
to husband Joshua Pennell 50 shillings out of money arising from
sale of lands left me by my mother Mary Waln. To son Evan 50
shillings. To my other 3 children Hayes and Joshua Pennell and
Hannah Yarnall the remainder of said money.
Executor: Friend William Fell of Springfield.
Wit: Danl. Hoopes, Mary Kirk, Mealchi Effinger.

EVANS, JOHN. Uwchlan.
No date. Oct. 15, 1771.
To grandson John son of David Evans gun and a chest. To son
Jonathan £10 and 5 shillings to each of his children. All
remainder to son David for support of wife Mary during life.
Executors: Son David and friend Griffith John, Jr.
Wit: Saml. Lightfoot, Benj. Parvin, Jane Wily.

ASKEW, LAZARUS. Chester. Oct. 29, 1771. Adm. to Joseph and Mabel
Brown.

DAVIS, JAMES. East Bradford. Nov. 1, 1771. Adm. to Mary and
Daniel Davis. [Moore crossed out and Davis added.]

ALLEN, JOHN. Londongrove.
12/7/1769. Nov. 5, 1771.
Provides for wife Amy. To son William plantation on which I now
dwell containing 63 acres and my right in grist mill, also part of
200 acre tract in New Garden, also tract of 68 acres lying west of
the other, he paying to his late deceased brother John's children,
Hannah £5, Amy £5, Ann £20, John £20 and Samuel £20. To son Joseph
5 shillings and wearing apparel. To son Benjamin remainder of 200
acre tract in New Garden. Tract of 37 3/4 acres between land of
Stephen Ailes deceased and Jas. Greenfield, to sons Wm., Joseph and
Benjamin. To daughter Elizabeth Dixon £50. To daughter Phebe
Thompson £40. To 4 grandchildren William, Emey, Ruth and Hannah
Moode £5 each. To granddaughter Elizabeth Ward 1 shilling. To 2
grandsons Thomas and Philip Ward £15 each. To grandson John
Fraizer £20 at 21.
Executors: Son-in-law Wm. Chandler and his wife Rebecca.
Wit: Saml. Sharp, David England, Lewis Lemert.

MILLER, SAMUEL. Sadsbury.
6/8/1769. Oct 1. Nov. 16, 1771. [Oct 1 written at top of Nov 16,
but not crossed out.]
To grandson Samuel Miller £10. To grandson Robert Cooper £10. To
grandsons Calvin and William Cooper £5 each. To granddaughter Mary
Miller bed and bedding. To Sadsbury Meeting £2 toward repairing

grave yard fence. Remainder to only son Robert Miller.
Executors: Jos. Williams and Thos. Truman. Letters to Truman.
Wit: William Moore, James Hennen.

THOMPSON, HENRY. East Caln. Nov. 26, 1771. Adm. to Richard Downing.

WOODWARD, ENOCH. East Marlborough. Nov. 27, 1771. Adm. to Zachariah and Catherine Shuggart.

PYLE, JOHN. Kennett.
7/5/1771. Nov. 16, 1771.
Provides for wife Sarah. To son John plantation I now live on, also small tract lately purchased of Michael Gregg except as hereafter devised paying to his brother James £160 at 21. £60 to sons John and William in trust for use of daughter Lidy Daharty. Remainder of personal estate to 8 children, viz., John, Mary, Abigail, Elizabeth, Olive, Lidy, William and James. To son William part of my said plantation 73 acres, also about 2 acres adj. To son James 20 acres adj. above and 2 acres meadow below Geo. Mason's saw mill on Red Clay Creek when he is 21.
Executor: Son John.
Wit: Geo. Sharp, Isaac Gregg, Robt. Lamborn, Jr.

KINKEAD, JOHN. Sadsbury.
Nov. 29, 1770. Nov. 29, 1771.
Provides for wife Mary. To son Charles all real estate paying legacies. To sons David, John and Samuel £20 each. To 4 sons-in-law Adam Hope, Thos. Kirkpatrick, John Simral and Josiah Crawford £12 each. To son James £50.
Executors: Sons David and John. Letters to John, David renouncing.
[Wit: none mentioned here.]

MATLACK, JOSEPH. Goshen.
11/9/1771. Nov. 30, 1771.
To son Isaiah £10. To son Nathan £75 in trust for his son Nathan when he is 21. To daughter Jemima widow of James Pennell £50. To daughter Ruth wife of Thos. Sheward £35. To daughter Esther wife of Geo. Brinton £50. To son Amos tract of land in Goshen containing 120 acres. All remainder of land I now live on to son Jonathan containing 170 acres.
Executor: Son Jonathan residuary legatee.
Wit: Wm. Dunwoody, Jr., Thomas Butler, Ralph Forrester.

STARRETT, JOHN. East Nantmeal. Dec. 3, 1771. Adm. to Anne and James Starrett.

EVANS, ANNE. East Whiteland. Dec. 4, 1771. Adm. to James Williams.

PILKINGTON, EDWARD. Lower Chichester. Dec. 13, 1771. Adm. to Margaret Pilkington.

GRIFFITH, MARY. Widow. Willistown.
Aug. 15, 1766. Dec. 4, 1771.

To daughter Sarah John all wearing apparel and £15. To granddaughters Susanna, Margaret and Mary £5 each. To great-granddaughter Ann daughter of said granddaughter Susanna £4 at 18. [no last names given for granddaughters.] To kinswoman Rachel Lewis that lives with me £15 and to her son Joel Lewis £20 and to her daughter Lydia Lewis £5. To Hannah Owen daughter of said Rachel Lewis £5 at 18. To Enoch Lewis son of Rachel £2.10. To Nathan Lewis son of ditto. £2.10. To Jacob Lewis £5. To Jane wife of Wm. Atherton of West Whiteland £5. To Thomas John of Willistown 5 shillings. To Rachel Lewis and Joel Lewis all remainder of estate.
Executors: Randle Melin and Jos. Williams.
Wit: Thomas Lewis, Moses David, David John.

EYRE, LEWIS. Bethel.
11/25/1771. Dec. 16, 1771.
To brother John Eyre messuage and lot of land in Chester Borough and all lands in Upper Chichester. To mother Mary Eyre £12. To brother Isaac £200. To brother Wm. all my staves and cooper tools. Remainder to mother, brother Wm. and sister Ann. Land brother Robert lives on to him during life and then to his son John.
Executors: Brothers Wm., John and Isaac. Letters to Isaac, the others renouncing.
Wit: John Askew, Francis Dutton.

HUGHES, ELISHA. East Nottingham. Dec. 20, 1771. Adm. to Mary Hughes and Timothy Kirk.

BARTRAM, ELIZABETH. Widow. Marple.
10/30/1771. Dec. 17, 1771.
To granddaughter Elizabeth wife of Isaac Maris furniture. To granddaughter Eliza Bartram wife of John Bartram, Jr. furniture and £100 at 21. To granddaughter Sarah Howell household goods. To my nurse Margaret Easton £10. To great grandchild Mary Maris £5. To great grandchild Elizabeth Maris £5 at 21. Remainder to 3 grandchildren Elizabeth Maris, Eliza Bartram and Sarah Howell.
Executors: Lewis Davis and James Rhoads.
Wit: Seth Pancoast, Elisha Worrall, Isa. Pearson.

WILLIAMSON, HANNAH. Willistown.
9/24/1771. Jan 8, 1772.
To daughter Margaret Bishop and daughter Abigail Lewis household goods. To granddaughters Hannah and Jane Harris pewter. To son-in-law Richard Harris and wife Hannah all remainder of household goods and wearing apparel. Remainder divided among all children share of daughter Abigail in trust.
Executor: Son-in-law Thomas Bishop.
Wit: George Miller, Thos. Smedley.

CHEYNEY, ANN. Thornbury.
8/27/1771. Jan 10, 1772.
To son Thomas Cheyney £140. To son John £80. To son Joseph £80. To son Richard 5 shillings over and above what he owes me. To granddaughters Lucy, Ann and Mary furniture and wearing apparel and £10. To Hannah Garton furniture. Remainder to sons Thomas, John, Joseph, Richard and daughter Mary Riley and granddaughter Ann

daughter of Thomas.
Executors: Richard Cheyney and Richard Riley.
Wit: Thomas Howell, Jos. Gibbons.

CLOTHIER, ELEANOR. West Nottingham. Jan 13, 1772. Adm. to Thomas Brown.

WILSON, JAMES. West Caln.
May 28, 1771. Jan 10, 1772.
To son James £10. Remainder of estate to be divided into 5 parts -- one part to daughter Ann Elliot wife of John and her children born to James Fleming. To 3 daughters Mary, Jean and Mable 1/5 part each, the remainder 1/5, to 2 granddaughters Mable McMath alias Kelso and Martha Kelso.
Executors: Friends Robt. and Saml. Withrow.
Wit: Alexander Davidson, Wm. Withrow, Peter Hafan.

THOMPSON, MOSES. Marple.
Jan 1, 1772. Jan 16, 1772.
Provides for wife Veronica. All remainder to 3 daughters, viz., Martha (by first wife), Mary and Grace "and the child where with my wife is now enscint," to be equally divided when of age. Bequeaths the best of my wearing apparel to brother Thomas Thomson and the worst and oldest of ditto. to Wm. Mason.
Executors: Friends Joseph Rhoads and Isaac Rhoads.
Wit: Charles Linn, Nathl. Holland, Elisha Worrall.

IRWIN, ROBERT. East Caln.
Oct. 9, 1771. Feb. 27, 1772.
Provides for wife Isabel. To only son George all my real estate, viz., 200 acres in East Caln. To daughter Margaret £15 at 18. To daughter Mary £15 at 18. To daughter Isabella £15 at 18. To daughter Rebecca who was born blind in part her maintenance during life and if she marries £15.
Executors: Wife Isabel and son Geo.
Wit: Archibald Irwin, Geo. Irwin.

LEA, JAMES. Chester. Jan 27, 1772. Adm. to Isaac Eyre.

FAWKES, WILLIAM. Feb. 8, 1772. Adm. to Richard Fawkes.

GARVER, HENRY. West Nantmeal. Feb. 14, 1772. Adm. to Peter Garver and John Rup.

JOHNSTON, JANE. Westtown. Feb. 15, 1772. Adm. to William Johnston.

MORTON, THOMAS. West Nottingham. Feb. 25, 1772. Adm. to James and Robert Morton.

WOOD, ISAAC. Lower Chichester. Feb. 27, 1772. Adm. to Elizabeth Wood.

GREEN, EDWARD. Cooper. Thornbury.
Jan 19, 1772. Feb. 4, 1772.

To son Thomas 7 shillings 6, but if he shall fairly settle the account I have against him, I give him £10. To son Joseph such debts as are due from him to me. To son Edward £10. To daughters Sarah and Rachel £10 each at 21. To daughter Margaret £10. To daughter Rebecca £25 at 21. To children of daughter Margaret 7 sheep. Remainder equally divided. Mentions son-in-law Geo. Fryer. Executors: Friends Thos. Cheyney and Persifor Frazer.
Wit: Levi Pyle, John Reed, Hugh Reed.

HEALD, RACHEL. Kennett.
2/18/1772. Feb. 24, 1772.
To daughter Ann Welsh £20. To daughter Sarah Heald £25. To daughter Mary McKenny £10 and what her husband owes me. Remainder to grandchildren. To son Samuel's children Jacob and Rachel £4 each. Granddaughter Rachel Welsh bed.
Executors: Daughters Ann Welsh and Sarah Heald.
Wit: Jacob Heald, Jr., George Green, Thos. Carleton.

DOWNING, THOMAS. East Caln.
9/9/1769. Feb. 28, 1772.
Provides for wife Jane including £8 per year which she is entitled to out of her former husband's estate. To son-in-law Joshua Baldwin piece of ground along north side of Conestogoe Road paying to Executors £25. Having given to son William dwelling house and grist mill where he now lives and 150 acres in Bart Twp., Lancaster Co., I now give him his bond for £50. To son Joseph plantation in East Caln containing 492 acres purchased of Saml. Gilpin, also remainder of tract bought of Noble Butler containing between 50 and 60 acres in East Caln, also farming utensils. To son-in-law Saml. Bond tract of land in Whiteland known by the name of *Thos. Blandfords*. To son Richard grist and fulling mill in East Caln with tract of land belonging containing 230 acres, also water right reserved in deed of land to son John. Saw and hemp mill in East Caln to sons Richard, Joseph and John and son-in-law Saml. Bond in equal shares. To daughter Jane wife of John Roberts £50 having already advanced her. To son-in-law Saml. Bond £50. Having already advanced my daughter Sarah Baldwin deceased, I now give my granddaughter Sarah Baldwin £50. To Mary daughter of Thos. Alcott late of East Caln deceased £20 at 21. To Andrew Knox 10 acres of cleared land during life. Forgives all "poor people of all the Book debts that may stand in my Book against them."
Executors: Sons Richard and Joseph.
Wit: Robt. Valentine, Joshua Way, Isaac Jacobs.

WAYNE, SARAH. Tredyffrin. Feb. 27, 1772. Adm. to Joel Evans.

JONES, JOHN. East Bradford. Mar. 26, 1772. Adm. to Sarah Jones and Isaac Taylor.

ROWLAND, JANE. West Nottingham. Apr. 1, 1772. Adm. to John Smith.

ROWLAND, JAMES. West Nottingham. Apr. 1, 1772. Adm. to John Smith.

DAWSON, THOMAS. West Caln.
Aug. 12, 1771. Mar. 25, 1772.
Provides for wife Margaret. To daughter Rachel married to Jos. Park £70. To daughter Elizabeth £100. To son William £100. To son David tract of land containing about 450 acres. To daughter Ann £100, to daughter Mary £80, to daughters Margaret and Jean £100 each, to son Thomas £80 to be paid each of them at 21.
Executors: Wife Margaret and brother-in-law John Fleming.
Wit: Richard Hope, Francis Alexander.

ROWAN, JAMES. Lower Chichester. Apr. 6, 1772. Adm. to Elizabeth Rowan.

JACKSON, JOHN. West Bradford. Apr. 14, 1772. Adm. to Thomas Meteer.

ARTHUR, WILLIAM. Londongrove. Apr. 21, 1772. Adm. to Jane Arthur.

CAMPBELL, JOSIAH. West Caln. Apr. 27, 1772. Adm. to Robert Wilson, Jr.

SCANLAN, LUKE. Lower Chichester. May 7, 1772. Adm. to Martha McKnight.

PHIPPS, NATHAN. Uwchlan.
Apr. 24, 1772. Apr. 30, 1772.
Provides for wife Sarah. To son Samuel £13.12.6 and wearing apparel. To daughter Mary Malpus 20 shillings. To daughter Hannah Harriford 20 shillings. To daughter Ann Paker 5 shillings. To daughter Dames John 5 shillings. To daughter Asenath Griffith £14.12.6. To grandson Jehu John 92 acres of land where Wm. Griffith now lives at 21. To daughter Hannah wife of Jos. Harriford of Warrington Twp., York Co., remainder of land on death of wife. To grandson Jonathan Roberts £1.10 and to grandson Nathan Roberts 20 shillings. To grandson Isaac Thomas 5 shillings, and to grandsons Joseph and Jacob Thomas 5 shillings each. To grandson Wm. Harriford coat with silver buttons. Mentions brother Joseph Phipps.
Executors: Richard Thomas and Joseph Harriford.
Wit: Reuben John, Evan Evans, Thos. Evans.

HASTINGS, DAVID. West Fallowfield.
July 30, 1770. May 1, 1772.
Provides for wife Margery. Remainder to 2 children Joseph and Mary Hastings except £10 to my grandchildren James and Elizabeth Whray and son by the law John Whray 5 shillings.
Executors: Friends Thomas McLuce and Saml. Dale.
Wit: Saml. Futhey, Jos. Criswell, Elisha Criswell.

WORRALL, PETER. Middletown.
3/19/1772. May 20, 1772.
Provides for wife Abigail. To son John plantation in Middletown and 2 lotts in Chester given me in my father's will, at 21 years of age. Executors to sell plantation containing 90 acres in Edgmont.

To daughters Sarah, Rachel, Abigail, Mary and Elizabeth Worrall remainder to be equally divided at 21 or marriage. Provision made for possible posthumous child.
Executors: Wife Abigail and Joseph Talbot, Jr.
Wit: Nathan Yarnall, Abel Green, Benj. Sharpless.

FLEMING, ROBERT. Oxford.
Mar. 10, 1772. May 21, 1772.
To father David Fleming all that was willed to me in my grandfather's will and £20 more. To sister Jean 5 shillings. To brother John Fleming £3. To brother James £70, horse and books. To brother David £20. Remainder to brother John.
Executors: John Black and brother James.
Wit: Thomas Armstrong, Jas. Scott.

ROGERS, THOMAS. West Nottingham.
Mar. 18, 1772. May 27, 1772.
Provides for wife Catherine. To sons William and Thomas plantation I now live on. To daughter Rachel, son Saml., to daughter Elizabeth £20 each, the latter at 18. As there is a burying ground on my plantation my will is that 1/4 acre be set apart for that use forever and privilege of one perch wide to the great road south of the same to and from it.
Executors: Sons Wm. and Thomas.
Wit: Timo. Kirk, Wm. Knight, Jacob Brown.

YARNALL, MORDECAI. Springfield.
9/21/1769. May 29, 1772.
To wife Ann all estate, also Executrix.
Wit: William Fell, Edward Fell.

TODD, JAMES. East Nottingham.
Mar. 16, 1772. June 3, 1772.
Provides for wife Jennet. To son John £5 and bed. To son James £5 and I give him, his wife and children house room and diet since he came from Carolina and I allow that as recompense for what he has done for me. To son Hugh, daughters Hannah, Mary and Margaret £5 each.
Executors: Sons-in-law Gilbert Anderson and James McCorkel.
Wit: Andrew Lowrdey, James Willson.

KEYS, JAMES. West Caln.
Dec. 7, 1770. Codicil Dec. 18, 1770. June 9, 1772.
Provides for wife Sarah. On her death or marriage, plantation in West Caln to son William, he paying to my daughter Mary Keys £15. To daughter Margaret Keys £8. To daughter Barbara 1 shilling. To son James one crown and to Wm. Fulton, Wm. Clark, and Robt. Kinkead my sons-in-law 1 shilling each.
Executors: Son Wm. and wife Sarah.
Codicil gives to son John £5. To daughter Jennet Keys £5 and to grandchildren James and John Fulton 40 shillings each.
Wit: Robert White, Thomas Law, John Miller.

CHAMBERLIN, JOSEPH. Concord.
Apr. 26, 1772. June 9, 1772.

Provides for wife Susanna. To grandson Joseph Pennell plantation whereon he now dwells in Aston containing about 180 acres being the same which formerly belonged to my brother John. To grandson Thos. Pennell plantation where on I now dwell containing in all about 280 acres. To granddaughter Mary Fairlamb £200. To granddaughter Abigail Pennell £200. To granddaughter Lydia Pennell £200. To Hannah wife of Jonathan Haycock £5. Remainder equall[y] divided among 5 grandchildren.
Executors: Wife Susanna and grandson Jos. Pennell.
Wit: Mark Wilcox, Danl. Sharpless, Jno. Hannum.

PHIPPS, JOSEPH. Uwchlan. June 17, 1772. Adm. to Caleb Phipps and Isaac Lewis.

HEALD, SAMUEL. Kennett. June 19, 1772. Adm. to Ruth Heald. The administration accounts filed Oct., 1, 1783 by Ruth Langley mentions six children, but do not name them.

WILLS, THOMAS. Middletown. June 23, 1772. Adm. to Jacob Richards, Jas. and Jos. Hemphill.

JAMES, ISAAC. Willistown. 1/28/1772. June 11, 1772.
To mother Hannah James £125. To brother Jacob 5 shillings. To sister Jane Hibberd £5. To friend Jas. Gibbons of Westtown £5. Remainder to mother.
Executor: James Gibbons.
Wit: Isaac Hoops, Mary Hoops, Saml. Oliver.

CALDWELL, JOHN. Chester Borough. June 5, 1772. June 13, 1772.
Provides for wife Joanna Frances. To sons George and John all real estate, Geo. to have one share and John two shares. Remainder equally divided between 4 daughters Martha, Elizabeth, Joanna Frances and Mary.
Executors; Rev. Geo. Craig and son Geo.
Wit: Samuel Shaw, Thomas Keimer.

EDMESTON, DAVID. West Nottingham. Feb. 19, 1770. June 24, 1772.
Provides for wife Margaret Edmeston alias Donal. To daughter Mary Steveston 5 shillings. To son David my plantation paying legacies. To daughter Sarah Edmeston £20 and furniture to £36. To daughter Hannah Edmeston £20 and goods to value of £36. To son Samuel mare and colt.
Executor: Son David.
Wit: Samuel Scott, James McMillan.

BILLERBY, JOHN. East Bradford. Aug. 4, 1772. Adm. to Mary Grubb.

TRIMBLE, JOHN. Concord. 5/27/1772. July 4, 1772.
Provides for wife Lydia. To 3 sons Thomas, William and John all real estate to be equally divided when youngest shall arrive at 21. To daughter Phebe £100 and furniture at 18. To sister Rachel £20.

Remainder to wife and 4 children.
Executors: Brother Wm. Trimble and brother-in-law Richard Thomas.
Wit: Saml. Trimble, Thos. Newlin, Danl. Trimble.

TORTON, LETITIA. Widow. Ridley.
Apr. 16, 1772. July 6, 1772.
To daughter Margaret wife of Thomas Smith horses, cattle and sheep, also negro woman Meina and her 2 children. To grandson Thos. Smith £200 at 21. All remainder to 2 daughters Rebecca wife of Lawrence Garrett and Margaret wife of Thomas Smith.
Executors: Son-in-law Thos. Smith and his wife Margaret.
Wit: John Morton, Swan Culin.

SWAYNE, ISAAC. East Marlborough.
7/14/1772. Aug. 7, 1772.
Executors to sell plantation whereon I now dwell. Provides for wife Susanna. To 2 daughters Rachel and Sarah Swayne and the child my wife is now pregnant with, £120 to be divided. To brothers Edward, Jonathan, Jesse and Robert wearing apparel.
Executor: Friend Francis Swayne.
Wit: Wm. Swayne, Jos. Williams.

WELDON, JOHN. West Fallowfield. Aug. 25, 1772. Adm. to Sarah Weldon.

JAMES, JOSEPH. Westtown. Sept. 9, 1772. Adm. to Hannah James.
[James crossed out and Joseph added.]

OWEN, JOHN. Uwchlan.
Aug. 19, 1772. Aug. 25, 1772.
To mother Abigail Owen £60. Remainder to brothers and sister William and David Owen and Martha Miller.
Executor: Friend Cadwallader Jones.
Wit: Edward Owen, Jas. Guest, Thos. Evans.

VAUGHAN, ISAAC. Haverford.
8/20/1772. Sept. 17, 1772.
To daughter Amelia Vaughan all my personal estate with reserve to her 2 sisters Tacy Lawrence and Amy Lawrence. Also to said daughter Amelia all the portion which my father shall leave me with reserve to my 2 brothers John and Thomas Vehan (name is so spelled in the will but not by Testator).
Executors: Friend Wm. Lawrence and cousin Jesse Ellis.
Wit: Aaron Coates, Saml. Humphreys.

DAVIS, REBECCA. Widow. Darby.
1/6/1759. Sept. 25, 1772.
To 5 daughters, viz., Rebecca, Ann, Hannah, Mary and Sarah all wearing apparel. To son John £20. To Executors £50 in trust for use of daughter Hannah Smith during life. Remainder to children Lewis, John, Rebecca, Ann, Mary and Sarah.
Executors: Sons Lewis and John and 2 sons-in-law John Levis and Wm. Parker. Letters to above except John Davis who is deceased.
Wit: none given.

TAYLOR, JOSEPH. Ridley. Tinnecum.
Sept. 3, 1772. Sept. 25, 1772.
Provides for wife Frederica. To daughters Elizabeth and Lydia all real estate.
Executor: Friend John Morton.
Wit: Deborah Quandril, John Quandrill, John Taylor.

CURLE, JAMES. West Nottingham.
Dec. 14, 1770. Sept. 25, 1772.
To brother John Curle watch and silver shoe buckles. To brother-in-law James Lynn buckskin breeches. To sister's daughter Martha McEwen my Bible. To sister's son James Reed my wearing fur. To sister Jenet silver sleeve buttons. To brother-in-law Alex. McElhatten my buckskin gloves. To sister's son Joseph Reed pocket book. Remainder to be divided into 3 shares to wife Margery and sons John and James with reserve to my sisters Sarah and Mary.
Executors: Friends John Reed and Wm. Haines.
Wit: Job Haines, Thos. Coulson, Jr.

PHIPPS, JOSEPH. Now of County of Botetourt, Virginia.
Dec. 7, 1771. Feb. 12, 1772.
To son Joshua of Botetourt Co., Va. merchant mill in Uwchlan and 3 tracts adjoining containing by estimate 150 acres. All debts owing from sons Aaron and Caleb to be canceled. To daughter Mary wife of Isaac Lewis £100. To daughter Rachel wife of Owen Astin £100 she living in Cumberland Co. Pennsylvania. To granddaughter Mary Hubbard mulatto girl named Pugg. To daughter Hannah wife of Geo. Astin of Botetourt Co. £150 and to her husband all he owes me. To sons Aaron and Caleb 5 shillings each. To daughter Esther Crosby negro girl Dinah. If mill and plantation in East Caln on Brandywine shall be recovered by law, then the sum of £100 to be paid to Jonathan Phipps and £50 to his sister Anne Phipps, children of Joseph Phipps, Jr., but not otherwise. To Benj. Phipps son of Esther Crosby a plantation containing about 135 acres in Uwchlan. "£10 to be paid toward repairing Quaker graveyard in Uwchlan."
Proven in Botetourt County, Virginia.
Executors: Friends John Nowles of Ridley and Elisha Price of Chester. Letters c.t.a. Caleb Phipps and Isaac Lewis, Executors named renouncing.
Wit: Thomas Madison, Wm. Bowing, Rees Bowing.

LEWIS, PHINEHAS. East Caln.
5/8/1772. Oct. 1, 1772.
Provides for wife Rachel. To son John Lewis £5 and wearing apparel. To son Lewis Lewis part of plantation on which I now dwell to contain 16 acres not to be sold out of the family. To daughter Hannah Pim 20 shillings. To son Curtis 20 shillings. To daughter Martha Lewis £20. To son Obed all remainder of plantation whereon I now dwell supposed to contain near 200 acres paying legacies. To each of daughter Dinah Whitacre's 7 children 5 shillings when 21. Remainder to wife and son Obed, also Executors.
Wit: Joshua Baldwin, Richd. Downing, Thos. Stalker.

HUETT, EDWARD.
Sept. 17, 1772. Oct. 5, 1772.

Nuncupative will. Patrick Kelley to manage all my affairs after death. To Hannah Smedley one of my shirts. To Hannah Guiry one of my best shirts. To Hannah Harris one of my middling shirts. To Patrick Kelley 2 pair stockings and my sea chest. My hat Patrick Kelley must sell to defray the expenses of the Doctor and others for all will be little enough I expect.
Wit: Hannah Guiry, Hannah Smedley.

KIRK, JOHN. East Nottingham. Oct. 14, 1772. Adm. to Wm. Churchman.

GIVENS, ROBERT. West Nottingham.
July 30, 1772. Codicil Aug. 19, 1772. Oct. 21, 1772.
Provides for wife Lucie. To sons John and William £10 each. To daughter Hannah and her husband John Welch £10. To son Samuel £20 in case he returns home in 2 years after my decease. To 5 youngest children, viz., Sarah Mary, Jonathan Thomas, James, Jean and Robert Givens all remainder of real and personal estate. Plantation where I now live to be sold as soon as convenient.
Executors: Jonathan Hartshorn and son Wm.
Wit: Jas. Maxwell, Samuel Glasgow, Henry Hall.

LLOYD, THOMAS. [Place not given.]
May 6, 1760. Oct. 23, 1772.
To daughters Lydia and Elizabeth 5 shillings each. To daughter Margret £5. To son Erasmus Lloyd all my land and premises paying to son John £70 and to son Nicholas £30. To wife Elizabeth all remainder of estate.
Executors: Wife and son Erasmus. Letters to Erasmus, the other renounced.
Wit: Alice McCue, Sarah Douglas, Richd. Richison.

TAYLOR, JOHN. Pennsbury.
Aug. 8, 1772. Oct. 26, 1772.
Provides for wife Mary. To son Isaac £60 at 21. To 2 daughters Esther and Deborah £15 each at 18. To daughter Mary £30 at 18. To son Samuel all remainder. Plantation to be sold. Sons to be put to trade at 15.
Executors: Wife and cousin Isaac Taylor.
Wit: Jos. Buffington, Isaac Taylor.

TRIMBLE, HENRY. Ridley.
Nov. 3, 1772. Nov. 12, 1772.
Body to be buried by side of late wife in burial grounds of Friends at Haverford. To the Elders of said Meeting £10 to be applied toward repairing wall of burial grounds. To John Crosby, Jr., Coroner of this County £100. To Valentine Vanhold £20. To the Ministers and Elders of St. James Church in Kingsess £50 towards finishing the Church. To the daughters of my son Lewis Trimble, Alice, Mary and Abigail £50 each at 18 or marriage. To grandson Abraham Trimble my plantation in Providence containing 54 acres. To son Lewis my plantation in Ridley where I lately dwelt containing about 370 acres with 26 acres of meadow on river Delaware. To friend Thomas Lucas £60. To Mrs. Catharine Gurney daughter of friend John Ross, Esq. of Phila. £50. Remainder to son

Lewis.
Executors: Son Lewis and Thomas Bishop. Letters to Lewis, the other being absent.
Wit: John Ross, Jas. Sharpless, Nathan Taylor, Jos. Edwards.

EVANS, EVAN. Radnor.
May 12, 1772. Nov. 14, 1772.
To Elizabeth Evans of Radnor £5 and to her daughter Lydia Evans £5. To Anne wife of Dr. John Davis £5. To Rebecca, Hannah and Rose Evans, daughters of Elizabeth Evans £5 each at 18. To Benjamin son of Rees Davis of Philadelphia. £5. Remainder to Elizabeth Evans and her 5 daughters above named.
Executrix: Elizabeth Evans.
Wit: Griffith Evans, Jr., Evan Lewis, Owen Shelton, James Davis.

BAKER, ALICE alias PENNOCK. East Mar.[lborough] Nov. 14, 1772.
Adm. to Moses Pennock.

BOYLAND, JOHN. New Garden. Nov. 26, 1772. Adm. to Wm. Miller.

KIRKPATRICK, JOHN. West Nottingham.
Nov. 18, 1771. Nov. 20, 1772.
To grandson Wm. Given £10. To son Hugh Kirkpatrick £5. To granddaughter Hannah Welch £10. To grandson John Given £5. £10 to use of the Congregation to which I have belonged. Remainder in 5 parts one each to son John and daughters Margaret Evans and Elenor Evans, one in Executors hands for use of grandchildren James, John, Wm., Hannah, Mary and Jean Boyd to be divided when of age. Remainder part for use of grandchildren Lettice Charlton Kirkpatrick, Hannah and Wm. Kirkpatrick, children of son Wm. when of age.
Executors: Sons-in-law Robert and James Evans.

HORNE, WILLIAM. Darby.
3/15/1763. Codicil undated. Nov. 26, 1772.
All estate to wife Elizabeth until oldest son John comes of age. To son William £200 at 21. To son Edward £200 at 21. To son John all real estate and personal estate paying legacies at 21. Nathan Garrett and Abraham Bonsall of Darby to be Trustees and Guardians to my children.
Executors: Wife Elizabeth and son John.
Wit: James Jones, Lewis Davis, Hannah Davis.

PUGH, JEMIMA. Relict of James. Uwchlan.
June 5, 1772. Dec. 3, 1772.
To son David and daughters Mary Dybrimple, Margaret McClay, Jamima McCarty, Hannah Jenkins and Hizziah Pugh and equal share of my estate. Directs her plantation to be sold. In case daughter Hizziah should die before receiving her share directs that her son Daniel Plane receive it.
Executor: William Beale.
Wit: David Jenkin, Israel Whelon, Thos. Jenkins.

HIPPLE, JACOB. [Place not given.]
Nov. 10, 1772. Dec. 3, 1772.

Provides for wife Anna. To grandson Lawrence son of Henry Hipple
£3. Grandson Jacob Hipple is to have my Bible. Remainder to son
John Hipple and when he is arrived to the age "she is to let him to
the sacrament of the Prisbeterian Religion."
Executor: Cousin Frederick Hipple, and Lawrence Hipple "for my
guardian."
Wit: Henry Hipple, Conrod Sharar.

HIPPLE, HENRY. Pikeland.
Sept. 19, 1772. Dec. 4, 1772.
All estate to remain in possession of wife Elizabeth until the 1st
day of April 1777. To son Lawrence all my lands in Pikeland paying
£280 to wife and children as follows 1/9 to wife, 1/9 for his own
share, 1/9 to daughter Catherine, 1/9 to daughter Ommi, 1/9 to
daughter Elizabeth and 1/9 each to daughters Mary, Maryliz and
Christiana and son Jacob.
Executors: Wife Elizabeth and kinsman Lawrence Hipple of Vincent.
Wit: John Smith, Frederick Hipple, David John.

MOULDER, MARY. Lower Chichester. Dec. 7, 1772. Adm. to Robert
Moulder.

BOYLE, DORINTON. West Fallowfield.
May 4, 1771. Dec. 9, 1772.
Provides for wife Mary. To daughter Ann Boyle £100 at 21. To son
Robert plantation whereon I now live at 21. To daughter Mary Boyle
£100 at 21. To son Samuel my plantation of 107 acres adj. where I
now live at 21.
Executors: Wife Mary, brothers Gideon Irwin and John Irwin and
nephew Jas. Willson. Letters to 3 first named, Willson renouncing.
Wit: David Caldwell, William Holmes, James Taylor.

CAMPBELL, HUGH. New London.
Jan 22, 1770. Dec. 10, 1772.
(d. Oct 25, 1772, bur. at New London Presbyterian Church, aged 71.)
Provides for wife Margaret. To daughter Elizabeth Hagans 10
shillings. To son John my right to the plantation of 100 acres now
in his possession. To son Samuel 20 shillings. To son William
£10. To son Thomas my right of that plantation I now live on
paying certain legacies. To daughter Isabel King 10 shillings. To
daughter Mary Campbell £50. To son Benjamin £30. To grandson Hugh
Hagans £10. To niece Elizabeth Jordan £2.
Executors: Wife Margaret and sons John and Thomas. Letters to
sons, wife renouncing.
Wit: Joseph Moore, John Menough.

CLARK, WILLIAM. West Bradford.
June 9, 1772. Dec. 15, 1772.
Provides for wife Sarah. To 2 sons Samuel and William £50 each.
To son John all my plantation whereon I now dwell containing 120
acres.
Executors: Wife and Ebenezer Speakman.
Wit: John Carpenter, James Marshall.

ROSS, JOSEPH. Oxford. Dec. 15, 1772. Adm. to James Walker.

STERN, PAUL. Lower Chichester. Dec. 28, 1772. Adm. to George Stern.

LAWRENCE, MARGARET. Radnor.
Nov. 5, 1772. Dec. 21, 1772.
To sister Jane Lewis £15. To 3 sisters Mary, Ellen and Hannah £5 each. To sister Jane's children, viz., Abner, Rachel, Henry, Mary, Enos, Lewis and Hannah £5 each. To brother Henry's children, viz., Mordecai, Joseph, Samuel and all the rest £5 when of age. To cousin Edward Williams' 2 daughters £1 each. To cousin Thos. Lawrence's children £1 each when of age. Remainder to brother Henry and brother-in-law David Lewis, also Executors.
Wit: Jesse Jones, James Maris.

LINDSEY, WILLIAM. Uwchlan.
May 9, 1771. Jan 2, 1773.
To wife Jane 1/3 of estate as the law directs. To son Andrew, daughter Rose Lindsey, daughter Rachel Lindsey £20 each. To daughter Jane, wife of John Rees 5 shillings. All remainder to sons Jeremiah, Alexander and William share and share alike at 21. Executors: Richard Thomas, and Geo. Thomas.
Wit: Wm. Trimble, Jr., Hannah Thomas, Benj. Davis.

JONES, EVAN. East Bradford.
11/6/1772. Jan 2, 1773.
To housekeeper Margaret Redmond £20 and privileges of house room &c. while unmarried. To son Richard Jones and Ann his wife the income and profits of the plantation where I now dwell until my grandson Thomas Baily arrives to age of 21 at which time I give 1/2 thereof including mansion house to said Thomas Baily. The other 1/2 I give to son Richard and Ann his wife during life, at their death to their children if any. Otherwise to be sold and proceed divided among my residuary legatees. The 1/2 devised to Thos. Baily to go to same if he dies under 21. To daughter Ruth Hayes £50. To sister Jane Benson £20. To granddaughter Sarah Starr chest of drawers. To son John Jones £5 having done sufficiently for him heretofore. Executors to sell plantation containing 200 acres in West Whiteland. All remainder of estate to grandchildren: Sarah, Rachel and Hannah Starr; Jonathan, Nathan, Evan, Deborah, Jane and Ellis Haynes and Jos. Hunt, Evan Baily; Mary Evan; James and Sarah Jones; Sarah, Rachel and Hannah Hayes; [Haynes but crossed out and Hayes written in] to be equally divided.
Executors: Son Richard and friend Humphrey Marshall and James Gibbons. Letters to Jones and Marshall, Gibbons renouncing.
Wit: Adam Grubb, Nathl. Sellers, Miles McCarty.

HENRY, SAMUEL. West Caln. May 7, 1773. Adm. to Wm. Henry.
(Patent to Samuel Henry 14 Dec 1749 for 227 acres and allowance in West Caln. Left issue William, James, Samuel, Ebenezer, Catharine (m. Alexander Martin), Jean (m. Thomas Cowan), Margaret and Mary. James and wife Agnes, with the others, released to William, who conveyed 16 June 1777, 128 acres to Vincent Cromwell (B 2.217) and 23 July 1788, 115 acres to William Clingan (D 2.109). See also F 2.323.)

GREEN, THOMAS.   East Caln.   Jan 11, 1773.   Adm. to Lewis Weiss.

GREEN, SARAH.   Middletown.   Jan 11, 1773.   Adm. to Joshua Proctor.

WOOD, HANNAH.   Widow.   Darby.
2/29/1772.   Jan 18, 1773.
To 3 daughters Jane, Sarah and All all wearing apparel.   All remainder of estate to 4 children, viz., Jonathan, Jane, Sarah and Ann and to the 5 children of son George Wood deceased, viz., Hannah, Margaret, Mary, Henry and Harriet.
Executors: Son-in-law Henry Hayes and my daughter Ann his wife.
Wit: Jesse Bonsall, Jos. Pearson.

TAYLOR, ELIZABETH.   Widow.   Thornbury.
Mar. 30, 1772.   Jan 19, 1773.
To friend Danl. Calvert of Thornbury all estate real and personal, also Executor.
Wit: Daniel Calvert, Jr. Jas. Claypoole.

MILLER, JOSEPH.   Haverford.   Feb. 15, 1773.   Adm. to Mary Miller and John Lewis.

JACKSON, JOSIAH.   Londongrove.   Feb. 25, 1773.   Adm. to Ephraim Jackson.

PHILLIP[S], THOMAS.   Willistown.
June 20, 1772.   Feb. 20, 1773.
Gives £20 to Executors for a tombstone over his grave.   To children of niece Sarah James as follows -- to Mary James £30, to Margaret, Ann and Isaac James £20 each when of age.   To Ezekiel son of Owen Howell £20 at 21.   To Sarah widow of Peter Mathers £10 and £10 towards the support of her son, a deaf and dumb boy.   To the Church wardens of Radnor Church £5 for relief of poor.   To Rev. Mr. William Currie £2.   To Walter Williams, if living, £1.   Plantation in Willistown containing 135 acres to be sold.   All remainder of estate to brothers Evan and John Phillip and sister Dorothy Evans living in the Parish of Amleston, Pembrokeshire, Wales.
Executors: Friends James Massey and Joshua Evans.
Wit: John Harris, Elizabeth Melin, John Griffiths.

BENNETT, SARAH.   Pennsbury.
12/7/1772.   Feb. 25, 1773.
Son John to be discharged from all arrears of dower under will of his father, John Bennett, on payment of £50.   To son William £5.   To son James £20 and all household goods.   To grandson John Pennock £3.   To daughter-in-law Hannah Bennett all wearing apparel.   To sons Titus and James all remainder of estate.
Executor: Son James.
Wit: Susanna Quaintance, Joseph Pierce, Thos. Temple.

COOPE, JOHN.   East Bradford.
7/6/1769.   Mar. 12, 1773.
Directs that his body be buried in a plain coffin made of oak or poplar wood in its natural color and not be wrapped in new or costly linen or muslin.   To son Samuel 5 shillings in addition to

the plantation I have conveyed unto him. To son John £10. To son
Nathan plantation whereon I now live containing 100 acres. To
daughter Hannah wife of John Carter 20 shillings. To daughter Mary
Coope £10. All remainder of estate including lott of ground and
tenement in Philadelphia to 3 younger sons Caleb, Joshua and
Joseph.
Executors: Son Joseph and son-in-law John Carter. Letters to Jos.
Cope, the other being defunct.
Wit: Humy. Marshall, John Battin, Jas. Kenny.

JERMAN, LEWIS. Radnor.
Feb. 3, 1773. Mar. 19, 1773. ["3" crossed out and Feb. added.]
To wife Mary my plantation in Radnor containing 42 acres whereon I
now dwell and all personal estate, also Executrix.
Wit: Humphrey Wayne, Alex. Oliver, Hannah Davis.

ASHBRIDGE, GEORGE. Goshen.
3/3/1773. Mar. 26, 1773.
Provides for wife Jane. To son Joshua the plantation I now live on
that was given to me by my father containing 250 acres with grist
mill, also part of the land I bought of Wm. Hudson, also 20 acres
of east end of land bought of Francis Rawles with saw mill. To the
children of my daughter Mary late wife of Jesse Jones, that is to
Jane, Ezra, Priscilla, John, Israel, Mary and Isaiah Jones each an
equal share of what would have fallen to their mother. To son-in-
law and daughter Wm. and Susanna Gibbons the middle part of the
land I bought of Francis Rawles. To son-in-law and daughter Jesse
and Jane Maris plantation bought of James Day containing 163 acres
part of land bought of Wm. Hudson. My third part of tract in York
Co. containing 178 acres taken up in expectation of copper mine to
all children share and share alike. House and lotts in
Philadelphia, my right to land in Pikeland, my land in Newberry
Twp., York Co., my land in Virginia, my land where Mary Croxon now
lives, my 250 acres unlocated land, my 100 acres ditto, my 60 acres
that I have a warrant for and my lot in Chester, all to be sold and
proceeds divided among sons George, Wm. and Joshua, daughters Mary,
Susanna, Phebe and Jane. Daughters to have £100 more than half as
much as the sons. Having given to son Daniel full £1500, I give my
daughter-in-law Hannah Ashbridge and her daughter Jane £20 each.
Executors: Sons Geo. and Joshua.
Wit: William Garrett, Wm. Garrett, Jr.

REGAN, MICHAEL. Vincent.
Jan 11, 1773. Mar. 29, 1773.
Provides for wife Frances. To sons John, James, William and
Michael each 1/4 of remainder of estate.
Executors: Wife Frances and son James.
Wit: John Dillor, Hugh Strickland, Thos. Hunter.

LITTLER, THOMAS. West Caln. Apr. 12, 1773. Adm. to Ann Littler.

RHOADS, ELIZABETH. Darby. Apr. 21, 1773. Adm. to Sarah Hibberd.

HANNUM, JOHN. Concord.
Sept. 30, 1769. Codicil Apr. 20, 1771. Apr. 3, 1773.

Provides for wife Jane. To daughter Margery wife of Joseph Gibbons, Jr. £300 in trust during life and to her children at her death. To daughter Mary wife of Richard Cheyney £250 in trust as above. Also tract of land in Thornbury containing 125 acres to said daughter Mary in trust as before. To son John my plantation in East Bradford containing 400 acres purchased of Jacob Taylor and Mary Empson, also £100, also all his indebtedness to me. To son William plantation where I now dwell with land bought of John Riley and Jos. Nicklin containing 300 acres, also £200. To son James plantation in West Marlboro containing about 200 acres with 50 acres of woodland, also warrant right of 50 acres of land and £150. Executors: Sons John, William and James.
Wit: Edward Brinton, John Morton, Jno. Pedrick.

MC CRACKEN, JOSHUA. Londonderry.
Dec. 30, 1772. Apr. 13, 1773.
To wife Catharine 1/3 of all estate. To children William, Sarah, John, Thomas and Catharine the remainder of estate to be equally divided.
Executors: Wife Catharine and son Wm.
Wit: Jas. Ochiltree, Jno. Alexander.

THATCHER, THOMAS. Yeoman. Thornbury.
9/20/1772. May 13, 1773.
To brother William plantation where I now dwell in Thornbury and Concord containing about 111 acres, also all personal estate, he paying legacies. To sister Hannah Haynes £5. To sister Sarah Bailef £50. To sister Ann Canby £50. To sister Phebe Hiett £50. To brother Samuel £50. To brother Stephen £50. To sister Mary Thatcher £50. To brother Jonathan 5 shillings and to be discharged of what he owes me.
Executor: Brother Wm.
Wit: Charles Dilworth, Mary Dilworth.

IVES, THOMAS. West Whiteland. May 27, 1773. Adm. to Rachel and Wm. Ives.

JAMES, THOMAS. Tredyffrin. June 12, 1773. Adm. to Esther James.

EVANS, ANN. Widow. Vincent.
Feb. 27, 1768. May 26, 1773.
To son David Evans £20. To son James Evans £20. To daughter Jane Rees now living in Wales £20 if she comes to this province. To daughter Elenor Dotson £20. To daughter Ann Dotson £20. To granddaughter Mary daughter of son Wm. £10. To grandson John son of ditto. £10 at 21. To grandson John son of David £5 at 21. To all the rest of grandchildren 7 shillings 6 each. To Jane Collins "my old maid," £2. To son William Evan all remainder of estate, also Executor.
Wit: Humphrey Bell, John Jones, David John.

WASON, MATTHEW. Birmingham.
Oct. 24, 1772. June 12, 1773.
To wife Rachel all personal estate to bring up my 3 children to 16 years of age, also Executrix.

Wit: Saml. Russel, Thos. Milsom.

PUSEY, WILLIAM. West Marlborough.
1/10/1773. Mar. 18, 1773.
Provides for wife Mary. To 2 sons William and Enoch my plantation containing 150 acres. To daughter Betty wife of Wm. Wickersham 20 shillings. To daughter Elenor wife of John Pennock 20 shillings. To daughter Mary Pusey £65 at 18. To daughter Jane Pusey £65 at 18. To grandson Caleb Wickersham £5 at 21.
Executrix: Wife Mary.
Wit: Joseph Pyle, Joshua Pusey, John Pusey.

WEBB, WILLIAM. Kennett.
4/7/1773. June 14, 1773.
Provides for wife Sarah. To daughter Rebecca Webb £200 at 18, also messuage and 20 acres at death of wife, furniture. To Wm. Webb son of brother Stephen £3. To Wm. Webb son of cousin Isaac 40 shillings at 21. To my aunt Sarah Hall £2. Remainder to wife and daughter subject to maintenance of grandmother Rebecca Webb.
Executors: Wife Sarah and brother Ezekiel.
Wit: Thomas Johnson, Hezekiah Hemp, Daniel Webb.

SELLERS, SAMUEL. Weaver. Darby.
Jan 20, 1772. June 15, 1773.
To 2 sons-in-law John Hunt and David Gibson £10 each. To son-in-law Lewis Davis and son John Sellers £5, the above on account of moneys advanced to son Joseph some years ago. To son Joseph all wearing apparel, gun and £20. To son Samuel £5. To son John £3, also tract of woodland adj. his plantation. Provides for wife. Remainder divided into 3 parts. To daughter Hannah Davis £10 of one part, remainder to grandsons Isaac and Hugh Lloyd, 1/3 part to daughter (2) Elizabeth wife of John Hunt and the other 1/3 to daughter Mary wife of David Gibson.
Executors: Sons-in-law John Hunt and David Gibson.
Wit: Wm. Parker, Susanna Marshall, Isa. Pearson.

DUTTON, JOSEPH. Upper Chichester.
May 22, 1773. June 22, 1773.
To each of my children whose names are as follows, viz., Mary, Jacob, James, Susanna, Hannah, Elizabeth and Joseph a silver spoon a piece. 1/2 of estate to 3 sons to be equally divided and remainder to 4 daughters to be equally divided at 18.
Executor: Son Jacob.
Wit: Isaac Pennell, Richd. Dutton, Jeremiah Booth.

WEBB, DANIEL. Kennett.
6/17/1773. June 29, 1773.
Provides for wife Christiana. To daughter Naomi Lamborn 5 shillings. Executors to sell part of plantation in Kennett and proceeds to wife and 5 children, viz., Daniel, Ruth, Thomas, Orpha and Eli Webb to be divided when sons are 21 and daughters 18. Remainder to be sold at death of wife and divided among surviving children, sons to have double portion.
Executors: Wife and son-in-law Jesse Harry.
Wit: Stephen Webb, Thos. Johnson, Ezekiel Webb.

CUTHBERT, JOHN. West Whiteland.
Aug. 20, 1772. July 19, 1773.
To oldest daughter Catharine Beane 5 shillings. To oldest son Allen Cuthbert £5. To son Thomas £10 and part of tract of land whereon I now live. To youngest son John all remainder of estate real and personal excepting £5 to be paid my step-daughter Elizabeth wife of Joshua Evans in Carnavan Twp., Lancaster Co.
Executors: Son John and Persifor Frazer.
Wit: Danl. Thompson, Henry Bull, Henry Atherton, Sr.

HOSKINS, JOSEPH. Chester Boro.
12/31/1769. Codicil 4/2/1770, 11/16/1772. July 21, 1773.
Provides for wife Esther. To brother Stephen Hoskins £10 yearly during life. To brother John all wearing apparel and maintenance during life. To 2 daughters of brother Stephen, viz., to Mary Warner £50 and to Ruth Wilson £25. To the 2 daughters of sister Mary deceased, viz., Ruth wife of Charles Thomson and Jane widow of Paul Jackson £25 each. To cousin Ann Trego £5. To cousin Saml. Taylor £10 and to friend Mary Shaw £10. I give £10 for enclosing the burial grounds of Friends at Chester to be paid to John Eyre. To Chester Preparative Meeting £30 for school purposes and gives (2) lott of ground in Chester for building a school house on. 1To nephew John Hoskins of Burlington all remainder and reversions, also Executor. Codicil gives house and lot, part of reversionery estate to wife's niece Lydia wife of Tristram Smith. Lewis Ferrell, Alex. Mitchell, Lydia Beakes at proving she was wife of Tristram Smith. To Codicil Wm. Swaffer.
Wit: John Eyre, Robt. Cobourn, Thomas Pedrick.

YEARSLEY, ISAAC. Thornbury.
5/1/1765. July 28, 1773.
Provides for wife Phebe. To brother Thomas silver watch. To brother Nathan ivory headed cane. To Jacob Yearsley son of brother Jacob deceased £20 at 21. At wife's decease plantaton in Thornbury containing 118 acres to be sold and £200 of the proceeds to be set apart for use of cousin Allen Key son of Wm. if living, otherwise to children of brother Thomas Yearsley. All remainder of estate to children of brother Thomas and children of late sister Elizabeth Heald.
Executors: Wife Phebe and brother Thomas. Letters to wife Phebe, Thomas being deceased.
Wit: George Eavenson, Stephen Taylor.

MINSHALL, AARON. Providence. July 29, 1773. Adm. to David and Danl. Broomall.

HODGETS, TOWNSEND. West Bradford. Aug. 5, 1773. Adm. to Joel Baily.

GREGG, HANNAH. Kennett. Aug. 16, 1773. Adm. to Benjamin Gregg.

URIAN, BENJAMIN. Darby.
July 2, 1773. Aug. 5, 1773.
To brother Andrew all personal estate and real estate during life and at his death to his son Benjamin with reserve to his brother

Israel.
Executors: Brother Andrew and Sketchley Morton.
Wit: Peter Hooff, Daniel Humphreys.

HALL, THOMAS. Willistown.
1/9/1771. Aug. 14, 1773.
Provides for wife Sarah. To son Samuel £6 yearly during life. To son Thomas plantation I now live upon in Willistown containing 177 acres, also tract adjoining containing 49 acres. To daughter Elizabeth wife of Michael Wayne £20. Remainder to 5 daughters Jane, Sarah, Mary, Elizabeth and Susanna.
Executors: Son Thomas and wife's son Wm. England.
Wit: Josiah Garrett, Thomas Garrett.

COOPER, THOMAS. Oxford.
Jan 14, 1772. Aug. 18, 1773.
Provides for wife Jane. To son John all remainder of real and personal estate paying legacies. To daughter Jane £30. To daughter Mary Cooper 5 shillings. To granddaughter Jane Inglis £5. To grandson Thomas Inglis £5. To granddaughter Jane Young £15 when of age. To grandson Thos. Cooper £15 at 19. To grandson Andrew Cooper £10 at 17. To granddaughter Betty Cooper £3 at 16. To servant Janet McLaughlin £3 when free.
Executors: Friend James Cooper and son John. Letters to John, the other renouncing.
Wit: James Henry, Thos. Cooper, James Cooper.

DURROUGH, JOHN. Aston. Aug. 20, 1773. Adm. to James Crage and Jas. McClaskey.

BALDWIN, ROBERT. West Marlboro. Aug. 21, 1773. Adm. to Hannah Baldwin.

WORRALL, EDWARD. Upper Providence.
June 27, 1773. Aug. 19, 1773.
Provides for wife Esther including use of plantation in Upper Providence devised to me by brother Thomas containing about 72 acres until son Abel is 21, when I give the said plantation to him. To daughter Martha Worrall the land in Upper Providence which my father deeded to me containing about 70 acres, at 21 or marriage. Reserve of real estate to brother John, also with wife Esther, Executors.
Wit: George Miller, Wm. Swaffer.

MEASE, JOHN. Oxford.
Sept. 11, 1772. Aug. 31, 1773.
Directs body to be buried in graveyard at Thunder Hill as near the grave of son John as may be. Provides for wife Janet. To son Matthew £10 and to his son John £40 at 21. To son-in-law Wm. Carlile 5 shillings and my daughter Mary his wife 20 shillings and to their son John Mease Carlile £20. To Elizabeth Sparks a cow or £4. Appears to leave real estate to son Thomas with reserve to grandson John Mease. To son James' daughter Janet 5 shillings.
Executor: Son Thomas.
Wit: Jas. Law, James McDowell.

MEEK, WILLIAM. Radnor. Aug. 21, 1773. Adm. to Adam Siter.

THOMAS, AZARIAH. Newtown. Sept. 1, 1773. Adm. to David Thomas.

LLOYD, HUMPHREY. Uwchland. Sept. 20, 1773. Adm. to Griffith John and John Jacobs.

FLEMING, JAMES. Londonderry. Oct. 1, 1773. Adm. to Archibald Fleming. (Sureties John Ramsey, George Copeland. Inv. by John Kinkead, Stephen Cockran sworn to Oct. 1, 1776. His wearing apparel £4.9.6; Books and Sundrys £0.4.0; One chest £0.12.6; Tools £0.4.0; 9 lb. wool £0.13.6. Total £6.2.6.) [has 1776 with 6 crossed out and 3 added.]

JOHNSTON, JAMES. East Nottingham. Oct. 22, 1776. Adm. to Susanna Johnston and Archd. Job.

SMEDLEY, FRANCIS. Willistown.
8/16/1773. Sept. 25, 1773.
To 2 brothers Thomas and George Smedley plantation where I now live which I had of my father containing about 223 acres at death of my wife. To brother John £5. To sister Sarah wife of John Minshall £15. To cousin Abiah Taylor £5. To cousin Hannah daughter of Isaiah Matlack £10 at 18. Provides for wife Ann plantation formerly belonging to Lawrence Cox, James Trevilla and John James in Willistown containing about 353 and to her heirs forever.
Executors: Wife Ann, brother George and friend Josiah Lewis.
Wit: Joshua Hoopes, Joseph James, Joseph Hoopes.

WHITE, THOMAS. Londonderry.
May 19, 1773. Sept. 20, 1773.
To sister Elizabeth wife of Henry McCadden deceased £30. To 2 brothers Matthew and Robert £30 each. To Mary wife of Wm. Cumings £5. To Margaret wife of James Moore £20. To nephew Robt. McCadden £20 and my watch. To nephew Hugh McCadden £20. To nieces Elizabeth, Ann and Rebecca McCadden £20 each. Orders a tombstone to his grave.
Executors: Stephen Cochran and Robert Finney.
Wit: John Ross, John Kinkead.

BABB, PETER. West Caln.
May 13, 1773. Oct. 27, 1773.
To wife Mary all estate during widowhood. To son Thomas 10 shillings being already advanced. To daughter Bathsheba Trego 5 shillings. To daughter Mary Willson £100. To son Peter that part of my plantation whereon I now live containing by estimate. 150 acres paying to daughter Elizabeth Bishop £100. To grandson Joseph now living with me. To daughter Ann Peirsoll 5 shillings. To daughter Susanna Babb £100. To son Sampson that part of my real estate on which he now lives paying certain legacies.
Executors: Wife Mary and son Thomas.
Wit: Wm. Kennedy, Wm. Neeley, Robt. Brown.

PARKE, ROBERT. East Caln. Nov. 8, 1773. Adm. to Ann Parke.

HUNTER, JAMES.   Bethel.   Nov. 20, 1773.   Adm. to Sarah Hunter.

TENNENT, JANE.   Widow.   Springfield.
Aug. 28, 1773.   Nov. 23, 1773.
To nephew Galbreath McCay my plantation in Springfield containing about 111 acres, at 21 on this condition, that he shall not at any time hereafter keep or entertain on the said premises John McCay or Wm. McCay, which if he do, I hereby revoke the devise to him and give the plantation to my nieces Mary McColough and Hannah Lord. I give to my first husband John Galbreath's sister Sarah £50 and to his sister Ann £10.   To niece Mary McColough £60.   To cousin Mary Calhoon £5.   To Mary Martin £5.   To Margaret wife of Rev. James Anderson wearing apparel.   To Francis Allison, Jr., son of Rev. Frs. Allison silver punch strainer.   To Ann McCausland daughter of Rev. Allison silver 1/2 pint can and to Mary Allison daughter ditto. wearing apparel.   To Rachel daughter of Jas. Crozer silver ware.   To niece Hannah Lord bond of £150 from Wm. McCay.
Executors: James Crozer and Benjamin Brannen.
Wit: Rachel Crozer, Elizabeth Crozer.

KIRK, JOSEPH.   Darby.
11/6/1771.   Nov. 27, 1773.
To son-in-law Jonathan Evans and daughter Sarah his wife 40 acres of my plantation whereon I dwell in Darby.   To son Samuel Kirk 30 shillings.   To daughter Mary Kirk £20.   To son Jesse 30 shillings. To daughter Martha Thomas £20.   Remainder of personal estate to grandson Joseph son of Saml. Kirk.   To son Isaac the remainder of plantation whereon I live containing 46 acres.
Executors: Son-in-law Jona. Evans and Wm. West of Darby.
Wit: Nathan Garrett, Wm. Garrett, Thomas Garrett.

LOWNES, BENANUEL.   Springfield.
10/26/1773.   Nov. 29, 1773.
1/2 of estate to be divided between mother and brother Hugh Lownes and the other half to my sisters Sarah, Alice, Mary and brother George Lownes share and share alike at interest until of age. Nothing left to brother Joseph "because he is otherwise provided for."
Executor: Friend Thomas Levis.
Wit: Lewis Davis, Abraham Garrett, Wm. Fell.

DAVIS, JAMES.   Tredyffrin.
Feb. 27, 1773.   Codicil Oct. 25, 1773.   Nov. 30, 1773.
Mentions settlement already made for wife Elizabeth during life. To son Jacob Davis £50.   To son Israel 1 shilling.   To grandson Methuselah Davis £40.   To grandson Jas. Davis £57 at 21.   To grandson Joseph Davis £40 at 21.   To grandson Israel Davis £40.   To granddaughter Rachel Davis £40 at 18.   To granddaughter Leah Davis £63 at 18.   To grandson Joshua Davis £40 at 21.   To Beninah Davis youngest daughter of son Israel £50 at 18.   To grandson James Davis plantation in Charlestown where my son Israel now lives, his father to have same until he is 21.
Executors: Joshua Evans of Willistown and grandson James Davis.
Wit: David Griffith, Eb. Griffith, Jno. Griffith.

WILLIAMS, DAVID. Uwchlan. Dec. 1, 1773. Adm. to Richard Thomas.

JONES, JANE. Goshen.
8/21/1773. Dec. 2, 1773.
To sisters Priscilla Jones and Mary Jones wearing apparel. Legacy left me by my Grandfather Geo. Ashbridge to be equally divided between brothers and sisters, that is, Ezra, Priscilla, John Israel, Mary and Isaiah Jones.
Executor: Uncle Geo. Ashbridge.

MINOR, THOMAS. New London.
Aug. 3, 1773. Aug. 31, 1773.
To wife Mary 5 shillings in lieu of her dower "and that because she hath been guilty of several elopements from me and of many other great misdemeanors to my great grief and loss." To son John Minor all estate real and personal after the legacies are paid. To daughter Agnes £70. To daughter Jean Bell 5 shillings. To daughter Elizabeth Davis 5 shillings. To daughter Francis Torrel £30. To daughter Mary McCalmont 5 shillings. To son Thomas 5 shillings. to daughter Susanna £70.
Executors: Son John and Wm. Montgomery. Letters to Wm. Montgomery, John Minor being deceased.
Wit: Andrew Boyd, James Hughes, Alexander Hughes.

MINOR, JOHN. New London.
Aug. 12, 1773. Aug. 31, 1773.
Refers to the devise to him in his father Thomas Minor's will dated Aug 3, 1773. To each child of my sister Elizabeth Davis £10 when of age. To nephew Joseph Bell £20 and to the other children of sister Jean Bell £10 each. To each of the children of sister Mary McCalmont £10. To each of the children of sister Frances Torrel £10. Remainder to brother Thomas and sisters Agnes and Susanna Minor to be equally divided.
Executors: Uncle Saml. Floyd and Wm. Montgomery.
Wit: Walter Davies, Andrew Boyd.

MINOR, SUSANNA.
Aug. 18, 1773. Aug. 31, 1773.
To brother Thomas Minor £30 if he returns within 7 years of this date. To nephew John Davis and niece Jenet Davis £20 each. To niece John Torrel's oldest daughter £20 when of age. Remainder coming to me from estate of my father and brother John deceased to be equally divided among children of sisters Jean and Mary which is now born.
Executors: Uncle Saml. Floyd and Walter Finney.
Wit: Andrew Boyd, Walter Davies.

MORRIS, MARK. Easttown.
Nov. 4, 1773. Nov. 23, 1773.
To son James Morris plantation whereon I now live containing by estimate 125 acres during life and at his decease to his sons with reserve to daughters. To granddaughter Mary Morris case of drawers. To granddaughters Sarah and Margaret Morris household goods. To Eleanor Llewlin alias Delany £15. Remainder to son James.

Executors: Son James and friends John Morris and Wm. Griffith.
Wit: Andrew Steel, John Evans, Joshua Evans.

GUTHERY, JAMES. Oxford. Dec. 8, 1773. Adm. to Sarah Guthery.
(At Orphans Court 20 June 1775, on petition of Sarah Guthery court appoints John Stewart guardian of Ann Guther, daughter of James, deceased, of Oxford.)

GILPIN, GEORGE. Birmingham.
Aug. 8, 1773. Dec. 2, 1773.
Provides for wife Sarah. To son George plantation in Birmingham purchased of brother Thos. Gilpin containing 214 acres, also 1/2 of my marsh in Cherry Island in New Castle Co. containing about 10 acres, also house and lot in Wilmington. To son Isaac plantation in Birmingham purchased of Nathaniel Ring containing 140 acres, also house and lot in Wilmington adj. that the devised to son George, also remaining 1/2 of marsh in Cherry Island, also marsh in Chichester containing 9 acres when he is 21. To daughter Betty Gilpin lot of ground in Birmingham containing one acre, also £100 at 21. Remainder equally divided between 2 sons and daughter. To each of 5 children of Saml. Crossley of Birmingham 20 shillings at interest until they are 21.
Executors: Son George and cousin Vincent Gilpin.
Wit: Gideon Gilpin, Robt. Chamberlin, Jos. Pierce.

KIRK, JESSE. Taylor. Darby.
May 17, 1772. Dec. 13, 1773.
To daughter Susanna Kirk £5 at 18, also furniture. To son Abner Kirk all remainder real and personal.
Executors: Brothers Samuel and Isaac Kirk.
Wit: Wm. Garrett, Thomas Lewis, Rebecca Camaran.

PRICE, JOHN. Lower Chichester.
Dec. 12, 1770. Dec. 13, 1773.
Provides for wife Elizabeth. To daughter Ann wife of Robert Eyre use of my plantation in Brandywine Hundred containing about 100 acres during life of her husband and then to her and her heirs. To son Samuel plantation whereon I now live in Chichester consisting of several contiguous tracts containing in the whole about 100 acres with grist and saw mills, also plantation adj. bought of Jno. Pierce containing about 80 acres. To daughter Hannah Price £900. To daughter Sarah Price £900 at 21 or marriage. To son John all that tract of land in Lower Chichester purchased of Thomas Clayton containing 32 3/4 acres and lot of woodland containing 2 acres, also messuage and lot in Chichester at wife's decease, also £900 at 21. To daughter Elizabeth £700 at 21 or marriage. To my sister Sarah Price £25. Remainder to Hannah, Sarah, John and Elizabeth. Rev. Geo. Craig guardian of 2 youngest children, John and Elizabeth.
Executors: Friend Elisha Price and son John.
Wit: John Smith, Richard Riley, Levi Lloyd.

ECKOFF, DAVID. Newlin.
Oct. 23, 1773. Dec. 15, 1773.
To son David all real and personal estate on payment of legacies.

To son Michael £50. To son William, to son Joseph, to daughter Phillis Eckhoff £50 each. To daughter Elisa Scott £3. To daughter Ann Eckoff maintenance during life. To heirs of daughter Susanna Barnard deceased £6.
Executors: Son David and Abel Wickerhsam.
Wit: Wm. Cloud, Jas. Wickersham, Sampson Wickersham.

DOUGLASS, JAMES. East Nottingham. Dec. 28, 1773. Adm. to David Junkin.

RICHARDS, WILLIAM. New Garden. Aug. 31, 1773. Adm. to Jane and Isaac Richards.

DAVIS, SAMUEL. Easttown. Dec. 31, 1773. Adm. to Wm. Lewis.

GIBSON, ALEXANDER, JR. Jan 17, 1774. Adm. to Alexander Gibson.

BLACK, BENJAMIN. Chichester. Jan 21, 1774. Adm. to Emanuel Grubb.

RAY, THOMAS. East Nantmeal. Jan 24, 1772. Adm. to Wm. Millhouse.

BEAN, WILLIAM. East Nottingham.
Sept. 8, 1772. Aug. 24, 1773. Jan 27, 1774. [written like this.]
Provides for wife Jean. To son-in-law and daughter James and Mary Galt 10 acres of the lower end of the land bought of Hugh Allison and £10. To daughter Abigail Bean £130 and furniture. To son-in-law John McNit Alexander 5 shillings and to his wife my daughter Jean 5 shillings and to their son Wm. Bean Alexander the plantation I have in Carolina near Broad River. To son Wm. Bean plantation I now live upon, also plantation bought of Hugh Allison, also remainder of personal estate paying debts and legacies.
Executors: Wife Jean and son Wm. Letters to Wm., the other renouncing.
Wit: Jas. Finley, Mary Duncan, John Quinn.

GREEN, JOHN. Wilmington, Delaware.
1/21/1774. Feb. 1, 1774.
To brother Job Green new suit of clothes. To brother-in-law Joshua Proctor remainder of wearing apparel. All remainder of estate to brother Job, sister Margaret Proctor and cousins Elijah, Sarah and Job Proctor.
Executor: Uncle Abel Green.
Wit: George Miller, William Regester.

SHARP, MARY. Widow. Easttown.
Dec. 12, 1773. Feb. 14, 1774.
To son Thomas Sharp £2. To daughters Mary and Margaret 5 shillings each. To grandchildren William son of Thomas £5 at 21. To Thomas McKean my milch cow in trust for use of son Thomas' children. Rachel and Mary mentioned. To grandchildren William and Esther Dunging and Margaret Peasley the children of my 2 daughters Margaret, Rachel, Thomas and Mary children of son Thomas all remainder of estate when of age.
Executor: Thomas McKean.

Wit: Robt. McGugan, Jas. Davis.

DAVIES, ELLIS. Goshen. Jan 24, 1774. Adm. to Lydia Davis and Richd. Thomas.

RUSSELL, WILLIAM. Edgmont. Feb. 1, 1774. Adm. to Wm. and Thos. Russell.

LAMPLUGH, SAMUEL. Lower Chichester. Feb. 15, 1774. Adm. to Elizabeth Lamplugh and Isaac Dutton. (Sureties John Smith, Jacob Richards. Inventory. by John Brown, Nathl. Squibb £49.0.6.)

HEACOCK, JOSEPH. Marple. Mar. 5, 1774. Adm. to Jesse Maris and Jone Heacock.

KENNEDY, DAVID. Londonderry.
Mar. 9, 1773. Feb. 23, 1774.
Provides for wife Margaret including £100 (mentioned in contract of marriage between us). To son Montgomery Kennedy £1. To son Samuel £100. To son David £100. To son John £100. To son Joseph £80 on condition he returns here within 5 years after my decease. To daughters Agnes Finley and Isabel Willson £40 each. To daughter Jean Fryer £60. To the use of "the Jersey College" £10. Executors to sell all estate.
Executors: Sons Saml. and John and son-in-law Michael Finley. Letters to sons, the other being absent.
Overseer: Son Montgomery.
Wit: Saml. Creswell, Archibald Fleming, Hugh Hamilton.

HAMPTON, SIMON. Concord.
Mar. 1, 1774. Mar. 12, 1774.
To wife Sarah all estate real and personal except following legacies — To son Walter, daughter Rebecca Pyle, son Thomas and daughter Sarah Baldwin 1 shilling each. Testator died before signing will.
Executor: Son-in-law John Baldwin.
Wit: Nicholas Newlin, Wm. Bell, Nathanl. Newlin.

BAKER, JOHN. West Marlborough. Mar. 15, 1774. Adm. to Hannah Baker.

HENDERSON, JOHN. New London. Mar. 16, 1774. Adm. to David Mackey.

SMEDLEY, MARY. Middletown.
8/3/1772. Mar. 16, 1774.
To son-in-law Joshua Smedley walnut chest and pewter dish which was his mother's. To sons Ambrose and Thomas 7 shillings 6 each. To 2 daughters Jane Larkin and Sarah Moore all wearing apparel. Remainder into 4 equal shares: one I give to son Caleb Smedley, one to daughter Jane Larkin, one to children of son Wm. Smedley and one to children of daughter Sarah Moore.
Executor: Son Thomas.
Wit: Thos. Minshall, Agnes Minshall.

ELLIOTT, JOHN. Darby.
Jan 11, 1774. Mar. 16, 1774.
To brother Benjamin Elliott 1 shilling. To brother Christopher 5 shillings sterling. To Martha daughter of Robert Henvis £10 and to her sister Elizabeth Henvis £10. To George son of Jonathan Wood of Darby £10 at 21 with reversion to my 2 above mentioned nieces. Remainder of estate including plantation my father gave me to wife Amy during life.
Executors: Aaron Oakford and wife Amy. Letters to Amy Elliott, the other being absent.
Wit: Richard Humphreys, John Humphreys, Jona. Wood.

SHIRARDIN, JACOB. Vincent.
Jan 9, 1773. Mar. 25, 1774.
To wife Otilia plantation and all movables during widowhood. Mentions her 8 children. "My children that ar married." Susanna, Johaneta, Paul, Jacob, Catharin, Margaret, Magdalen and Mary is to have her living in the house and garden as long as she (if she should not go to Stoffel Teny again), also mentions my 4 youngest children Henery, Abraham, Yustin, Elizabeth.
Executors: Wife Otillia and son-in-law Adam Gider.
Wit: Jonas Heck, John Miller, Conrad Sharrar.

CAMPBELL, JOHN. West Caln. Mar. 28, 1774. Adm. to Charles Campbell.

YOUNG, HUGH. East Fallowfield. Mar. 30, 1774. Adm. to Elizabeth Young.

TAGGART, JOHN. Vincent. Apr. 1, 1774. Adm. to Jane and Jas. Taggart.

BELL, WILLIAM. Easttown.
Nov. 6, 1773. Apr. 6, 1774.
Provides for wife Margaret including remainder of Wm. McNeal's time. To son David plantation on which I now dwell on death of wife except 4 acres now occupied by Thos. Welch and wife Elizabeth, to daughter Mary on decease of Elizabeth Welch. To son William, plantation in Upper Merion bought of Abel Roberts. To sons Edward and Samuel 5 shillings each and to daughter Hannah McGee 5 shillings.
Executors: Wife Margaret and son Wm. (when 21). Letters to Margaret.
Wit: John Steel, Thomas Massey.

THORNTON, ROBERT. West Bradford.
1/7/1773. Apr. 9, 1774.
To son Samuel £5. To daughter Mary McVey £5 and an ox chain. To daughter Abigail White £5. To grandson Daniel Freeman £5 and book. To grandson Nathan Freeman £5. To grandson Saml. Freeman £20. To daughter Hannah Freeman 2 iron potts and my Bible. Remainder to daughter Hannah and her younger children, names not known. Real estate to be sold. Letters to Jos. Martin, the other renouncing.
Executors: Friend and kinsman, Peter Taylor of Upper Providence and Joseph Martin.

Wit: Robt. Spear, John Buffington.

SILL, JAMES. Edgmont.
July 3, 1772. Apr. 15, 1774.
Provides for wife Ann. To son James plantation in Edgmont subject to wife's life interest. To son Joseph £20. To son Richard £20, also all interest due me at my decease. To sons George and Michael £20 each. To daughters Mary Morris, Martha Holston and Ann Kennedy £20 each. To grandson James Regester £20 for services he did for me. Executors to sell plantation in Willistown. Remainder to wife Ann and son James, also Executors.
Wit: Nehemiah Baker, Lydia Baker, Nathan Baker.

GEST, DANIEL. East Bradford.
2/25/1774. Apr. 16, 1774.
Provides for wife Hannah. To son Joseph plantation in East Bradford containing 200 acres, also watch. To my 4 daughters Mary, Phebe, Ruth and Jane £200 each, also all remainder of estate. Land purchased of Geo. Strode containing 50 acres to be sold.
Executors: Son-in-law Joseph Temple and Emmor Jefferis.
Wit: Geo. Carter, Isaac Mendenhall, Jas. Marshall.

CAMPBELL, ALEXANDER. Londonderry.
Mar. 1, 1766. Apr. 19, 1774.
Provides for wife Elizabeth. To son John 1/3 personal estate and all real estate at wife's decease. To daughter Elizabeth Campbell remaining 1/3 of personal estate and £40 to be paid by son John. To grandson Alexander Campbell who now lives with me, £20 at 21. To daughter Janet Campbell £5. To wife remaining time of Samuel Boyd who now lives with me.
Executors: Wife and son John. Letters to John, wife renouncing.
Wit: Saml. Ramsey, Wm. Pinkerton, David Ramsay.

GREGG, BENJAMIN. Kennett. May 3, 1774. Adm. to Sarah Gregg.

REGISTER, JOHN. Edgmont. May 6, 1774. Adm. to Rebecca Register and Thos. Minshall.

HURFORD, JOHN. New Garden.
3/21/1774. May 5, 1774.
To son Samuel £1. To son Joseph all the interest now due me on a £40 bond. To daughter Elizabeth £1. To daughter Sarah £20. To son Caleb £100. To son Isaac £100. Joshua Pusey to be Trustee for him until he "be restored to his former or natural senses." To son Nicholas plantation where I now dwell containing about 100 acres subject to wife's life interest. To daughter Hannah 1/2 of all personal estate. Remainder of lands to be sold.
Executors: Wife Hannah and son Nicholas.
Wit: Nathaniel Scarlett, John Pusey, Lewis Pusey.

DAVIS, MARY. Wife of John. Charlestown.
Dec. 24, 1773. May 23, 1774.
Refers to marriage contract dated 27 March 1749 giving right to will £60. To Rev. Mr. John Davis £4 and to his brother Thomas Davis 20 shillings. To Mary daughter of David Davis, my stepson,

4 pewter plates. All remainder of goods and chattels to husband John Davis during life and then to his son David.
Executors: John Davis and son David. Letters to David, the other being absent.
Wit: Nicholas Pergrin, Benja. Thomas. John Pergrin.

MAXFIELD, SAMUEL. Chester Co.
Sept. 14, 1773. May 26, 1774.
To wife Jane 1/3 of all real and personal estate. To son Wm. £50. To daughter Mary £10. To daughters Margaret, Janet, Ann and Rebecca £10 each. To daughter Isabel £30. To daughter Elizabeth £40. To son Robert £50. Executors to sell real estate. Remainder to Wm., Robt., Elizabeth and Isabel.
Executors: James Henry and son Wm. Maxfield.
Wit: John Stewart, John Ross.

MILLER, HUGH. Blacksmith. Oxford.
Sept. 24, 1773. May 30, 1774.
To father Hugh Miller all my property this side the river Susquehanna, also all rent due me from Robert Curry in Baltimore Co. which is £20, also what is due from brother Francis's estate, and what is in sister Agnes' hand due me I give to brother-in-law's son Hugh Smith £20 and to his second son John Smith £20 at 21. Remainder which is £6 I give to herself. Remainder due me in Baltimore Co. to my brother-in-law Robert Smith.
Executors: Saml. McNeal and Hugh Miller, Sr. Letters to Miller, the other renouncing.
Wit: Robt. Criswell, Robt. Smith, Charles Dougherty.

SCOTT, JAMES. East Nottingham.
Mar. 2, 1774. May 31, 1774.
Directs body to be buried at Oxford graveyard. Provides for mother during life, not named. To sister Margaret £40. Saml. Scott, son of brother John, to be brought up on the place and learned to read, write and cipher and put to trade at 16 or 17. To sister Rebecca plantation whereon I now dwell paying what is still due thereon to my brother Philip and taking a deed from him as per agreement dated Mar. 5, 1768, it being my will she have the land as she has not received her part of our father's estate, also residuary legatee and Executrix.
Wit: James Steel, Archibald Job.

TURNER, ROBERT. Vincent.
Aug. 11, 1772. June 2, 1774.
To grandsons Isaac and Daniel Turner £50 each. To granddaughters Sarah, Rebecca, Ruth, Mary and Elizabeth £10 each, the boys at 21 and the girls at 18. Remainder if any to grandsons Abraham and John Turner.
Executors: Good friends Isaac Turner and Edward Jones.
Wit: Constantine O'Neill and Daniel Pickerd.

BLACKBURN, MARY. West Nottingham.
Oct. 20, 1773. June 2, 1774.
To son Robert Blackburn 10 shillings. To son John £1. To son Samuel £3. To son Ephraim £3. To son James 5 shillings. To son

Nathaniel £5. To daughter Susanna Cooper £1. To daughter Elinor McClannaughan £3. To daughter Jean Blackburn £7 at 21 or marriage. To daughter Mary Blackburn £7 at 21 or marriage. Remainder to Nathaniel, Jean and Mary.
Executors: Patrick Mulloy and John McMillon.
Wit: Saml. Ewing, Edward Brodely.

MILLER, JAMES. New Garden.
12/3/1772. June 13, 1774.
Provides for wife Ann. To son James plantation I now live upon and all other lands and stock paying the following legacies. To daughter Mary £4. To daughter Ann wife of Joshua Spikeman £20. To daughter Sarah wife of Thos. Barnet £4. To daughter Hannah wife of John Kerans £20. To son Joseph Miller's children £20 each as they come of age. To son William £30. To grandsons Wm. and Isaac Barns £5 each. To daughter-in-law Ann Miller and her children £180. To son-in-law Edward Dougherty 1 shilling and to daughter-in-law, son Joseph's widow, 1 shilling sterling.
Executor: Son James.
Wit: Thomas Hutton, Benja. Hutton, Wm. Miller.

HARTT, THOMAS. East Caln.
Nov. 19, 1770. June 13, 1774.
Provides for wife Mary. To brother John Hartt £5. To sister Martha Brooks £10. To nephew Thos. Brooks 1/2 part of my lands in East Caln to be taken off the eastern end adjoining lands of Moses and Isaac Coates, the other 1/2 of lands of Henry Fleming I give to wife Mary and her heirs. To brother John Hartt my house in Phila.
Executrix: Wife Mary.
Wit: Warrick Miller, Alex. Fleming, John Fleming.

PENNOCK, NATHANIEL. West Marlborough.
May 20, 1772. Codicil 6/6/1774. June 15, 1774.
Provides for wife Sarah. To daughters Susanna, Mary, Sarah and Alice £100 each at 21, also £100 each in trust for use of said daughters. To my 4 sons John, Joseph, Samuel and William as tenants in common, plantation where I now dwell containing about 500 acres, also plantation in Londongrove containing 500 acres purchased of Saml. Smith, also plantation in Springfield containing about 270 acres. Executors to sell grist mill and 10 acres in New Castle Co., also tract near by containing 50 acres, also 11 acres with 90 acres adj. the meadow and the money to be divided among my 4 sons. To son John all my right interest in about 100 acres of land in Birmingham which descended to me in right of my former wife, his mother.
Executors: Two oldest sons John and Joseph, brother Levis and brother-in-law Humphrey Marshall.
Codicil authorizes Executors to sell such lands devised to sons as shall be necessary to pay obligations.
Wit: Joseph Ashbridge, E. Price, Nathan Sellers. Jonathan Morris, Joseph Williams to Codicil.

HOPE, WILLIAM. East Caln. June 25, 1774. Adm. to Thomas Hope.

SWAFFER, JOSEPH. Chester Twp.
Oct. 4, 1770. Codicil 4/26/1774. July 4, 1774.
Provides for wife Elizabeth including "my family Bible that was bought from England." To son Richard 2/3 of my real estate during his life and at his death to his children with reversion to children of my daughter Ann, wife of Richard Maris, viz., Elizabeth, Richard, Tacey and Rebecca and other lawful issue, her son Jonathan only excepted. The remaining 1/3 of real estate to children of daughter Ann Maris. To sister Hannah wife of Danl. Humphrey at Merion £20. To niece Catharine Davis £10. To sister Ann Ellis £5. To Trustees of free school in Borough of Chester £10. To brother Wm. Swaffer all my law books and wearing apparel. £3 towards fencing Friends graveyard at Chester.
Executors: Brother Wm. and nephew Nehemiah Davis.
Codicil names nephew Roger Dicks, executor, instead of Nehemiah Davis.
Wit: John Morton, James Barton.

CHANDLER, SAMUEL. Kennett. July 5, 1774. Adm. to Thomas Johnson.

FISHER, ROBERT. Pennsbury.
4/15/1774. July 25, 1774.
Provides for wife Martha including right and interest in estate of her late father, Wm. Edwards. To daughter Hannah plantation in Pennsbury containing about 133 acres at 21 and all remainder of estate not otherwise disposed of. In case of her death, property to be sold and money divided as follows — To cousin Hannah daughter of Saml. and Hannah Cook and remainder to cousin Wm. son of Thomas Fisher.
Executors: Wife Martha and uncle Thos. Fisher. Letters to wife Martha, the other being absent.
Wit: Thos. Fisher, Jeremiah Cloud, James Bennett.

PAINTER, ELIZABETH. Birmingham.
6/1/1772. Aug. 8, 1774.
To son Saml. Painter and daughter Ann Chamberlin 5 shillings each. To granddaughter Elizabeth daughter of Robt. Chamberlin £30. To granddaughter Patience Holiday £20. Household goods to 3 granddaughters Mary Green, Hannah and Elizabeth Chamberlin. Remainder to daughter Ann and her children.
Executor: Trusty friend Danl. Green.
Wit: Thomas Thatcher, Saml. Painter, Thos. Woodward.

PEDRICK, JOHN. Appoquinimink Hundred, New Castle Co.
Mar. 28, 1774. Aug. 8, 1774.
To brother Adam silver watch. To sister Rachel silver shoe buckles. All remainder real and personal to wife Ann, also Executrix.
Wit: Zedekiah Wyatt Graham, Abigail Graham.

ZUCK, RUDULPH. East Caln.
Aug. 16, 1774. Adm. to Veronica Zuck.

DAVIS, THOMAS. Tredyffrin.
Nov. 17, 1773. Aug. 22, 1774.

"Shortly intending a voyage to the Island of Jamaica in the West Indies." To my mother Elizabeth Davis plantation whereon I now live in Tredyffrin during life, at her death to my sister Sidney Davis during her life and then to her male heir with reversion to her other children, she, he or they paying to my cousin Mary Hubbert £100 and to my cousin Mary Cambell £100.
Executors: Mother Elizabeth Davis and friend Lewis Gronow.
Wit: Saml. Davis, John Maxwell, Cornelius Dempsey.

EACHUS, DANIEL. Joiner. East Marlborough.
July 4, 1772. Aug. 23, 1774.
To cousin Daniel Eachus son of brother Robert £10 at 21. To sister Ann Wickersham and her husband Jas. all remainder of estate.
Executor: Cousin Abel Wickersham.
Wit: Caleb Baily, Abner Cloud, Sampson Wickersham.

HARLAN, JAMES. Londongrove.
5/9/1772. Aug. 30, 1774.
To son Solomon plantation I now live on containing 210 acres paying £105 as follows — To son Henry £50. To daughter Ann wife of John Updegraff £25. To daughter Susanna Harlan £25. To son-in-law Wm. Willis £5. Remainder to son Solomon.
Executor: Friend Richard Flower.
Wit: Joshua Pusey, John Pusey, Lewis Pusey.

MEREDITH, JOHN. West Whiteland. Sept. 2, 1774. Adm. to Mary Meredith. (Sureties Jos. Rea and James Hunter.)

MC CALLISTER, DANIEL. Concord. Sept. 5, 1774. Adm. to John Burnett.

SMITH, RICHARD. Springfield.
May 7, 1774. Aug. 30, 1774.
To sons Robert and James 20 shillings each and to grandson James Smith, Jr. 10 shillings. All remainder to wife Jane "altho my little substance is but a small gratuity to the said Jane Smith in respect to the great trouble and pains she has taken of me these several years past in my infirmities."
Executrix: Wife Jane.
Wit: Thomas Levis, Isaac Levis.

CLOUD, ANN. East Marlborough.
Apr. 18, 1774. Aug. 30, 1774.
To sons William, Jeremiah and Mordecai each 1/3 part of my estate. To granddaughter Lydia Troutten £10 and riding mare. To granddaughter Ann Reece 20 shillings and household goods. To grandson Jeremiah Underwood 20 shillings.
Executor: Son Mordecai.
Wit: Hannah Cloud, Betty Cloud, Jos. Davis.

MOORE, WILLIAM. Carpenter. West Fallowfield.
July 17, 1774. Sept. 7, 1774.
To brothers Robert, Francis, George, Howard and Andrew Moore and brother James Dunn and sister Rebecca Dunn each an equal share of all my estate and my brother James Devor and sister Elizabeth Devor

and my brother Thomas Karr and sister Jean Kerr have each of them 1/2 as much as the others.
Executors: Brothers Francis and Howard Moore.
Wit: John Dunn, James Dunn.

HUNTER, THOMAS. Upper Chichester. Sept. 19, 1774. Adm. to Elizabeth Hunter.

PETERSON, SOPHIA. Vincent. Sept. 19, 1774. Adm. to Henry Hethery.

LITTLER, WILLIAM. East Caln.
May 9, 1773. Sept. 27, 1774.
To daughter Rachel 106 acres to be surveyed off that place she now lives on. To daughter Elizabeth 100 acres of the west end of my plantation joining Ralstons and her sister Rachel's land. To daughter Cathrine £100. To 2 grandchildren Rachel and Elizabeth, daughters of son Thomas £100 each at 21. To daughter Ann wife or widow of son Thomas 5 shillings. Remainder of land to wife Elizabeth during life, also £100. To Mary wife of Hugh Cowan £15. Remainder equally divided among wife and children, daughter Ann, son Thomas' widow, to have no part therein.
Executors: Robt. Withrow and John Walker.
Wit: Saml. Withrow, Wm. Withrow, James Withrow.

WATKINS, AARON. Vincent.
Aug. 24, 1769. Oct. 1, 1774.
To wife Ann 1/3 of clear estate. To son Jacob 1/6 of clear estate at age 21. To daughter Jane 1/6 ditto at age 18. To son William 1/6 ditto at age 21. To daughter Margaret 1/6 ditto at age 18. To son Robert 1/6 ditto at age 21. To son Benjamin 1/6 ditto at age 21.
Executors: Wife Ann and brother-in-law Robt. Ralston. Letters to Ann Watkins, the other renouncing.
Wit: Joseph Cox, John Ralston, John Ralston.

THOMAS, THOMAS. Radnor.
2/14/1772. Oct. 1, 1774.
To my grandchildren by my daughter Margaret Lewis 40 shillings each. To my grandchildren by son Michael Thomas 40 shillings each. To daughter Margaret Lewis 20 shillings. To daughter-in-law Ester Thomas 20 shillings. To cousin Elizabeth Meredith £4. To Nathan Lewis and his son Levi wearing apparel, also all the books of Divinity Physic. To grandson Levi Lewis all remainder of estate, also Executor.
Wit: Lewis Lewis, Nathan Matlack, Joshua Clever.

VERNON, AARON. Newtown.
8/15/1765. Oct. 1, 1774.
To eldest son Edward Vernon £10. To second son Aaron £10. To third son John £10. To daughter Sarah wife of Samuel Bishop £10. To daughter-in-law Rebecca wife of Jos. Tenyear £3. Provides for wife Margaret. To youngest son Abraham plantation in Newtown as the same was conveyed to me by Jacob Edge and Wm. Wall being near 100 acres of land, also all remainder of personal estate subject to

legacies.
Executors: Wife Margaret and son Abraham.
Wit: Joshua Smedley, Geo. Smedley, Jr., Hannah Smedley.

HUNTER, ELIZABETH. Upper Cheter.
Sept. 20, 1774. Oct. 3, 1774.
To son William Hunter £4. To daughter Ann Hunter £10. All remainder to son Thomas.
Executor: Saml. Withrow of Aston.
Wit: Andrew Hunter, James Crage.

SMITH, JOHN. New London.
June 18, 1765. Oct. 4, 1774.
To grandsons John Smith and John Menoch £5 each. To daughter Janet Morrison in Ireland £10. To wife Martha and daughter Margaret Smith 1/2 of real and personal estate during their lives and the other 1/2 to my son John Smith.
Executors: Son John and John Scott. Letters to Smith, the other renouncing.
Wit: James Elder, James Scott.

CLOUD, ESTHER (alias HARRY). Pennsbury. Oct. 10, 1774. Adm. to Jeremiah Cloud.

CHAPMAN, JOHN. Goshen. Oct. 11, 1774. Adm. to Geo. Brinton and Caleb Peirce, Jr. (Left 3 daughters Ann, Mary m. John Henderson, Phebe m. John Robinson. Wife named Ailce, 1773. See Deed Book F 2.174.)

ROMAN, JOSEPH. East Caln. Oct. 18, 1774. Adm. to Ruth Roman.

MASON, WILLIAM. East Marlborough.
July 20, 1774. Oct. 11, 1774.
Provides for wife Margaret. All remainder of estate to 2 children Mary and William to be equally divided when son is 21.
Executor: Abel Wickersham.
Wit: Jas. Wickersham, David Eckhoff.

GRIFFITH, JOHN. East Nantmeal.
Sept. 25, 1774. Oct. 17, 1774.
Provides for wife Mary. To son William £100. To son Samuel £100. To daughter Anna Wickersham £35. To son-in-law Samuel Fisher 1 shilling. To son John all real estate and remainder of personal estate, also executor.
Wit: Stephen Phillips, Arthur Cunningham, Wm. Griffith.

PARKER, SEBELLAH. Kennett.
6/9/1774. Oct. 24, 1774.
To daughters Hannah Way, Sebbelah Cooper and Margaret Parker household goods and wearing apparel. To son Elisha one iron square.
Executor: Friend and neighbor Wm. Lamborn.
Wit: John Morgan, Hannah Way.

WAGGONER, JOHN. West Caln. Nov. 1, 1774. Adm. to Barbara Waggoner.

GRANTHAM, WILLIAM. Ridley.
Dec. 1, 1772. Oct. 31, 1774.
To nephew Charles Grantham son of brother George deceased the plantation I now dwell, also tract of 8 acres of woodland at 21, with reversion to his brother George. To my brother Isaac Hendrickson all the marsh meadow on my plantation. To niece Lydia Grantham £100 at 21. To friend Sketchley Morton £50. To St. James Church in Kingsess £15. To my 2 negroes Ceaser and Wm. remainder of my plantation lying next Crum Creek, also house and lot in which Simon Rice now dwells during their lives, they to be free at my decease. To nephew George Grantham my plantation lying next Crum Creek except what is devised to Isaac Hendricksen at 21.
Executor: John Morton, Esq.
Wit: Robert Colven, Michael Kets.

BUFFINGTON, JOHN. Yeoman. West Bradford.
Oct. 11, 1774. Died 10/23/1774. Nov. 4, 1774.
To wife Jane 1/3 of estate real and personal she bringing up her youngest daughter Phebe without any charge upon my estate. To 4 sons Robert, Richard, Jacob and Joshua 1/3 of whole estate. To other son John and 4 daughters, viz., Mary, Elizabeth, Jane and Phebe the other 1/3 of estate to be equally divided after making allowance for bringing up daughter Jane.
Executors: Wife Jane and son Richard. No record of letters.
Wit: Jas. Marshall, Wm. Cooper, Robt. McElheny.

VERNON, LYDIA. Spinster. North Providence.
Apr. 16, 1773. Nov. 7, 1774.
To sons Jonathan, Nathaniel, Mordecai and daughter Esther Aston household goods. To daughters Esther Aston, Hannah Calvert and Mary wife of Mordecai Vernon all wearing apparel. To Nathaniel son of Thos. Vernon £1 and to Thomas son of Nathl. £1 and to John son of Nathl., gold sleeve buttons. To Lydia wife of Jas. Walters, to granddaughters Ann and Esther Vernon, to granddaughter Elizabeth daughter of Mordecai Vernon and to granddaughter Hannah Calvert furniture.
Executors: Abraham Aston of Chester and John Hinkson. Letters to Aston, the other being absent.
Wit: Jona. Vernon, Jr., Thos. Hinkson, Frederick Vernon.

LEWIS, JOHN. West Bradford. Nov. 15, 1774. Adm. to Samuel Worth.

MOORHEAD, ANDREW. Birmingham. Nov. 16, 1774. Adm. to Andrew McKee.

O DAVILLEN, HUGH. Thornbury. Nov. 17, 1774. Adm. to George Fryer.

MASON, GEORGE. Kennett.
1/8/1770. Nov. 12, 1774. Buried at New Garden 10/26/1774.
To sons Joseph, Benjamin and Mathew one guinea each. To daughter Mary £20 "when my hay is sold which is at Risborough in Yorkshire."

To daughter Rachel one guinea. To daughter Jane £10 at 21. To wife 1/3 of estate during life. To sons John and James and daughter Grace all my lands in Maryland when 21. To son George all the land I now live upon and all remainder of estate, also Executor.
Wit: T. Woodward, Elizabeth Woodward.

ROWLAND, HUGH.
Aug. 10, 1774. Nov. 29, 1774.
To wife Ann 2/7 of whole estate. To son John 1/7 of whole estate, also watch and still. Remainder to be equally divided among my other 4 children (not named).
Executors: Wife Ann and Wm. Rowland. Letters to Ann, the other renouncing.
Wit: Samuel Ewing, John Smith.

HOLMES, JOHN. West Nottingham. Nov. 29, 1774. Adm. to Jane Holmes.

HANNA, JANE. West Nantmeal. Dec. 9, 1774. Adm. to James Hanna.

TREVILLO, PRICE. East Fallowfield. Dec. 23, 1774. Adm. to Alice Trevillo.

SPEARY, JAMES. Uwchlan.
11/26/1774. Dec. 9, 1774.
To John Evans farmer and miller of Caernaroon Twp., Lancaster Co. £20. To Edward Hughs of same place £20. To David Jones of Carnaroon, Berks Co., £10. To Rebecca widow of John Thomas of Warrinton, York Co. £100 being the bond due me from her son Jehu. To James Hockley £9. To Friends of Uwchlan Meeting £60 for walling graveyard. Remainder to executor for his trouble.
Executor: Friend Cadwallader Jones.
Wit: Joseph Phillip, Evan Evans, Josiah Phillip.

PATTON, DAVID. West Nottingham.
Nov. 24, 1774. Dec. 12, 1774.
To son William £7 and to his son David 40 shillings and to his son Wm. 20 shillings. To daughter Cathrin Lyon and her husband 30 shillings. To daughter Agnes Mackey and her husband 10 shillings. To granddaughter Mary Caldwell furniture. To granddaughter Agnes Caldwell furniture. To grandson Robt. Caldwell, a colt. To granddaughter Elenor Meck 10 shillings. To son David 1/2 of land and improvements I now possess and remainder of real and personal estate to son Thomas.
Executor: Son Thomas.
Wit: Jas. Maxwell, David Patten, Thomas Finly.

DAVIS, ELIZABETH. Darby.
10/12/1771. Dec. 24, 1774.
To eldest son Isaac £20 and clock. To son Jesse £20. To son William £5. To son James £100. To son Asa £20. To my daughter Elizabeth wife of Mordecai Moore £15. To daughter Hannah £20.
Executors: Sons Jesse, James and Asa.
Wit: Lewis Davis, Jr., Danl. Lawrence, John Hibberd.

WILLIAMS, SAMUEL. Lower Chichester. Dec. 28, 1774. Adm. to Andrew Forsyth. d.b.n.c.t.a.

FORDHAM, JOSEPH. Darby. Jan 5, 1775. Adm. to Jesse Bonsall and Lydia Fordham.

STARR, JEREMIAH. Londongrove. Jan 6, 1775. Adm. to Moses Starr.

ROWAN, WILLIAM. New Garden. Jan 11, 1775. Adm. to James Rowan. Sureties Geo. Sharp, James Milhous.

LAMPLUGH, JACOB. Upper Chichester. Jan 20, 1775. Adm. to Wm. Lamplugh.

MATHER, JOSEPH. Chester. Feb. 6, 1775. Adm. to David Jackson.

GIBBS, JAMES. West Caln.
Oct. 31, 1774. Jan 2, 1775.
To son Gilbert Gibbs my whole estate real and personal paying legacies. To wife Cathrin £50. To son Wm. £5. To son Hugh £20. To daughter Ann Marten £15. To daughter Mary Baxter £15. To daughter Margaret Gibbs £20. To daughter Isabella Gibbs £15. To grandson James Baxter £5.
Executor: Son Gilbert.
Wit: Thomas Kennedy, Patrick Porter.

SIDWELL, ABRAHAM. West Nottingham.
Mar. 27, 1774. Feb. 10, 1775.
Provides for wife Charity. To each of children (who are not named) an equal share of estate when they come of age.
Executors: Brother Hugh, William Allen and Nathan Harris. Letters to Sidwell, the others renouncing.
Wit: George Gartril, Joshua Haines, John Erwin.

LLOYD, ENOCH. Vincent.
May 29, 1773. Mar. 15, 1775.
To wife Sarah 1/3 of estate. To daughter Elizabeth all remainder of estate at 18. Executors to sell land in Virginia.
Executors: Wife Sarah and neighbor Saml. Morris. Letters to Sarah, the other renouncing.
Wit: John Adam Miller, Frederick Marsteller, John Neal.

REESE, WILLIAM. Willistown. Feb. 13, 1775. Adm. to Mary Reese and Nehemiah Baker. (At Orphans' Court 19 Sept, 1775 Enoch Yarnall and Nathan Baker were appointed guardians of Lydia, Hannah, Nehemiah and William Reece, children of William.)

PYLE, JOHN. Kennett. Feb. 27, 1775. Adm. to Judith Pyle.

THOMPSON, JAMES. Willistown. Feb. 28, 1775. Adm. to Geo. Smedley.

HOPE, ROBERT. Sadsbury. Feb. 28, 1775. Adm. to Hannah Hope and Robt. Withrow.

REED, HUGH. Londonderry. Mar. 1, 1775. Adm. to Wm. Montgomery.

DAVIS, ISAAC. Thornbury. Mar. 11, 1775. Adm. to Catherine and Geo. Davis.

THOMAS, JAMES. "of the 500 tract" in Chester Co.
May 18, 1773. Mar. 21, 1775.
Provides for wife Mary. To son Nathan at 21, 1/2 of all my lands and tenements paying to daughter Sarah £20. To son Isaac at 21 the other 1/2 of my lands paying to daughter Rachel £20.
Executors: Wife Mary and friend David John of Charlestown. Letters to Mary, the other being absent.
Wit: James Adams, Thomas Thomas, George Chapman.

HARRIS, JAMES. West Nottingham.
Apr. 28, 1774. Mar 21, 1775.
To mother Martha Harris £12 yearly during life. To brother William £50. To cousin Elizabeth Harris £80 at 18. To cousin John Oglebe's son James Harris Oglebe £10.
Executors: Brother William and cousin Elizabeth Harris. Letters to Wm., the other renouncing. (Elizabeth was daughter of William, she renounced her rights.)
Wit: Saml. Scott, James Barclay.

MUSGROVE, ABRAHAM. Londongrove.
Feb. 22, 1775. Mar. 24, 1775.
To step-father William Edens £50 and my mother the interest of £200 during life and at her death to sister's children, Elizabeth and Hannah Coats when 18. To brother-in-law Moses Coats £50 and to his wife Hannah my sister £200.
Executor: Thomas Pim of East Caln.
Wit: Jas. Lindley, Jonathan Lindley, Thomas Corse.

ANDERSON, JOHN.
9/12/1757. Mar. 25, 1775.
My share and interest in lands in Juniata I leave to James Alexander and my lands in Cumberland Co. to be sold and all remainder of estate I leave to my mother Mary Anderson if living, otherwise, to my sister Susanna Queaf. Said Mary Anderson and Susanna Queaf lives in Parish of Thomastown, Co. Kilkenny, Ireland.
Executor: Wm. Allen.
Wit: John Gartril, John Glasgow.

PORTER, JAMES. Blacksmith. West Nantmeal.
Aug. 23, 1774. Mar. 27, 1775.
Provides for wife Elizabeth. To son William £20. To my 5 daughters, viz., Rebecca, Isabald, Elizabeth, Elenor and Violet £20 each. To son Nathaniel all remainder of estate on paying above legacies and £15 additional to daughter Isabald.
Executors: Wife Elizabeth and son Nathaniel. Letters to Nathl., the other renouncing.
Wit: Wm. Porter, Francis Gardner.

DAY, JOHN. Nottingham (or so reputed)
May 18, 1774. Mar. 28, 1775.

Provides for wife Lydia. To eldest son John my plantation in York Co. which he now lives on. To second son Joseph my land and tanyard in Virginia bought of Stephen Ross. To eldest daughter Rebecca wife of Jacob Reynolds £10. To daughter Catharine wife of Jos. Wood £10. To youngest son George plantation I now live on in East Nottingham with tanyard. To grandson John Day son of John £25 at 21.
Executors: Wife Lydia and son George.
Wit: Timo. Kirk, John White, Jr., Jonathan Ross.

CHALFANT, JOHN. West Bradford. Apr. 3, 1775. Adm. to Ann Chalfant.

ROGERS, DAVID. East Nantmeal. Apr. 3, 1775. Adm. to Hannah Rogers.

DUTTON, THOMAS. Aston. Apr. 15, 1775. Adm. to Hannah and Jonathan Dutton.

ELDRIDGE, JONATHAN. Goshen. Apr. 22, 1775. Adm. to Sarah Eldridge.

LINN, CHARLES. Miller. Upper Providence.
Oct. 31, 1774. Mar. 29, 1775.
Mills and land belonging in Providence and Marple to be sold. Provides for wife Mary. To son Andrew £250 in full. To son John (doctor) £10. To daughter Margaret wife of Nathan Haycock £25. To daughter Martha £80. To daughter Mary £80. To daughter Esther £80. To son Charles £160 at 21. To daughter Hannah £80 at 18. To daughter Jean £80 at 18. To daughter Sarah £80 at 18. To grandson Hugh son of my son Hugh deceased 5 shillings at 21.
Executors: Son Andrew and daughters Martha and Mary.
Guardian for 4 minor children: Henry Hale Graham.
Wit: Joseph Rhoads, Isaac Rhoads.

YARNALL, JOHN. Willistown.
8/26/1765. Apr. 25, 1775.
Provides for wife Mary. To 2 sons Joshua and Caleb that part of my plantation on the west side of Providence Road. To son John 5 shillings. To son Nathan £10 and 4 sheep. To daughter Ann Edwards £10. To my sister Sarah Askew £3. To son Isaac the remainder of plantation where I now live, also all remainder of estate and Executor.
Wit: Joseph Thomas, Mary Thomas.

GOODWIN, THOMAS. Chester Co.
2/17/1775. May 1, 1775.
Provides for wife Ann. To son Richard my plantation on which I now dwell in Goshen containing 130 acres paying £500 to my estate. To son John £70. To son Thomas £70. To son Richard £70. To son Isaac £100. To daughter Jane Massey £100. To son-in-law Jesse Williams 5 shillings. Executors to sell land bought of Lewis Jones containing 53 acres.
Executors: Wife Ann and son Richard.
Wit: John Mechem, Jane Mechem, Margaret Forrester.

PEOPLES, WILLIAM. East Fallowfield.
Feb. 21, 1775. May 5, 1775.
Provides for wife Martha. To daughter Agnes Peoples £20 when of age. To daughter Sarah Peoples £20 when of age. To daughter Martha £20 when of age. To son Robert £30 at 21 to be bound out at 16. To son Alexander all real estate and remainder of personal.
Executors: Wife Martha and William McKey. Letters to Martha, the other renouncing.
Wit: Davison Filson, Hugh Jordan.

HENDERSON, MARGARET. New London.
Apr. 21, 1775. May 9, 1775.
To daughter Margaret Crawford all wearing apparel. To son John Henderson £40. To granddaughter Margaret Henderson, Edward's daughter, cow and furniture. Orders a large tombstone for self and late husband. All remainder to son Edward, also Executor.
Wit: Francis Allison, Jr., David Mackey.

TEMPLE, WILLIAM. Kennett.
6/10/1769. May 9, 1775.
To sons-in-law Wm. Seal, Benj. Hutton, John Pyle and Benj. Jones 5 shillings each. To grandson Stephen Webb £40. To son-in-law Caleb Seal 2 lotts in Borough of Wilmington. To son Benjamin plantation whereon I now dwell in Kennett containing 234 acres, also 9 acres in East Bradford purchased of John Collier, also all furniture and stock. Remainder equally divided between sons Thomas and Benjamin and daughter Hannah, wife of Isaac Miller.
Executors: Jas. Bennett and James Marshall.
Wit: Jos. Martin, Robt. Woodward, Abrm. Ford.

FOULKE, ENEAS. Bethel. May 24, 1775. Adm. to William Gest.

ZINK, MICHAEL. Coventry. May 30, 1775. Adm. to Mary and Jacob Zink.

TURNER, ROBERT. Oxford.
Aug. 30, 1774. May 31, 1775.
To son James all lands, tenements and remainder of personal estate after legacies are paid. To daughter Sarah wife of Wm. Rutherford £30. To son-in-law George Creswell £20 which he owes me and to his wife Mary £20. To grandson Robert All £10. To granddaughter Mary Turner, daughter of Moses deceased, 30 shillings.
Executor: Son James.
Wit: John White, John Curle, Wm. Miller.

WORRALL, JONATHAN. Marple.
3/11/1773. June 5, 1775.
To wife Mary 1/3 of estate. To daughter Patience McClaskey £10. To son William 5 shillings. To son Samuel £10. To son Jacob 5 shillings. To daughter Anne Elliott £15. To son Elijah £85. To son Joseph 5 shillings. To daughter Mary Moore £30. To daughter Martha Moore £30. To sons Benjamin and Seth plantation I now live on and all remainder of estate, also Executors.
Wit: John Morton, Daniel Culin, Jr.

WOOD, WILLIAM. Londongrove. June 5, 1775. Adm. to Margaret and Thos. Wood.

HARPER, SAMUEL. Kennett. June 14, 1775. Adm. to John McCullough.

JONES, SARAH. Widow. East Bradford.
Jan 13, 1775. June 10, 1775.
To son Edward Jones £5. To sons John and Benjamin £15 each. To daughters Hannah wife of Thomas Temple and Lydia wife of Jas. Jefferis £5 each. To 3 youngest daughters Elizabeth Harlan, Cordilla Webb and Ann Chandler £50 each.
Executor: Son Benjamin.
Wit: John Jones, Betty Jones, Jas. Marshall.

SHARPLESS, JAMES. North Providence.
Feb. 18, 1775. June 19, 1775.
Provides for wife Elizabeth. To grandson James son of Jas. Sharpless £5 at 21. To son Joshua 1 shilling sterling as for my daughter Rebecca and granddaughters Elizabeth Sharpless, Mary Richards, Sarah and Abigail Dicks, I do not see cause to give anything, but love and good will. To son Nathaniel my plantation whereon I now dwell in North Providence containing about 161 acres and all remainder of estate.
Executors: Wife Elizabeth and son Nathaniel.
Wit: James Crozer, Jos. Gibbons, Jr., Caleb Davis.

WHITE, JOHN. Oxford.
May 23, 1772. June 20, 1775.
Provides for wife Margaret. To son Saml. £15. To daughter Janet Love £15. To son James £6. To son Edward £16. To son Thomas £16. To son Isaac £16. To daughters Sarah and Rebecca their beds and saddles. Remainder equally divided.
Executors: John Ross and Thos. Love.
Wit: David Fleming, Thos. Armstrong, John Black.

BEATTY, DAVID. Uwchaln. July 24, 1775. Adm. to Elizabeth and Robt. Beatty. (See Deed Book A 2.252, 4/1/1777. Daughters Esther m. John Elliot, Agnes m. Samuel Culbertson, Rachel m. Samuel McClure.)

GEST, HANNAH. East Bradford.
6/12/1775. June 20, 1775.
To daughter Mary Dilworth £20. All wearing apparel to 3 daughters. Remainder of estate to 3 youngest children, Joseph, Ruth and Jane to be equally divided, sons at 21, daughters at 18.
Executor: Brother Benjamin Mendenhall.
Wit: Jos. Pierse, Jesse Mendenhall.

SHARPLESS, JACOB. Concord.
7/9/1775. July 26, 1775.
Provides for wife Ann. To son John £20. To daughter Lydia wife of David Dutton £50 in trust during life of her husband. All remainder of estate to be equally divided amongst 8 of my children, viz., John, Nathan, Joseph, Jesse, Ann, Jane, Martha and Hannah Sharpless, the sons at 21, daughters at 18.

Executors: Son Nathan and cousin Isaac Sharpless.

TAYLOR, BENJAMIN. Pennsbury.
--- 1775. July 29, 1775.
To son Isaac all that tract of land my father Joseph Taylor bought of Ruth Harlan and conveyed to me in Pennsbury containing 100 acres paying to wife Sarah £300. To son Benjamin tract of land my father bought of James Underwood and conveyed to me containing 140 acres he paying to daughter Elizabeth wife of Emmor Jefferis £250 and to daughter Ann wife of Joseph Cope £250 and to wife Sarah £100. To wife Sarah lot of ground in Wilmington, also plantation whereon I now live containing 100 acres during her life and at her decease sons to sell the same and the money to be equally divided among 5 children, Isaac, Benjamin, Elizabeth, Hannah and Ann. All remainder to wife Sarah, also Executrix.
Wit: Thos. Temple, Titus Bennett, Jas. Bennett.

POWELL, JOSEPH. Marple.
Mar. 13, 1773. Aug. 7, 1775.
To son Thomas 27 acres of land part of the land whereon I now live in Marple. To son Joseph 50 3/4 acres of same land. To son George 27 acres of same land. To daughter Elizabeth Pannol 5 shillings and to son-in-law Evan Pennol 1 shilling 6. To daughter Mary Powell 5 shillings. To daughter Sarah McAffee 5 shillings and to her husband David Macaffee 1 shilling 6. To daughter Hannah Bonsall 5 shillings. To daughter Jane Gracy 5 [shillings] and to her husband Samuel Gracy 1 shilling 6. To daughter Susanna Griffith 5 [shillings] and to her husband Lewis Griffith 1 shilling 6. To daughter Patience Hayworth 5 shillings and to her husband Geo. Hayworth 1 shilling 6. Provides for wife Patience.
Executors: Sons Thos. and Joseph. Letters to Jos., the other being absent.
Wit: David Ellis, Philip Moore, Jacob Beery.

GRUBB, MARY. East Bradford.
7/15/1775. Aug. 8, 1775.
To Isaac son of my cousin John Billerby in England all that plantation in St. George's Hundred, New Castle Co., Delaware, containing 360 acres. To cousin Isaac Grubb formerly of Pennsbury £30. To cousin Mary Grubb of Pennsbury £30. To cousin Mary daughter of Richard Thatcher £30. To cousin Mary Flower £30. To cousin Thos. Thorpe his bond of £21. To Saml. and Mary children of Edward Jones £10 each. To cousins Mary and Elizabeth Buffington £20 each. To Temperance Clayton £10 and table linen. To Saml. son of John Martin £20. To Elizabeth daughter of John Buffington £20. To Frances wife of Jos. Smith £20. To Geo. Turner £3 per annum during life. To Jane daughter of Thos. Themple, Esq., £30. To my maid Mary Martin £100 and furniture. To cousin Mary Gladley £100. To cousin Saml. Grubb of Pennsbury all remainder of estate, also Executor.
Wit: Thos. Temple, Jos. Temple, John Nethery.

CULIN, DANIEL, JR. Ridley. Aug. 10, 1775. Adm. to Wm. Worrall.

TODD, JOHN.   New London.
7/16/1774. Aug. 18, 1775.
To son William Todd now supposed to be in Carolina £100.   To
daughter Jane wife of Henry Hayes £35.   To son James £15 and all
wearing apparel having advanced him to the value of £115 in my
lifetime.   To daughter Margaret wife of James Willson £15.   To
grandsons John and James, sons of John Todd, £30 each.   To 3
grandchildren Martha, Mary and Sarah Willson £20 to be divided. To
daughter Sarah McKee £10 and to grandson John McKee £15.   To
daughter Elizabeth Hodgson £5. To grandson John Willson £5.   To
grandson Isaac McKee £5. To grandson Wm. son of Jas. Todd £5.   To
daughter Margaret wife of son James £10. Reversion of legacy to
son Wm. to sons-in-law John Morton and Wm. Hutton of York Co.
Executors: Son John of Phila. and son-in-law Henry Hayes.
Wit: John Waugh, James Puntle, Reobert Caien.

NIVIN, ISABEL. Londonderry.
Sept. 9, 1771. Aug. 21, 1775. (See Deed Book J.201.)
To aged mother all the profits of whole estate during life.   To
sister Mary Montgomery's daughter Margaret, my sister Agnes
Sample's daughter Margaret and sister Martha Nivin's daughter
Isabel, brother Wm. Nivin's daughter Isabel and to my brother-in-
law Wm. Montgomery's 2 daughters Mary and Margaret by my sister
Margaret my whole estate real and personal to be equally divided
considering Wm. Montgomery's 2 daughters as one party.
Executor: Brother in law, Wm. Montgomery.
Wit: Ebenezer Brooks, Edwd. Crooks.

MORRISON, MARY. Widow. Concord.
6/23/1775. Aug. 21, 1775.
To son Nathaniel, daughter Agnes, sons Robert and Joseph, daughter
Mary and son James 5 shillings each. To daughter Elizabeth
household goods. To son John £5 at 21. To daughter Priscilla
household goods. To granddaughter Letitia Brice 40 shillings at
18, also all remainder of estate.
Executors: Brother Nicholas Newlin and John Walter.
Wit: John Arment, John Palmer, Nathan Yarnall, Jr.

GIBSON, ALEXANDER. Late Chester Co., now of Rowan Co., N.C.
Oct 26, 1773. Nov. 1, 1774. Jan 6, 1775, letters.
To father and mother £50. To brother Dr. Isaac Gibson £40.   To
nephew Alexander, son of brother John Gibson £15. To nephew
Alexander son of brother James £15. To my sister's son Alexander
Fleming £15. To each of my nephews excepting the above named £10.
Remainder to 3 brothers John, James and Samuel and brothers-in-law
Wm. Dizart, James Fleming and Andrew Newberry.
Executors: Brother James and Andrew Newberry. Letters to Jas.
Gibson, the other renouncing.
Wit: James Morrison, Thos. Morrison, Joseph Steel.

WEBB, REBECCA. Widow of Wm. Kennett.
9/25/1764. Aug. 29, 1775.
To grandson Wm. Webb £75. To grandson Stephen Webb £30. To
granddaughter Rebecca Taylor £30. To grandson Ezekiel Webb £50.
To granddaughter Jane Webb £35. To grandson Wm. Webb's daughter

named Rebecca £20 at 18. To Benj. Taylor, Jr. son Joseph £15 at 21 and to his son Wm. £15 at 21. To granddaughter-in-law Wm. Webb's wife Sarah £8. To cousin Jane, wife of Robt. Brown, to cousin Rebecca Blackburn £5. To servant girl Mary Carson case of drawers. To grandson-in-law Benj. Taylor, Jr., to daughter-in-law Wm. Webb's widow Elizabeth walnut table. To grandson Wm. Webb all remainder of estate, also Executor. Letters c.t.a. to Stephen Webb.
Wit: Thos. Boyle, Phebe Carter, Jehu Hollingsworth.

MILHOUS, SARAH. Pikeland.
8/7/1770. Aug. 29, 1775.
To oldest son John Milhous £9. To son James £10. To son Thomas £9. To each of my grandchildren, viz., Sarah, Mary, Ruth, Lydia and Thomas (children of son John) and Paschall, Hannah, Samuel, Phebe, Deborah, Enos, Susanna and Elizabeth children of son Thomas and John, Dinah, and Jesse (the children of son Robert) and George son of my daughter Sarah Parker and Mercy daughter of son William £4 each at 21. To son Wm. riding chair. To daughters-in-law Ann Milhous, Margaret and Elizabeth Milhous all wearing apparel.
Executors: Sons John and Thomas.
Wit: Thomas Johnson, Sarah Webb, Phebe Johnson.

TEMPLE, THOMAS. East Caln. Aug. 30, 1775.
Adm. to John Temple (who affirmed).

SCOTT, JAMES. Easttown. Aug. 31, 1775. Adm. to Sarah Scott and Azariah Lewis.

KENNEDY, GEORGE. Chester Co.
May 19, 1775. Aug. 30, 1775.
To wife Elizabeth and 3 children William, Elizabeth and Rebecca all estate real and personal when son is 21.
Executors: Wife Elizabeth and brother-in-law Thomas White.
Wit: James Thompson, James McCalla, Warrick Miller.

BENTLEY, JEFFREY. Yeoman. Late of Polecat Settlement, Guilford Co., N. C. now Uwchlan.
Aug. 10, 1775. Aug. 31, 1775.
To wife Mary all personal estate and use of real estate until son Joseph is of age at which time I give to my children, viz., Joseph, Jonathan, and Eleanor an equal share in the same. Peter Dix, John Beals, Jr. and Joseph Leonard all of Guilford Co., N.C. guardians for my children.
Executors: Wife Mary and brother Banner Bentley. Letters to Banner, the other being absent.
Wit: Benjamin Davies, Israel Whelen, James Packer.

SHARPLESS, DANIEL. North Providence.
7/29/177?. Sept. 7, 1775.
Provides for wife Sarah. To eldest son Thomas several lotts of ground in Chester, also his note of £10. To son Daniel the land my father devised to me on the north side of Ridley Creek in North Providence containing about 200 acres and the land I purchased of Nathan Vernon containing about 40 acres and marsh in Ridley containing 8 acres, also stock and farming utensils. To daughter

Rebecca wife of John Eyre £150. To daughter Abigail £200.
Remainder to wife and 4 children.
Executors: Sons Thomas and Daniel.
Wit: Wm. Swaffer, Isaac Weaver, Roger Dicks.

RALSTON, JOSEPH. Upper Chichester. Sept. 11, 1775. Adm. to Wm. Lamplugh.

SCOTT, JOHN, JR. Easttown. Sept. 19, 1775. Adm. to Elizabeth Scott and Wm. Garrett.

PRATT, JOSEPH. Edgmont.
7/26/1775. Codicil 8/3/1775. Sept. 7, 1775.
To son Abraham plantation purchased of Jonathan Ashbridge in Goshen containing about 217 acres paying to my daughter Jane Hoopes £200 and to my daughter Mary Pratt £50. To son Joseph messuages and tracts of land where I now dwell in Edgmont containing 209 acres paying to my daughter Mary Pratt £250. To son David plantation in Marple, late of Joshua Pennell, Jr., containing about 172 acres paying to daughter Priscilla Pratt £250. To son Thomas plantation purchased of Nathan Yarnall in Marple containing about 113 acres and about 79 acres of the Pennell tract. To daughter Priscilla Pratt £50. To daughter Sarah Pratt £50 at 18 and £250 at 21.
Executors: Sons Abm. and Joseph.
Wit: George Miller, William Russell.

RUSSELL, EDWARD. Chester Borough.
June 29, 1770. Sept. 26, 1775.
Provides for wife Dinah. To daughter Mary wife of Adam Grubb £300. To grandson Edward Russell £150 at 21. To my 2 granddaughters Elizabeth and Jemima £100 each at 18 or marriage. I give my share in the Chester Library to the first of my grandchildren who shall come to live in Chester. All remainder to son Joseph.
Executors: Wife Dinah and son Joseph.
Codicil May 17, 1774 gives to granddaughter Mary Russell £100 at 18 and to niece Sibella Coppock, bed &c.
Wit: Jno. Pedrick, Edwd. Bettle.

GRAHAM, MICHAEL. West Nantmeal.
Jan 24, 1759. Oct. 11, 1775.
To eldest son John Graham 200 acres to be laid off the north side of my plantation. To son Michael all the remainder of my plantation together with what vacant land is between it and Robt. Lusks. Provides for wife Elizabeth Smith, otherwise Graham. To son James £30 when of age. To son Abraham £30 when of age. All personal estate to sons James and Abraham and daughters Susanna, Margaret, Elizabeth and Eleanor Graham and what other children may be born to me.
Executors: Friends Jason Cloud and Michael Graham and son John.
Wit: Jarett Graham, James Anderson, Hannah Graham.

ROE, WILLIAM. New Garden.
Apr. 14, 1775. Oct. 18, 1775.
To daughter Jane wife of Alex. McMonigal all rents and profits of plantation I now live upon lying partly in New Castle Co. (partly

for schooling and clothing my grandchildren James and Elizabeth Bell) until my grandson comes to age of 21, she paying following legacies — To her niece Annable wife of Moses Montgomery £50 and to all the rest of my son-in-law David Robinson's children 5 shillings each. To daughter Annable wife of Jos. Robinson and to my daughter David Robinson's wife 1 shilling each. To granddaughter Jane daughter of Moses Montgomery and to my grandchildren James and Elizabeth Bell, children of my daughter Jane, all this my plantation aforesaid to be divided or sold if necessary.
Executors: Daughter Jane and Wm. Miller of New Garden.
Wit: Andrew McAntier, William Whiteside, Hannah Whiteside.

PIERCE, GEORGE. Newlin.
9/12/1775. Oct. 24, 1775.
To son Joshua tract of land in Newlin purchased of John Newlin containing 23 acres together with 80 acres adjoining, to be taken off the land I had by deed of my father lying on south side of Brandywine, also about 50 acres of same land lying on north side of said Creek paying to son Thomas £80. To son Robert £60. To daughter Hannah Martin £100. To son George all that land in Newlin purchased of John Stanton containing about 100 acres, also all lands purchased of Nathl. Newlin about 32 acres adjoining with a part of land I had of my father paying to son Robert £80. Executors to convey to Sarah Stubbs 2 lotts of land in Newlin purchased of Wm. Thompson containing 12 acres and 18 perches according to bargain made with her. All remainder of lands to sons Caleb, Jesse and David. To son Thomas £25 and his debt of £30 owing to me. Remainder to sons Joshua and Caleb, also Executors.
Wit: Wm. Cloud, Jos. Pierce.

BOON, ANDREW. Darby.
Sept. 2, 1771. Oct. 31, 1775.
Provides for wife Bridget. To son Joseph messuage where he now lives and 60 acres of land to be laid off the northern end thereof and 1/2 of meadow. To son Hans messuage where I now live and 70 acres to be laid off the middle of my tract and other 1/2 of meadow paying to my daughter Barbara, wife of John Bryan, £50. To son Andrew the messuage and 20 acres where he now lives and meadow now occupied by him. Remainder to son Hans, also Executor. Letters to Joseph and Andrew Boon, Hans having relinquished.
Wit: John Morton, Andrew Urian, Andrew Boon, taylor.

HOOPES, BENJAMIN. Goshen. Nov. 4, 1775. Adm. to Betty and Joshua Hoopes.

DONAHEY, WILLIAM. Oxford. Nov. 20, 1775. Adm. to Martha Donahey.

BOURNE, THOMAS. West Marlborough. Nov. 28, 1775. Adm. to Robt. Lamborn d.b.n.c.t.a.

PUGH, WILLIAM. East Nottingham. Nov. 30, 1775. Adm. to Patience Pugh.

LAMBORN, ROBERT. Londongrove.
11/3/1775. Nov. 27, 1775.
To youngest son Thomas a tract of land being part of the plantation I now live on at the north end thereof containing about 16 acres. All remaining real and personal to wife Sarah during life. To son Wm. and 3 daughters, viz., Ann Fisher, Elizabeth Fisher and Sarah Mendenhall 20 shillings each. Remainder at death of wife to 5 sons, viz., Robert, Francis, John, Thomas and Josiah.
Executors: Wife Sarah and son Robert.
Wit: Francis Lamborn, Samuel Gaskill.

WILLIAMS, JOSEPH. Sadsbury.
July 26, 1774. Dec. 1, 1775.
Provides for "once well beloved wife" Mary "while she behaves herself." To eldest son Amos 25 acres at S.W. corner of my land in Lancaster & Chester Counties. To second son Minshall 30 acres at S.E. corner of my land. To second eldest daughter Eleanor Williams £40. To third daughter Hannah Williams £40. To 3 youngest sons, viz., Joseph, John and Joshua all remainder of my land to be equally divided at 21 paying to my 2 youngest daughters Mary and Ann Williams £40 each. To grandson Joseph Moore £5 at 21.
Executors: Sons Amos and Minshall.
Wit: William Powell, Samuel Simmons.

BAILY, CHARLES. Dec. 1, 1775. Adm. to Cottrell Baily.

REECE, LEWIS. Newtown.
2/20/1769. Dec. 15, 1775.
Funeral charges to be paid by my son-in-law Geo. Garrett as specified in article dated 8/24/1757. To son David all wearing apparel and watch. To granddaughter Sarah Lewis £12. To granddaughter Mary Evans £8. To granddaughter Grace Craige £8. To grandson Mordecai Morris £8. To granddaughter Hannah Edwards £3. To grandson Reese Edwards £8. To grandson Joseph Edwards £8 at 21. To grandson Reece Garrett my biggest Bible at 18. To grandson Peter Garrett 20 shillings and to granddaughter Lydia Garrett 30 shillings at 18. Remainder to son David, also Executor.

BAILY, JOEL. West Marlborough.
May 7, 1773. Dec. 19, 1775.
Provides for wife Betty. To son Joel £25. To son Isaac tract of land in West Marlboro purchased of Edward Tatnel containing 130 1/2 acres with 61 acres adjoining the remainder of tract purchased of Aaron Baker (except 5 3/4 acres to son Joshua). To son Joshua tract of land whereon I now dwell containing 166 1/2 acres, also 5 3/4 acres of above tract. £150 received from sale of house and lott in Wilmington, Delaware, to son Joel to be divided between daughter Betty 1/4 part, daughter Ann 1/4, daughter Mary 1/8. To grandson Thos. Harlan 1/8 at 21, daughter Phebe 1/4. To grandson John Webster 5 shillings. Legacy to Ann, wife of David Hayes, in trust. If Thomas Harlan should die under age, his share to his brother Israel and sister Lydia.
Executors: Wife Betty and son Joel. Letters to Joel, the other being deceased.
Wit: James Kenny, Samuel Worth, Rachel Baker, Richard Baker.

STRINGER, JOSEPH. West Fallowfield. Dec. 28, 1775. Adm. to Elizabeth Stringer.

DAVIS, DAVID. Vincent.
Oct. 2, 1775. Jan 4, 1776.
To wife Eleanor 1/2 of real and personal estate during life. To son thomas the other 1/2 of estate and remainder at death of wife. To daughter Lettice, wife of James John, £30. To daughter Margaret Davis £30 and cow when married. To daughter Jane Davis £30 and cow. To daughter Hannah Davis £30 and cow. To son John £40.
Executors: Wife Eleanor and son Thomas.
Wit: Wm. Chiddick, Wm. James.

MORRIS, ROBERT. Marple.
May 2, 1775. Jan 11, 1776.
Mentions plantation in Marple now in possession of father and mother left to me by grandfather Robt. Taylor. To 3 youngest sisters Jane, Phebe and Hannah, all the said plantation containing 200 acres at expiration of time the same was left to my father and mother, they paying to my oldest sister Mary Moore £100.
Executor: Father John Morris.
Wit: Thomas Simon, Amos Yarnall, Jacob Beery.

DUNWOODIES, WILLIAM. West Nantmeal.
Apr. 7, 1773. Jan 11, 1776.
Provides for wife Janet. To eldest son Andrew the bay horse. To son James, a mare. To brother James Dunwoodies £20 if he stands in need thereof. To sister Martha Graham £20 with reversion to her children and children of my deceased sister Agnes McCoulough. My plantation and all remainder of to be equally divided between my 2 sons Andrew and James.
Executors: Wife Janet and sons Andrew and James. Letters to sons, Janet being absent.
Wit: Wm. Irwin, Jas. Anderson, Moses Scott.

PEIRCE, SARAH. Concord.
Dec. 31, 1775. Jan 11, 1776.
To daughter Hannah furniture. To son William £5. To son John £5, also Executor. To my 5 grandchildren 5 shillings each. To daughter-in-law Mary Peirce chest of drawers. Remainder to 2 daughters Hannah and Rachel. Testator died before signing on above date.
Wit: Thomas Millsom, Hannah Perkins.

HOBSON, MARTHA. Widow of Francis. New Garden.
11/23/1775. Jan 17, 1776.
To sons Francis and John 5 shillings each. To son-in-law Robert Boyce £2 and to his wife, my daughter Mary, £2 and to my granddaughter Martha Boyce £5. To granddaughter Isabel Boyce £20 and all household goods. To son-in-law Saml. Miller and to his wife Martha £2 each and to their children, viz., Joseph, Rebecca, Jane, Samuel, Lydia and Jacob Miller, £30 to be divided. To son Joseph 5 shillings and to his son Francis, Bible and weaver's loom and to his daughter Hannah a cow.
Executor: Son-in-law Saml. Miller.

Wit: Saml. Cherry, Isaac Jackson.

MILLER, ANN. New London. Jan 19, 1776. Adm. to Wm. Miller.

WAYNE, ISAAC. Newtown. Jan 31, 1776. Adm. to Elizabeth and Anthony Wayne.

POWELL, SAMUEL. Feb. 28, 1776. Adm. to Benj. Powell.

PASCHALL, JOHN, JR. Darby. Feb. 28, 1776. Adm. to Henry Paschall.

CAIN, JOHN. Londongrove.
Dec. 19, 1775. Feb. 16, 1776.
All estate real and personal to friend and cousin Charles Booth of Londongrove, also Executor.
Wit: David Hunter, David Mackey.

DAVIS, PHILIP. Uwchlan.
Nov. 4, 1772. Feb. 21, 1776.
To eldest son David 5 shillings having alreday received more than his share of my estate. To son Philip 3 acres off the N.W. corner of my land where he now lives during his life and at his death to my son Miles. To son Jerman 5 shillings. To daughter Sarah wife of Myrick Davis 5 shillings. Provides for wife Elizabeth. Remainder to wife and son Miles, also Executors. Letters to Miles, the other renouncing.
Wit: Humphrey Lloyd, Jno. Lloyd, David Thomas.

GRONOW, JOHN. Tredyffrin.
Oct. 9, 1775. Feb. 27, 1776.
Provides for wife Isabella. To grandson John Gronow Bull when 21 my plantation in Cumberland Co. containing 150 acres with reversion to granddaughter Mary Bull. To son Lewis Gronow £200 in trust for use of daughter Sarah Bull. To son Lewis my plantation in Tredyffrin containing 165 acres and all remainder of personal estate, also Executor.
Wit: David Davis, Issacher Evans, Joshua Evans.

ANDERSON, WILLIAM. Tredyffrin.
2/15/1775. Feb. 28, 1776.
To nephew Wm. Anderson £10 and wearing apparel. To my housekeeper Jane Meredith £20 and furniture. To Susanna Meredith, Jr., household goods. To Mary Meredith £5. To Friends of Radnor Meeting £5 to repair grave yard wall. Remainder to Jane and Mary Meredith.
Executor: Nathan Matlack of Radnor.
Codicil 9/14/775 revokes legacy to Radnor Meeting and gives it to nephew Wm. Anderson.
Wit: Jesse Meredith, Mary Jones, Hugh Griffith, Jr.

REED, ANDREW. Fallowfield.
June 11, 1773. Feb. 28, 1776.
To daughter Mary £7.10 which I am bound for on her husband's

account. To daughter Margaret £10. To daughter Lattice £20. To son John £15. To daughter Isabel bed and cow. To son Andrew the grey mare and all implements of husbandry. Remainder to 4 children, viz., John, William, Isabel and Andrew.
Executors: Sons Wm. and Andrew. Letters to Wm., the other being absent.
Wit: James Liggett, James Noble.

KENNEDY, THOMAS. West Nantmeal.
Mar. 14, 1772. Feb. 28, 1776.
Provides for wife Dorety. To son Archibald 5 shillings. To daughter Jane's children by David Drennan 5 shillings. To daughter Nelly 5 shillings. To daughters Elizabeth and Mary, to son John, to daughter Isabella 5 shillings each. To son William after my wife's decease all my plantation.
Executors: Wife and son Wm. Letters to Wm., the other being absent.
Wit: Samuel Denny, William Logan.

THOMAS, DAVID. Vincent. Mar. 18, 1776. Adm. to Hazael Thomas.

LEWIS, ABRAHAM. Darby. Apr. 6, 1776. Adm. to Ann Lewis and Wm. West.

VIRT, FRAY. Relict of Aartin Virt. East Fallowfield.
Jan 23, 1776. Mar. 5, 1776.
To Mary wife of Joseph Arthurs all my personal estate, also Executrix.
Wit: Catherine Campbell, Wm. Dunley, Saml. Quinn.

CROSBY, SAMUEL. Londonderry.
Jan 23, 1776. Mar. 29, 1776.
To brother David my carpenter tools. Remainder to be sold and divided between mother Rachel Crosby and John, David, Rachel and Thomas Crosby, my brothers and sister.
Executors: Brothers John and David.
Wit: John Picken, Alex Lewis, John Hindman.

LINDSAY, WILLIAM. Lower Providence.
Mar. 27, 1776. Apr. 4, 1776.
To wife Margaret my whole estate during her natural life and after her decease as follows — To son John £5 and to his son John £5. To son James £5 and to his son Wm. £5. To son Wm. £5. To Thomas £5. To son-in-law James Ewing £5 and to his son Wm. £5. To son Robert £40. To son Samuel £20. To son Joseph £10.
Executors: Sons Robert and Samuel.
Wit: James Anderson, William Anderson.

DARLINGTON, ABRAHAM. Birmingham.
5/6/1772. Apr. 13, 1776.
To son Abraham plantation whereon I now live in Birmingham, also furniture he paying legacies. To daughter Deborah, relict of Saml. Taylor, £50. To daughter Elizabeth wife of Isaac Pyle £50. To daughter Hannah wife of Wm. Jefferis £50. To daughter Rachel relict of William Seal £50. To 2 grandchildren John and Rebecca,

children of John Brinton by my daughter Rebecca, his former wife,
£20 each. To son Thomas £20. To son John plantation whereon he
now lives in East Bradford and £20. To grandson Abraham son of
Moses Pyle £20. To granddaughter Lydia wife of Simeon Woodrow £20.
To nephew John Darlington £5. To niece Mary Darlington now wife of
John Slack £5. All my books of Physic and Chirurgery to son Thomas
and daughter Rachel Seal.
Executors: 3 sons Abraham, Thomas and John.
Wit: Wm. Jefferis, Jno. Townsend, Samuel Osborne.

PRATT, MARY. Widow. Edgmont.
8/18/1758. Apr. 15, 1776.
Directs body to be buried in Friends burying ground in Middletown.
To son-in-law Joseph Pratt £30 and to his wife Jane £10 and to
their 3 sons Abraham, Joseph and David £6 each at 21. To my
granddaughter Jane Pratt bed. To my nieces Mary and Elizabeth
Hinds all my pewter and £6 each, to their brothers James and John
Hinds £6 each. To Ann widow of Thomas Watkins £3. Remainder of
goods to 4 daughters-in-law Rose, Alice, Sarah and Ann, daughters
of my late husband Joseph Pratt.
Executor: Son-in-law Joseph Pratt. Letters c.t.a. to Abraham and
Joseph Pratt.
Wit: John Gribble, Thomas Russell, Cadwallader Evans.

MORRISON, ELIZABETH. Spinster. Concord.
Oct. 30, 1775. May 3, 1776.
To natural daughter Letitia Brice all my estate.
Executrix: Sister Agnes Morrison.
Wit: Sarah Morrison, Jos. Newlin, Nathl. Newlin.

NICHOLS, WILLIAM. Newlin.
2/13/1776. May 4, 1776.
Provides for wife Hannah. To son Amos plantation in Newlin
containing 125 acres and all remainder of personal estate paying to
each of his brothers William, Jonathan and James £60 and to my
daughter Elizabeth, wife of Edward King, £25. To daughter Mary
wife of Geo. Martin £25. To daughter Hannah wife of George Gregson
£25 and to daughter Emey £25. Son Amos paying the expense of
building a stone wall around one square perch of land to enclose my
grave in the Church yard in West Marlborough.
Executors: Son Amos and friend Charles Wilson. Letters to
Nichols, the other being absent.
Wit: Thomas Wilson, Alexander Patterson, Thos. Woodward.

SWAYNE, EDWARD. East Marlborough.
6/16/1775. May 11, 1776.
To wife Sarah plantation whereon I now dwell during life and at her
decease to be sold, also all household goods. To son Edward 5
shillings. To son Jonathan £20. To daughters Jane Calvert and
Hannah Yarnall 5 shillings each. To son Jesse £45. To daughter
Sarah England £5. To son Robert £45. To daughter Elizabeth Ailes
£25. To daughter Martha Swayne £30. Remainder to 3 daughters
Sarah, Elizabeth and Martha.
Executor: Friend William Swayne.
Wit: Jesse Miller, Frs. Swayne.

CULIN, SWAN. Ridley. May 20, 1776. Adm. to John Crosby, Jr.

LINN, CHARLES. Concord. May 28, 1776. Adm. to Eleanor Linn.

COATES, HANNAH alias MUSGRAVE. East Caln. May 30, 1776. Adm. to Moses Coates.

JAMES, SAMUEL. West Whiteland.
5/10/1776. May 30, 1776.
Provides for mother Rachel James. To brother-in-law Jacob Humphreys horse and bridle, wearing apparel and to my sister Sarah Humphreys £30, also all money due to me from my cousin Jos. James of Newtown from my right in the plantation where he now resides. To sister Hannah James £30, also 2/7 of a lot of ground in Wilmington, Delaware. I give the plantation whereon I now live containing about 200 acres to Edward Humphreys, a minor, son of Jacob and Sarah Humphreys, if he lives to 21, otherwise to my 2 sisters Sarah and Hannah. To step(half)-sisters Elizabeth Yarnall, Rachel Ring and Magdalen Johnson 20 shillings each.
Executors: Saml. Bond and Richard Thomas.
Wit: William Lawrence, John Jacobs.

PEIRCE, RACHEL. Widow. East Marlborough.
5/13/1775. May 30, 1776.
To sons Joshua and Caleb articles of furniture. To son Isaac his bond of £50. To grandson Joshua, son of Joshua, large Bible. To granddaughter Rachel Marshall all my pewter. To granddaugher Rachel, daughter of Joseph, furniture. To Lydia daughter of son Joseph ditto. To Lydia daughter of son Isaac saddle and bridle. To sister Sarah Cooke wearing apparel. To Ann wife of son Joshua and Hannah wife of son Isaac wearing apparel. Remainder to son Joseph, also Executor.
Wit: Jane Temple, Joshua Newbrough, Ann Broomhall.

ASHBRIDGE, AARON. Goshen.
4/30/1776. May 31, 1776.
Provides for wife (not named). To Jane and Elizabeth wives of Thomas and Isaac Starr and their brother David Ashbridge £30 each. Also to children of John Ashbridge late of Lancaster £30 each at 21. To Penna. Hospital £30. £300 towards the setting up a school chiefly for the help of the poorer sort of Friends. To brother Joseph Ashbridge of Chester £400. Remainder of estate real and personal to children of brother Joseph, viz., Aaron, Joseph, George, Sarah, Priscilla and Jane Ashbridge.
Executor: Geo. Ashbridge.
Wit: Joseph Garrett, Joshua Ashbridge.

EDWARDS, CALEB. West Marlborough.
11/23/1775. June 4, 1776.
To 5 brothers, viz., Joshua, Moses, John, Thomas and Nathan all my estate to be equall divided.
Executor: Friend Isaac Pyle.
Wit: Josiah Baily, Joshua Pusey.

HENDERSON, DANIEL. West Nantmeal.
June 29, 1772. June 6, 1776.
To eldest son Samuel 1/2 of tract of land whereon he lives. To second son James 5 shillings. To third son John £40. To daughter Mary Henderson £60 and horse at 21. Provides for wife (not named). To other sons Daniel, William, David, Joseph and Benjamin all remainder of estate real and personal in equal division.
Executors: Sons Saml. and Danl.
Wit: William Denny, William Moore.

BARR, WILLIAM. West Nantmeal.
Apr. 30, 1776. June 6, 1776.
To wife Sarah and sons Samuel and Moses Barr all my lands in Cumberland, also all moveables. To sons John, Robert, Andrew and James and daughters Mary and Jane Barr 1 shilling sterling each. To son William 1 shilling and new coat.
Executor: James McClure.
Wit: Francis Alexander, Jennet Alexander.

MATSON, MORRIS. Aston.
May 21, 1776. June 11, 1776.
Provides for wife Margaret. To son Levi plantation whereon I now dwell, he paying my 3 grandchildren Mary, Phebe and William children of son Moses £10 each, also paying his brother Moses £70, also paying his brother Aaron £100, also his 2 other brothers Nehemiah and Enoch £100 to be divided. To son Nehemiah tenement and lot of land containing 10 acres, also 1 acre of meadow. To son Enoch tract of land where John Matson now dwells containing about 60 acres purchased of Geo. Peirce, also 2 acres of meadow. To 5 daughters Margaret Vernon, Elizabeth Petterson, Sarah Matson, Mary Ratew and Rachel Matson £30 each and £5 addition to daughter Margaret Vernon for her former kindness unto me.
Executors: Sons Aaron and Levi.

SMITH, WILLIAM. West Nantmeal.
May 6, 1776. June 12, 1776.
Provides for wife Rebecca. To three children John, Robert and Sarah Smith all estate to be equally divided. Directs tombstone to be placed over Hannah Smith's grave. Wearing apparel to brother James Smith.
Executors: Rebecca Smith and Jas. Anderson, also residuary legatees.
Wit: Matthew Brown, George Wallace.

BOND, JOSEPH. East Whiteland.
June 25, 1776. Aug. 8, 1776.
To mother my plantation in East Whiteland which my father left me containing 108 acres during her life and at her decease to be sold, proceeds divided as follows — £150 to my relatives, viz., Ann Bond my brother's daughter, my sister Hannah and 4 of her children Benjamin, Ann, Hannah and Elisha Garrett, share and share alike. All remainder to the use of the Meeting of Goshen.
Executor: Friend James Garrett.
Wit: Joseph Rea, Enoch Lewis, Joshua Evans.

FILSON, DAVISON. East Fallowfield.
Aug. 2, 1776. Aug. 23, 1776.
Provides for wife Agnes. To son John 2 cows along with the land he got be deed from me, £50 of his indebtedness on the land to be forgiven him, the next £50 to be paid to daughters Ann and Elenor Filson when of age. To son Robert horse and cow along with the land I gave him by lease. Place bought of Wm. Filson to be sold except the 50 acres made over to son Robt. and proceeds with remainder of personal estate equally divided between children Ann, Elenor, Moses, Jean and Elizabeth Filson and "the last one born and not named yet." I confess the land I bought of James Harlan is to be Betty Ring's after she pays John Passmore the money he has against me.
Executors: Son Robert and friend Wm. Grant.
Wit: Wm. Moode, Joseph Filson.

VAUGHAN, THOMAS. Darby.
Aug. 19, 1773. Aug. 24, 1776.
To son John £5 and to his 4 children £20 to be divided when of age. To granddaughter Amelia daughter of son Isaac deceased £50 at 21 or marriage. To son Thomas messuage and land I now live on in Darby, also remainder of estate real and personal, also Executor.
Wit: George Dunn, Wm. Davis, Lewis Davis, Jr.

WHITE, JOSEPH. Goshen.
Aug. 8, 1776. Aug. 28, 1776.
Proven by Geo. Ashbridge, Ezekiel Griffith and Francis Hickman. Non-cupative will. "My will is that Bill (meaning a bound boy then living with him named Wm. Harding) shall have £30 and I leave all the rest to Abigail (meaning his wife)."
Letters to Abigail.

BUCKWALTER, JOHN. Charlestown.
June 3, 1772. Codicil Oct. 29, 1774. Sept. 2, 1776.
To 2 sons John and Daniel tract of land bought of John Morgan and David Harry in Charlestown to be valued at £1000. To son David plantation I now live on to be valued at £700. All estate real and personal, land at above valuation to be equally divided between my daughters, viz., Mary Wagoner, Ann Leap, Barbara Kysinger, Susanna Bussard, Louisa Allebach, Elizabeth Gobble, Catherine Latshaw, Magdalena Brower, Esther and Hannah Buckwalter and youngest son Jacob, said son to have £150 more than daughters, daughter Ann Leap's share in trust.
Executors: Son John and son-in-law Frederick Bussard. Codicil states "having an inclination to marry a certain Charlotte Slaughter thinks it reasonable to make provision for her after my decease."
Witnesses to codicil: Peter Holman, Jona. Coates, David Longacre, Peter Lester.

GARRETT, WILLIAM. Goshen. Sept. 2, 1776. Adm. to Mary Garrett.

MARTIN, JOEL. Charlestown. Sept. 4, 1776. Adm. to Anna Martin and Benj. Thomas.

BOGGS, JOHN. Willistown. Oct. 21, 1776. Adm. to Margaret and Jos. Boggs.

SHERADON, PRISCILLA. Vincent. Oct. 24, 1776. Adm. to Henry and Abm. Sheradon.

ROBINSON, JAMES. East Bradford.
Apr. 28, 1773. Oct. 5, 1776.
To son William £5. Provides for wife Mary. To 2 sons John and James plantation where I now dwell in East Bradford and all remainder of estate subject to wife's life interest.
Executors: Wife and son John.
Wit: Joshua Hoopes, Abiah Taylor, James Kenny.

OGDEN, STEPHEN. Springfield.
10/8/1776. Oct. 25, 1776.
To mother Hannah Ogden £40. To brother John Ogden £6. Wearing apparel to brother Aaron. All remainder to brothers and sisters Aaron, Mary Horne, Hannah, Martha and Abigail Ogden.
Executor: Brother Aaron.
Wit: Jesse Maris, Jane Maris.

MILES, JOHN. Uwchlan.
Sept. 25, 1776. Oct. 25, 1776.
All estate to wife Mary and 2 children Sarah and Ann. Wearing apparel to brother James.
Executors: Wife Mary and father-in-law Isaac Lewis.
Wit: Wm. Owen, David Pugh.

RHOADS, JOSEPH. Marple. Nov. 19, 1776. Adm. to Rachel Rhoads and Enoch Taylor.

PHILLIPS, ELIZABETH. Darby. Nov. 21, 1776. Adm. to Griffith Phillips.

REESE, CALEB. Willistown. Nov. 28, 1776. Adm. to Hannah Reese.

DERRICK, ZACHARIAH. Lower Chichester. Dec. 6, 1776. Adm. to Zachariah Derrick.

CHERRIE, AARON. Lower Chichester, late of Bucks Co.
Oct. 3, 1776. Oct. 29, 1776.
All estate of every description to brother Isaac Cherry, also Executor.

WILLS, ANN. Widow. Thornbury.
Oct. 10, 1775. Nov. 23, 1776.
To grandson Wills Hemphill son of daughter Ann and his brother Thomas, coat with silver buttons, silver shoe buckles and books. To daughters Jane Burns, Ann Black, Elizabeth Oliver, Mary Black, Elizabeth Hemphill, Christian Baker, Susanna Richards and Ann Hemphill all remainder of estate to be equally divided.
Executrixes: Daughters Christian Baker and Ann Hemphill.
Wit: Patrick Dougherty, Martha Baker, Persifer Frazer.

YARNALL, JOSEPH.
4/8/1775. Nov. 28, 1776.
To brother Amos all wearing apparel when free. To brother Samuel silver watch at 21. To brother Aaron silver buttons and my buckles to brother James. Also to Aaron and James 20 shillings each at 21.
Executors: Josiah Garrett and Enoch Yarnall.
Wit: Amos Yarnall, Aaron Garrett.

BAKER, MARGERY. Widow. Chichester.
6/3/1773. Dec. 11, 1776.
To daughter Mary Dickey the cow and to son Richard Baker the large Bible. My slave Adam to be free at my decease and £20 given for his maintenance if he should become incapable. All remainder to be divided among my children, viz., Mary Dickey, Sarah Reynolds, Richard, Robert and Wm. Baker and Lydia Grubb.
Executors: Son Richard Baker and Benj. Reynolds.
Wit: Jacob Dingee, Samuel Carpenter.

KELLY, JOHN. Darby. Dec. 20, 1776. Adm. to John Knowles.

COBOURN, WILLIAM. Lower Chichester. Jan 9, 1777. Adm. to Joseph Cobourn.

SMITH, ROBERT. Darby. Jan 13, 1777. Adm. to Wm. Smith.

MC CONNAUGHY, ROBERT. West Nantmeal. Jan 14, 1777. Adm. to Jas. McConnaughy.

GLENN, JAMES. Concord. Jan 14, 1777. Adm. to Margaret Glenn.

COCHRAN, ANDREW. Chester. Jan 16, 1777. Adm. to Joshua Cowpland.

JAMES, MORDECAI. East Nottingham.
8/26/1771. Dec. 24, 1776.
Provides for wife Susanna. To daughter Hannah Churchman £10. To 2 sons Micajah and George 1/2 of a lott of ground in Charlestown, no. 46 in plan of said Town. Remainder to be sold and net proceeds equally divided between above 3 children.
Executor: Friend David Brown.
Wit: Thos. Barrett, Arthur Barrett, John Kirk.

BARTHOLOMEW, MARGARET. Widow of Thos. Willistown.
Dec. 6, 1776. Jan 14, 1777.
To friend Rowland Evans £30. To Rev. Wm. Currie £1.10. To brother-in-law John Williams and his wife Mary all other personal estate, also my house in Philadelphia during life and after their decease to Benjamin Bartholomew, Jr.
Executors: Rowland Evans of Philadelphia Co., Joel Evans and John William Jr. of Tredyffrin. Letters to Joel Evans and Williams.
Wit: Jacob Bough, Thos. Simmons, Joshua Evans.

WAY, JACOB. Pennsbury.
6/21/1776. Jan 28, 1777.
To son Joseph plantation in Pennsbury on which I now dwell containing about 150 acres, he allowing to wife Mary the privileges

mentioned in certain Articles of agreement Tripartite 13th of 6th mo. 1767 between us before our marriage. To son John 20 shillings and to his son Jacob the 2 vols. of Anthony Pervers translation of the Bible. To son-in-law Jesse Taylor and wife Ann 20 shillings. To son-in-law John Bennett and wife Ruth 20 shillings. To son-in-law John Hawk and wife Sarah 20 shillings. To son James £30. To son-in-law Thomas Harry and wife Rachel 20 shillings. To son-in-law Stephen Hayes and Betty his wife lott of ground in Borough of Wilmington containing 2 acres. To daughter Hannah £70. To granddaughter Mary Logan 1/2 of my marsh meadow on Christiana Creek, also 20 shillings and to her mother Jane Logan 20 shillings. To son Amos 5 shillings. To son-in-law John Holahan and wife Phebe £70. To granddaughter Hannah Hayes 1/4 of marsh meadow. To granddaughter Ann daughter of son James 1/4 of marsh meadow. Remainder divided among daughters, share of daughter Sarah in trust.
Executor: Son Joseph.
Wit: Amos Davies, Thos. Woodward, Jas. Wickersham.

COPPOCK, JOHN. Chester. Jan 25, 1777. Adm. to Abner Coppock.

SALKELD, JOHN. Chester Twp.
Dec. 14, 1776. Jan 29, 1777.
Provides for wife Elizabeth. To grandson John Gest £10 at 21. To nephew Joseph Salkeld £5 at 21. To Elizabeth Dutton £5 at 21. Remainder divided as follows — To son John 2/8 to son Isaac 1/8. To daughter Elizabeth 1/8. Daughters Ann and Sarah 1/8 each. Reversion of share of son John to grandson John, son of son Isaac.
Executor: Son-in-law Joseph Larkin.
Wit: Miles Macarty, John Thompson.

BRYAN, JOHN. Ridley.
Jan 8, 1777. Feb. 4, 1777.
(Marriage license July 27, 1763 John Bryan and Barbara Boone.)
Provides for wife Barbara. To son William plantation on which I now live and all other lands. To mother Diana £5 per annum during life.
Executors: Wife Barbara and friend Isaac Hendrickson.
Wit: John Archer, Danl. Broom, Sketchy Morton.

BARKEFILE, THOMAS. West Nantmeal. Feb. 13, 1777. Adm. to Dan Griffith.

GORDON, WILLIAM. Vincent. Apr. 4, 1777. Adm. to Robt. Fullerton, Alex McClister and Geo. Fitzsimons.

FORGESON, MARY. Apr. 8, 1777. Adm. to Alex. Fleming and John Graham.

FORGESON, WILLIAM. Apr. 8, 1777. Adm. to Alex. Fleming and John Graham.

SCOTT, JOHN. Sadsbury.
Feb. 14, 1777. Apr. 10, 1777.
To grandson John son of Thomas Scott all my land on which I now

live in Sadsbury being about 200 acres at 18, except 50 acres to son Thomas during his life. To son Patrick £50 and to his son John £50. To son Thomas £50. To daughter Sarah Mitchell £25. Remainder equally divided. Letters to Scott surviving Executor.
Executors: Son-in-law Jos. Cowan and son Thomas.
Wit: John Fleming, John Wilken.

OLIVER, SAMUEL. Goshen.
Oct. 27, 1776. Apr. 10, 1777.
Provides for wife Elizabeth. Remainder equally divided among all children James, Andrew, Nathaniel, Saml. and Alexander Oliver. Youngest child Alexander to have £15 more than the others. Daughter Jane wife of John Bowen to have but 10 shillings of estate.
Executors: Wife Elizabeth and brother-in-law Jas. Hemphill.
Wit: John Beaumont, John Jacobs.

MC PHERSON, ROBERT. Sadsbury.
Sept. 25, 1776. Apr. 10, 1777.
Provides for wife Agnes. All estate to be equally divided between wife and 9 children except son Thomas who is to have £10 more.
Executors: Wife and brother-in-law Arthur Park.
Wit: Alex. McPherson, Wm. Wilken.

BENSON, JAMES. Uwchlan. Apr. 14, 1777. Adm. to Hannah and Jas. Benson.

HOPE, THOMAS. Sadsbury.
Feb. 11, 1775. Apr. 10, 1777.
To son Richard £100 and to his son Thomas £5. To son Adam £100 and to his son Thomas £5. To daughter Agnes £50 and to her son Thos. McPherson £5. To daughter Gennet £50 and to her son Thomas Park £5. To daughters Sarah and Mary £50 each. To son-in-law Robt. Cowan's son Thomas £10 and to all the rest of his children £40 to be divided. To daughter-in-law Hannah Hope the use of the place I now live upon for 7 years to enable her to bring up the children. To grandson Thomas son of Robert deceased the plantation I now live upon at 21, he paying £50 to his father's estate and renouncing all claim to a share in his father's real estate with reversion to his brother Robert.
Executors: Son Richard and son-in-law Robt. McPherson. Letters to son Richard, surviving Executor.
Wit: Wm. Wilken, John Wilken.

GRANT, WILLIAM. East Fallowfield.
Feb. 10, 1777. Apr. 10, 1777.
Provides for wife, not named. To son James plantation I now live on after my wife's decease being about 90 acres. All the rest of land adjoining the above to daughter Abigail, wife of John McMichen, and daughter Mary to be equally divided. Son James to pay to my 2 daughters £10.
Executor: Friend John Fleming.
Wit: Robert Filson, Jr., Patrick Shields.

WADDEL, JAMES. West Nantmeal.
Mar. 29, 1777. Apr. 14, 1777.
To wife Elizabeth 2/3 of estate. Remainder to children who are not named.
Executors: Charles Reed and Robert Wallice.
Wit: Jas. McEachren, Gayen Wallace.

LIVESTON, JOHN. Sadsbury. Apr. 19, 1777. Adm. to Wm. Leviston.

KENNEDY, WILLIAM. West Nantmeal. Apr. 23, 1777. Adm. to Mary Kennedy.

KIZER, ADAM. Apr. 26, 1777. Adm. to Henry Deem.

BEALE, JOHN. Apr. 10, 1777. Adm. to William Beale.

BOYER, MICHAEL. East Nantmeal.
Feb. 11, 1777. Apr. 21, 1777.
Provides for wife Margaret Elizabeth. To son Philip stock and farming implements. Place where I now live and 120 acres of land to be sold and money given to my daughters, viz., Catherine, Sarah, Rebecca, Susanna, Michal Magdelene and Juliana Terasia, which 6 daughters shall have £50 each and remainder to daughters Ann, Mary Elizabeth, Hannah and above named 6 in equal shares. Remainder of lands and other estate to son Philip.
Executors: Wife and son Philip.
Wit: Jacob Morets, Peter Kimes, Joseph Millard.

MC FALL, PATRICK. Charlestown.
Apr. 6, 1777. Apr. 22, 1777.
To daughter-in-law Sarah Griffith wearing apparel of late wife. To mother-in-law Barbara Davis and her daughter Hannah Davis remainder of ditto. To son John and daughters Ann, Hannah and Mary all remainder of estate to be equally divided when of age.
Executors: Friends Wm. Bodley and Alex McCarraugher.
Wit: Wm. Graham, Peter Christie, John Beaton.

SHUSTER, JACOB. East Nantmeal.
Feb. 1, 1777. Apr. 23, 1777.
To brother's son Philip Jacob £6. To brother's daughter Sievela £5. To sister's son Wm. Berat £6.10. To Geo. Keim £10. All other personal estate and lands to wife, also Executrix. Letters to Catherine Shuster.
Wit: Christopher Folkerth, Kiny. Beerbower.

PERRIE, MARTHA. Haverford. (Daughter of John and Hannah Parry of Haverford).
Mar. 12, 1777. Apr. 23, 1777.
To mother bed and clothes during life and at her death to my niece Martha Llewellin. To sister Hannah wife of David Llewelyn furniture and interest of £50 until niece Martha is 21 when it is to be divided between them. To nephew Joseph Hall £50 at 21. To nieces Susanna Holmes and Margaret Morgan and nephew Parry Hall £10 each. To Edward son of Thomas Vaughan £5. Remainder of cash to nephew Rowland Hall and nieces Margaret Lewis and Mary and Ruth

Hall. Gives various articles to niece Hannah Nice, Elizabeth
Duffield, cousin Catherine Duffield, niece Hannah Robins, sister-
in-law Prudence Vaughan, Rebecca Humphreys and brother-in-law Chas.
Humphreys.
Executor: Cousin Edward Duffield.
Wit: Philip Super, Jacob Humphreys.

PEIRCE, EDWARD. Westtown.
Oct. 15, 1776. May 3, 1777.
Provides for wife Frances. After her decease estate to be divided
between 2 sons Cromwell and George, they paying to their sister
Rachel Robeson £20.
Executors: Wife Frances, son George and Daniel Cornog. Letters to
Frances and Geo. Peirce.
Wit: Abraham Lewis, Jonathan Evans.

MC LURE, JOHN. Uwchlan.
Dec. 30, 1775. Apr. 23, 1777.
To daughter Esther wife of Alexander Williams £10. To son James
£30. To daughter Mary wife of Thomas McNeely £30. To daughter
Rachel wife of James Neal £10. To daughter Jane McClure £60 if she
remain unmarried until my decease, otherwise but £15. To sons
Joseph and Benjamin all remainder of estate real and personal.
Executor: Son Joseph.
Wit: John Rodgers, Wm. Milhouse.

BAINBRIDGE, EDMUND. Practitioner in Physic. Kennett.
Mar. 22, 1777. May 5, 1777.
All estate right and interest in lands in New Jersey as heir at law
to my father's estate to my brothers John and Absalom. To brother
John all wearing apparel which belonged to my father. To brother
Absalom my silver hilted sword, pistols, fiddle, flute and also
medical books and case of surgeon's instruments. All remainder of
estate to said brothers and sisters Elizabeth and Kezia.
Executors: Sister Elizabeth, Robert Henry and Robt. Cooper.
Letters to Henry and Cooper, the other renouncing.
Wit: Jos. Shippen, Jr., Peter Bell, James Walter.

THOMAS, CATHARINE. Widow. Vincent.
Sept. 23, 1775. May 7, 1777.
To son-in-law Humphrey Bell married to my daughter Anne £10. To
son-in-law Enoch Watkins married to my daughter Mary £10. To
grandsons Theophilus and Robert Watkins £5 from money owing me by
their father. To grandson Jonathan Thomas £3 at 21. To
granddaughters Margaret Bell and Catharine daughter of son John
dishes at 18. To son John Thomas all remainder of estate, also
Executor.
Wit: Christian Eberhard, James Barber, David Thomas.

HOLMAN, ADAM. Pikeland.
Mar. 17, 1777. May 30, 1777.
Provides for wife Elizabeth. To son John Holman £150. To son
Michael £25. To daughter Catherine Rooke £25. To son Henry £100.
To daughter Eve £100. To daughter Mary £90. To daughter Elizabeth
£90. To son Adam £100. To son Martin £100 to be paid them as they

arrive at age. Plantation in Charlestown to be sold, son John to have plantation where I now live for 6 years after my decease for support of younger children.
Executors: Sons John and Henry.
Wit: Michael Holman, Conrad Holman, Jona. Coates.

COWAN, JOSEPH. Sadsbury.
Feb. 26, 1777. Mar. 8, 1777.
To wife 1/3 of personal estate and profits of the whole until son James is 21. To son James £50 at 21. Remainder of personal estate to 6 daughters, viz., Jean wife of Geo. Richman, Ann wife of John Semple, Mary, Elizabeth, Margaret and Sarah. To son James all real estate at 21.
Executors: Wife Mary and son-in-law Geo. Richmond.
Wit: Nathl. W. Semple, Charles Kinkead.

FAGAN, JOHN.
Jan 31, 1777. May 9, 1777.
All estate to be sold and money to daughter Ann Fagan now living in Ireland. Friend Patrick Culbertson to be released from all debts he may have contracted with me.
Executors: Friends David Mackly of New London and David Mackey of Milford Hundred.
Wit: John McDowell, Robert Montgomery.

WILLIAMS, ROBERT. Uwchlan. May 12, 1777. Adm. to Ann Williams.

MORRIS, MORDECAI. May 10, 1777. Adm. to Morcecai Morris.

COWAN, ELIZABETH. Widow. West Caln.
May 8, 1775. May 10, 1777.
To grandson George son of Thomas Cowan £10 and to granddaughter Ann, Thomas Cowan's daughter, £20. Remainder to sons and daughters, viz., John, William and Henry Cowan, Jane Morgan, Margaret Dawson and Abigail Fleming, share and share alike.
Executors: Son Henry and son-in-law John Fleming.
Wit: Charles Kinkead, Wm. Crawford.

PORTER, PATRICK. West Caln.
Feb. 1, 1777. May 13, 1777.
To mother Mary Porter all estate during life and at her decease to brother John Porter £40. All lands and remainder of personal estate to brother Thomas and sister Margaret Porter.
Executor: Wm. Davidson of West Caln.
Wit: Gilbert Gibbs, John Bettay, Wm. Gill.

MARTIN, JAMES. Charlestown.
Apr. 13, 1777. Codicil Apr. 14, 1777. May 13, 1777.
To sister Rachel Martin lot of land containing about 7 acres in Charlestown and 2 cows. Provides for wife Margaret. To daughter Sarah plantation I now live on containing about 140 acres subject to her mother's life interest. To brother-in-law Saml. Lewis all wearing apparel. To mother-in-law Sarah Jones £3 per annum during life. Moses Coates guardian of daughter Sarah.
Executors: Wife Margaret and her brother John Jones.

Codicil gives reversion of plantation to wife Margaret.
Wit: John Pawling, Jacob Pennebacker, Rowland Evans, Wm. Jones.

USHER, MARY. Widow. Darby.
1/13/1775. May 22, 1777.
To granddaughter Ruth wife of Jesse Bonsall pewterware. To granddaughter Sarah Fordham ditto. To granddaughter Lydia Fordham all remainder of goods, also Executrix.
Wit: Isaac Pearson, Isaac Lloyd, Saml. Ashe.

SCOTT, JOHN. New London.
Apr. 11, 1775. July 1, 1777.
To Thomas Scott son of brother William all estate both real and personal except watch which I give to Jas. Scott.
Executor: Thomas Scott.
Wit: David Correy, John Smith.

COLHOON, JOHN.
July 8, 1776. July 3, 1777.
In a letter to James Hair states "I am now going to march out of this province and don't know if ever I shall return" and desires him to collect his accounts and dispose of them as follows — To sister Elizabeth Colhoon otherwise Crage £50 to each of her two children and £3.8.3 to Jas Hunter in Philadelphia and the remainder to my brother Adam's 2 children Robert and Jenet Calhoon. There is an account against Archibald Irwin of which I allow Mr. Carmichael 7 shillings 6 and Rev. Mr. Proudfoot the remainder. Account against John Thompson £4.7 I allow it to be blank.
Executor: Friend James Hair. Will proven by Jas. Mitchell, Thos. Baggs being absent at camp.
Wit: Jas. Mitchell, Thomas Baggs.

LONG, JOSEPH. East Caln.
Dec. 28, 1772. June 27, 1777.
To wife Mary rents of 3 plantations for maintaining and educating children. To eldest son Alexander £5 which for his disobedience I shew my dislike. To son David plantation I now live on in East Caln. To son Joseph plantation in West Nantmeal now in tenure of Wm. Scott. To son John plantation in West Nantmeal bought of Wm. Graham and mother now in tenure of Wm. Quaintance. To daughters Dorcas, Mary and Janet Long £145 each when of age. If son Alexander reforms so as to become a member of some Christian Society for one year or more, his is to have £150 and so continuing for another year shall have £150 more.
Executors: Wife Mary and friends Saml. Mackelduff and Dr. Moses Scott. Letters to wife and Mackelduff.
Wit: Wm. Scott, Andrew Spence, Francis Willson.

MOORE, NATHANIEL. Goshen.
May 17, 1777. June 25, 1777.
Provides for wife Hannah. To son Thomas £100 at 21. To son Emmor £100 at 21. To son Benjamin £100 at 21. To son Nathaniel £100 at 21. To son Joseph plantation where I now dwell in Goshen containing 200 acres subject to legacies.
Executors: Wife Hannah and eldest son Joseph.

Wit: Thomas Scholfield, Jona. Matlack, Levis Janney.

HANCOCK, JOSEPH. Vincent.
Mar. 13, 1777. May 23, 1777.
To wife Love Hancock my plantation in Vincent where I now live and all stock and household goods forever. To daughter Sarah Christy 5 shillings 6.
Executrix: Wife.
Wit: Hugh Strickland, Danl. Corker, David Evans.

QUICKLESS, HUGH. May 28, 1777. Adm. to David Watt and John Moore.

MC CORMICK, JAMES. May 28, 1777. Adm. to Sarah and Jas. McCormick.

BROWER, JOHN. May 30, 1777. Adm. to Danl. and Henry Brower.

ACORE, ANTHONY. May 30, 1777. Adm. to Mary and Jacob Acore.

OWEN, DAVID. Uwchlan. May 31, 1777. Adm. to Elizabeth Owen. Affirmed.

CARTER, EDWARD. Chester Twp.
June 8, 1776. May 27, 1777.
To daughter Mary Miller and her daughter Hannah all personal estate. To brother Abraham Carter all my land and premises in Chester Twp.
Executors: Brother Abraham and friend Saml. Armar.

RICHEY, WILLIAM. Oxford.
June 12, 1777. June 19, 1777.
To brother John Richey in the Parish of Bovery, Co. Londonderry, Ireland £30. To sister Jean Richey of same place £30. To brother Francis in Parish of Tamlaughfinlagen, Londonderry, £30. To nephew Mary Carrie of Winchester, Virginia £10. To nephew Thomas Smith of Cumberland Co., Pennsylvania £6. To Jannet and Margaret, David Simpson's 2 oldest daughters of Oxford Twp., £3 each. To nephew Wm. Leech of Little Britain, Lancaster Co., remainder of estate.
Executors: David Simpson and Wm. Leech.
Wit: Jeremiah Simpson, James Simpson.

WILDAY, OBADIAH. Haverford.
Nov. 13, 1769. Codicil Aug. 9, 1770. June 15, 1777.
Provides for wife Elizabeth. To eldest son Edward £8. To second son Thomas £15. To 3rd son John £50. To daughter Sarah 5 shillings. To daughter Phebe 5 shillings. To son Obadiah all my messuage and lands, also Executor. Codicil gives to daughter Phebe the house where she lives during life.
Wit: Evan David, Cloas Johnson, Isaac Davis.

HINKIN, HENRY. Coventry. May 31, 1777. Adm. to Margaret Hinkin.

DARLINGTON, ROBERT. East Caln. June 6, 1777. Adm. to Joseph Darlington.

DAVIS, JOHN. June 10, 1777. Adm. to Elizabeth and Griffith Davis.

ADAMS, WILLIAM. West Fallowfield. July 7, 1777. Adm. to Rebecca Adams.

BOYD, JOHN. Birmingham. Nov. 6, 1777. Adm. to William Boyd.

LEWIS, JOHN. Ridley.
Apr. 12, 1777. May 28, 1777.
To son Harvey Lewis my copper still and 8 day clock and all money he owes me, also lot of ground in Wilmington, Delaware, and all other real estate. To son Samuel negro lad James until he is 30. £200 in trust for use of daughter Margaret wife of John Maris and her 4 children Harvey, Saml., John and Mary. Remainder to 4 children, viz., Samuel, John, Mary and Margaret.
Executors: Son Harvey and friend Wm. Garrett.
Wit: Benj. Thomas, Thomas West, Isa Pearson.

ARNDOFF, PHILIP. Vincent.
Feb. 17, 1777. May 31, 1777.
Provides for wife Elizabeth. To son John £15 and 1/6 of remainder of clear estate. To son Lewis £15 and 1/6 of remainder. To son Philip £15 and 1/6 remainder, to go to a trade at 16. To daughter Mary wife of Cronomus Saylor 1/6 of estate. To daughters Margaret and Susanna 1/6 each.
Executors: Wife Elizabeth and son Lewis.
Wit: Matthias Keely, James John, David Thomas.

FUERY, ELIZABETH. New London.
Jan 9, 1765. June 6, 1777.
To son Wm. Kelley £10. To daughter Ann Woodward £10. To son Joseph Fuery and daughter Margaret Kelley plantation I now live on "and keep the tavern" and to Margaret £100 and bound servant Mary Kenan. To daughters Hillen Hair and Jane Arthur £20 each. To grandson Joseph Leach £10 when of age.
Executors: John Scott and Margaret Kelley. Letters to Margaret, Scott renouncing.
Wit: James Reed, Esther Brown.

MC CALL, BENJAMIN. Kennett. Aug. 11, 1777. Adm. to Abigail McCall.

WALLACE, THOMAS. West Fallowfield. Mar. 27, 1778. Adm. to John Wallace.

DEE, RICHARD. Sept. 1, 1777. Adm. to Mary Dee.

BOYD, JOHN. Sept. 6, 1777. Adm. to William Boyd.

STEIGER, PETER. Uwchlan. Nov. 26, 1777. Adm. to Jacob and Hannah Steiger.

ROATS, MARTIN. East Nantmeal.
June 26, 1777. Aug. 16, 1777.
To 6 daughters Mary, Elizabeth, Catharine, Hannah, Christina and

Margaret all moveable estate to be equally divided. To son Jacob when 21, 2 shares of real estate and the third share to 6 daughters above named.
Executors: Christopher Folkerth and Powell Pearson.
Wit: Phineas Bertbour, Geo. Gross.

KEELEY, SEBASTIAN. Vincent.
Nov. 3, 1777. Apr. 2, 1778.
To wife Elizabeth mills and plantation whereon I now live during widowhood to bring up and educate my younger children. Remainder equall divided among children, son John only mentioned. Plantation in Limerick Twp., Philadelphia Co. to be sold, also plantation in West Caln. Executors to release to brother Henry for any share or right I ever had to the plantation whereon he now lives in Skippack and Perkiomen Twps., Philadelphia Co. being the place where my father formerly dwelt.
Executors: Wife Elizabeth, son Matthias and brother-in-law Geo. Christman.
Wit: Thomas Heimberger, Jonathan Coates.

MENTZ, CHRISTOPHER. Pikeland. Feb. 16, 1778. Adm. to Barbary Mentz and Peter Shuman.

PAUL, JOHN. Vincent. Mar. 7, 1778. Adm. to Mary Paul.

HIPPLE, JOHN. Vincent. Mar. 12, 1778. Adm. to Mary Hipple and George Deery.

HADDEN, JOHN. Pennsbury. Mar. 23, 1778. Adm. to Mary Hadden.

HOUNSTOW, JACOB. Apr. 7, 1778. Adm. to Catherine Hounstow.

JACKSON, SAMUEL. Apr. 13, 1778. Adm. to Gennett Jackson and Robt. Thomson.

KYLE, WILLIAM. West Fallowfield.
Jan 4, 1775. Apr. 15, 1778.
To son John Kyle 20 shillings and big Bible. To son-in-law Robt. Rogers 20 shillings. To son-in-law Geo. Sloan 20 shillings and to his daughter Mary Sloan bed and cloths. To son-in-law John Kirkpatrick £3. To son Joseph all lands and tenements and personal estate paying legacies, also Executor.
Wit: Wm. Steward, Saml. McNeal, Robt. Hamill.

STEWART, WALTER. Sadsbury.
July 20, 1777. Apr. 29, 1778.
To son Andrew plantation I now live on and all belongings, except otherwise devised. To son James £30. To daughter-in-law Martha widow of son Alexander £5. To grandsons Walter and William Stewart £5 each at 21.
Executor: Son Andrew.
Wit: Thomas Boyd, Joseph Powell.

EBERHART, CHRISTIAN. Vincent.
Sept. 9, 1777. May 13, 1778.

To wife Sarah 1/2 of clear estate during widowhood. To son Benjamin the other 1/2 of clear estate paying legacies. To daughter Sophia Eberhart £50. To son James £15 at 21 to learn the weaver trade. To son Samuel £20 at 21. To daughter Mary Eberhart £15 at 18. To daughter Sarah £15 at 18. To daughter Elizabeth £15 at 18.
Executors: Wife Sarah and friend John Thomas. Letters to Sarah, the other renouncing.
Wit: John McFarland, David Thomas.

ELTON, JOHN. Sadsbury. Apr. 4, 1778. Adm. to Thos. and Robt. Elton.

REGAN, JOHN. Vincent. Apr. 13, 1778. Adm. to Wm. Regan.

HAGIN, JOHN. West Fallowfield. Apr. 14, 1778. Adm. to Robert Bell.

WHITE, THOMAS. East Caln. Apr. 14, 1778. Adm. to Rachel White.

DAVIS, ISAAC. Tredyffrin. May 23, 1778. Adm. to Elizabeth and John Davis.

MC KINLEY, JOSEPH. East Caln. May 30, 1778. Adm. to Elizabeth McKinley.

WAGGONER, BARBARA. West Caln.
Feb. 7, 1777. May 25, 1778.
All real and personal estate left at the death of my husband to be equally divided among 7 children, 5 sons and 2 daughters (not named). To son John 5 shillings of my personal estate and to daughter Catharine bed and bedding.
Executors: Son John and Harman Skyles.
Wit: Gilbert Gibbs, John Boyd, Philip Lynch.

HAMILTON, JAMES. West Nantmeal.
Feb. 3, 1777. May 27, 1778.
To daughter Janet wife of Andrew Barr and to daughter Agnes wife of Saml. Henderson all estate real and personal. To brother John Hamilton's son James 5 shillings and all wearing apparel.
Executors: Sons-in-law Andrew Barr and Saml. Henderson.
Wit: John Tode, Joseph Darlington.

STEUART, ROBERT. East Nantmeal.
May 18, 1778. May 28, 1778.
Provides for wife Eleanor. Margaret Ray to hold and enjoy the house which she formerly enjoyed on my land during life. To Wm. Steuart 10 shillings. Remainder to be sold and the money paid to my nephew Robert son of George Steuart of Litterkenny, Co. Donegall, Ireland. Orders grave stones to his grave.
Executors: Friend John Lewis and Robert Wallace.
Wit: Hugh Johnson, Alex. Mecke.

ARBUCKEL, JAMES. Coventry.
Apr. 4, 1778. June 6, 1778.

Provides for wife Esther. To son John plantation in Coventry when 21. Remainder to 4 daughters Anna, Esther, Mary and Eleanor in equal shares at 18.
Executors: Wife Esther and brother-in-law Jacob Switzer. Letters to Esther Arbuckel.
Wit: Abraham Grub, David Grub, Joseph Evans.

BALLA, HANNAH. Charlestown. June 6, 1778. Adm. to Elizabeth Balla.

COOPER, JAMES. Oxford. June 9, 1778. Adm. to Wm. Cooper and John Andrews.

STOCKMAN, JAMES. May 12, 1778. Adm. to Isabell Stockman.

HARVEY, SAMUEL. Charlestown. May 22, 1778. Adm. to Martha Harvey.

HETHERLIN, JACOB. Coventry. June 6, 1778. Adm. to Orsila Hetherlin.

WESLER, JOHN. Charlestown. July 2, 1778. Adm. to Margaret Wesler.

MC MILLAN, JOHN. West Nottingham.
Feb. 6, 1777. June 17, 1778.
To wife Rachel bed and bedding, also horse and saddle. To daughter Jane McMillan £4 and to her child, my granddaughter Rachel Perry 20 shillings. To son James best great coat. To daughter Martha McMillan £10. To daughter Mary McMillan furniture. To son Ephraim fur hat. To son John 20 shillings. Remainder in 9 shares. To wife Rachel 2 shares and one share each to son James, daughter Agnes, daughter Mary, son Robert, son Joseph, son Ephraim and son John.
Executors: Son James and son-in-law John Perry. Letters to Perry, the other renouncing.
Wit: John Dickey, David Edmiston.

CULIN, DANIEL. Ridley.
June 12, 1777. Aug. 27, 1777.
Directs body to be laid by side of wife in Wickes burying ground. To son John £15 yearly during life and to his daughter Rebecca £50 and household goods at 21. To son Isaac's daughter Elizabeth £20 at 18. To daughter-in-law Rebecca Culin £30 to be paid the day she removes off the premises. To cousin Swan Culin's daughter Margaret £10 at 18. To son Isaac all my messuages and lands, also Executor.
Wit: John Ducke, Peter Matson, Hugh Lloyd.

LEWIS, WILLIAM. Darby. Aug. 6, 1778. Adm. to Wm. Lewis.

GRIFFITH, JOHN. Tredyffrin. Aug. 26, 1778. Adm. to Esther James.

JAMES, JOSEPH. Aug. 26, 1778. Adm. to Mary James.

SHEWMAN, PETER. Aug. 21, 1778. Adm. to Elizabeth Stewman, Geo. Deery and Peter Miller.

ROMAN, JACOB. Chichester. Aug. 18, 1778. Adm. to Andrew McIlwain.

ENGLE, FREDERICK. Chester. July 20, 1778. Adm. to Abigail Engle. (She m. Wm. Briggs. Children Mary (m. Edward Woodward), John, Frederick, Elias, Abigail, Isaac, Joseph and Edward.)

KENNEDY, SAMUEL. Practitioner of Physic. West Whiteland.
June 15, 1778. July 24, 1778.
Provides for wife Sarah. To oldest son Thomas Ruston Kennedy 2 parts of all my estate paying £500 to his younger brother at 21. To youngest son John one part of estate. To eldest daughter Mary Kennedy one part ditto. To youngest daughter Sarah Kennedy one part ditto when 21 or married. To the congregation to Charlestown (where I intend to be interred) £15 provided they surround graveyard with a stone wall.
Executors: Wife Sarah and brother Montgomery Kennedy.
Wit: Alexander McCaraher, Thomas Marshall, Alvery Hudgson.

LONG, JOHN. West Caln.
June 30, 1778. Aug. 4, 1778.
To son William all my lands which I hold in this Twp. of West Caln. To daughter Gennet Long £200 and furniture. To daughter Elizabeth wife of Jas. Alexander £100. To daughter Martha wife of Jesse Steward £100. Remainder to son Wm.
Executors: Son Wm. and daughter Gennet.
Wit: Elizabeth Jack, John Carmichael.

MORTON, JOHN. Ridley.
Jan 28, 1777. Aug. 26, 1778.
Provides for wife Ann. To son Aaron the other part of messuage and tract of 120 acres devised to me by my father (except 15 acres). To son Sketchley brick messuage and tract to 60 acres purchased of John Hendrickson, also 41 acres purchased of Jonas Morton, 1/2 of books and surveying implements. To son John messuage and 60 acres purchased of Matthias Hendricksen, also 15 acres reserved from land devised to son Aaron. To 3 sons my marsh meadow containing about 30 acres. To daughter Mary negro boy Joe with what she has already had. To daughter Sarah £250 and negro boy Tom. To daughter Lydia £270. To daughter Ann £270. To daughter Elizabeth £270. Remainder to wife and 5 daughters Mary, Sarah, Lydia, Ann and Elizabeth.
Executors: Wife Ann and son Sketchley.
Wit: James Wood, Thomas Smith.

PHILLIPS, GRIFFITH. Aug. 26, 1778. Adm. to Ann Phillips and Wm. Garrett.

LEWIS, ABNER. Sept. 2, 1778. Adm. to Margaret Lewis.

ASH, JOSHUA. Darby. Sept. 18, 1778. Adm. to Joshua and Caleb Ash.

ROBINSON, JOHN. West Caln. Sept. 22, 1778. Adm. to Samson Babb.

SMITH, JOHN. West Whiteland. Sept. 11, 1778. Adm. to Hannah Smith.

MARIS, MARGARET. Springfield. Sept. 15, 1778. Adm. to John Maris.

SKETCHLEY, MARY. Widow. Ridley.
Apr. 14, 1777. Aug. 26, 1778.
To 3 youngest granddaughters Lydia, Ann and Elizabeth Morton £50 each and all remainder of personal estate to 5 granddaughters, viz., Mary Justice, Sarah Currie, Lydia, Ann and Elizabeth Morton to be equally divided. To Sarah Price £20. To grandson John Morton all real estate except 4 acres to grandson Aaron Morton. Executors: Daughter-in-law Ann Morton and grandson Skitchley Morton.
Wit: H. H. Graham, William Price.

CULIN, ANDREW. Darby.
May 17, 1774. Aug. 26, 1778.
Plantation where I now dwell to be sold. Provides for wife Lydia. To daughters Rachel and Rebecca £5 each. To son Andrew £100.
Executor: Friend Sketchley Morton.
Wit: John Bryan, Israel Longacre, Benj. Richards.

ALEXANDER, FRANCIS. West Nantmeal. Sept. 24, 1778. Adm. to Jane Alexander.

BAKER, LYDIA. Edgmont. Oct. 21, 1778. Adm. to Jos. and Nehemiah Baker.

BOYD, THOMAS, ESQ. Nov. 9, 1778. Adm. to Catherine Boyd.

JONES, WILLIAM. Westtown. Nov. 3, 1778. Adm. to Mary Jones and Jos. Dilworth.

GIBSON, JOHN. Oxford. Nov. 30, 1778. Adm. to Isabel Gibson and Robt. Smith.

COWPLAND, DAVID. Chester Borough.
Dec. 3, 1777. Codicil Jan 5, 1778. Aug. 26, 1778.
To wife Isabel all personal estate, also lands and tenements during life, except as hereafter devised and after her decease as follows — To son David messuage and part of tract of 200 acres in Chester Twp. To 2 daughters Sarah Cowpland and Agnes Bevan the remainder of aforesaid 200 acres, also messuage of Inn in said borough and 12 acres of marsh with reversion to grandson Caleb son of Joshua Cowpland deceased and grandson David Bevan. To granddaughter Ann Bevan lot of ground in said borough, also £100. Devises other real estate to said 2 daughters.
Executrix: Wife Isabel.
Wit: John Lownes, Joseph Palmer, Martha Davis Price.

TAYLOR, THOMAS. Springfield.
Oct. 20, 1776. Sept. 16, 1778.
Provides for wife Mary. To son Robert plantation on which I now dwell paying legacies. To sons Israel, Elisha and Thomas £40 each. To daughter Sarah, if living, £30. If deceased to be divided between granddaughters Lusenda Hall and Tacy Johnson at 18.
Executors: Wife Mary and son Robert. Letters to Robert.
Wit: Jesse Maris, Jesse Maris, Jr.

PEARSOLL, JOHN. West Nantmeal.
Apr. 23, 1773. Sept. 11, 1778.
Provides for wife Alice. Plantation where I now dwell to be sold at wife's decease and proceeds equally divided between 4 daughters Sarah Porter, Alice Trego, Rebecca Brown and Elizabeth Pearsoll. Plantation bought of Wm. Carruthers and Saml. Culbertson to be sold and money divided as follows - To granddaughters Saah and Mary Persoll daughters of son John £5 each. To daughter-in-law Bathsheba Pearsoll 5 shillings. To grandson Mordecai Pearsoll, granddaugher Hannah Pearsoll, grandson Peter Pearsoll, granddaughter Mary Pearsoll and daughter-in-law Dinah Kennedy 5 shillings each. Remainder to be divided between 4 daughters above named and grandson John Davis son of daughter Mary Davis and Zacheus Pearsoll son of my son John. To son-in-law David Davis 1 shilling sterling. I release unto son-in-law Joseph Trego all debts due me from him before 8th Mar. 1771. Letters to Jos. Trego, the others renouncing.
Executors: Wife Alice, Joseph Trego and Wm. Gibbons.
Wit: Wm. Trego, Wm. Smith, Samuel Thomas.

DAVIS, SAMUEL. July 27, 1778. Adm. John Bartholomew and David Davis.

YARNALL, FRANCIS. Willistown.
8/8/1775. Sept. 21, 1778.
Provides for wife Mary. To daughter Hannah wife of Caleb Reece tract of land where she now lives containing 50 acres, also 7 acres adj. during life and at ther decease to grandson Caleb Reece, he paying to his 3 brothers Thomas, David and Francis £10 each and £20 each to his sister Hannah and brother Joseph and £5 each to his brother Wm.'s 4 children SLydia, Hannah, Nehemiah and William at 21. To grandson Isaac son of late son Joseph 100 acres of eastwarly part of my land adj. Corum Creek, he paying to his sister Jane £100 and to his mother Elizabeth £6 yearly during life. Remainder of lands in Willistown at death of wife to son-in-law Joseph Thomas and wife Mary paying to daughter Jane wife of Wm. Williams £120 and £10 to grandson John Reece and £20 to daughter Hannah Reece. To Griends of Newtown Meeting £5 for repairing graveyard or meeting house.
Executors: Stepson John Morris and kinsman Enoch Yarnall.
Wit: Isaac yarnall, Caleb Yarnall, Richard Howell.

BENTLEY, JOSEPH. Uwchlan.
Sept. 6, 1774. Sept. 25, 1778.
To sons Jeffrey, Ellis, Eli and Banner 20 shillings each. All remainder of estate real and personal to wife Mary to dispose of

among my other children as she shall see proper, sons Caleb, George and Joseph and daughter Jane Bentley.
Executrix: Wife Mary.
Wit: Thomas Evans, James Packer, Danl. Bowen.

KNOWLES, JOHN. Ridley.
Sept. 9, 1777. Aug. 26, 1778.
To Hannah Crozer £50 "for faithful services in my family." To my 3 children James, John and Hannah plantation where I now dwell in Ridley and all other lands in Ridley and Darby, all lands in Kingsess, likewise my land in West New Jersey and plantation in Oley Twp., Berks Co. and all other estate to be divided equally when they come of age.
Executors: Kinsman Wm. Garrett of Darby and friends Wm. Jones of Philadelphia and John Crozer.
Wit: Henry Paschall, Hannah Crozer, Sarah Wood.

WALKER, NATHANIEL. Londonderry.
Aug. 24, 1778. Sept. 13, 1778.
Provides for wife Hannah. To son Benjamin £40 and "all the benefits of the Continental hides now in my tanyard." To son Nathaniel £20 and wearing apparel. To son John £50. To daughter Elizabeth £5. Plantation to be sold in 10 years and proceeds divided 1/3 to wife during life, 1/3 to son Isaac and remaining 1/3 with all other personal estate to be divided among daughters Mary, Jane, Ruth, Isabel, Hannah and Rebecca.
Executors: Wife Hannah and son Benj.
Wit: Wm. Gilliland, John Kinkead.

JEFFERIS, WILLIAM. East Bradford.
Dec. 10, 1777. Sept. 21, 1778.
Provides for wife Hannah. To son Wm. at 21 all my plantation he paying £250 each to my sons Abraham and Job when 21, also £25 each to my daughters. To daughters Jane, Betty, Rachel, Hannah, Rebecca, Agnes and Lydia £25 each to be paid by son Wm.
Executors: Wife Hannah and brothers-in-law Abm. Thomas and John Darlington. Letters to Hannah.
Wit: Joseph Buffington, Nathl. Jefferis, Richard Strode.

JOHN, GRIFFITH. Uwchlan.
8/19/1774. Sept. 16, 1778.
Provides for wife Ann. To son Joshua John £25. To son Abel £15. To son Reuben £15. To 4 daughters, viz., Ann Benson, Hannah Davis, Jane Meredith and Esther McClean £15 each. To grandson Jehu son of Robert John deceased 10 shillings at 21. To the 4 children of daughter Rachel Benson deceased, viz., James, Benjamin, Jonathan and Ann Benson 10 shillings each. To Friends of Uwchlan Meeting 10 shillings. To son Griffith messuage and plantation whereon I now live and all remainder of estate, also Executor.
Wit: Cadwallader Jones, Evan Jones, Rudolph Haines.

BENARD, PAUL. Vincent.
Jan 26, 1778. Oct. 16, 1778.
Provides for wife Elizabeth. To daughter Barbara Barnard £40. To daughter Mary Benard £40. To daughter Rebecca wife of Jacob Smith

£40. To daughter Hannah Benard £40. to son John part of the upper end of my plantation paying to his brother George £150. to son Abraham the part of my plantation where house stands. To daughter Catherine Benard £40. To son Jacob 50 acres of the lower end of plantation at 18, also £50. To son George £400 at 21.
Executors: Wife Elizabeth and neighbor John Ralston.
Wit: Wm. Melchioz, James Ralston.

GILLELAND, JAMES. Londonderry.
Apr. 4, 1778. Codicil May 20, 1778. Sept. 29. 1778.
To daughter Elizabeth £20 and furniture. To daughter Agnes £20 and furniture. Remainder of estate real and personal to be sold and proceeds equally divided among all children, not named.
Executors: Sons thomas and James.
Wit: Benjamin Walker, John Kinkead.

JOHNSON, JOHN. Haverford.
Feb. 25, 1776. Sept. 30, 1778.
To brother David Johnson plantation whereon I now dwell in Haverford containing 110 acres paying legacies. To wife Elizabeth 10 shillings. To daughter Susanna Johnson £5. To my mother Mary Johnson £20, also £100 to sister Martha Johnson. All remainder of estate to 2 brothers Saml. and Wm. Johnson.
Executors: Saml. and David Johnson.
Wit: Edward Humphreys, John Davis.

WELLS, PETER. Charlestown. Oct. 2, 1778. Adm. to Jona. and Edward Wells.

JEFFERIS, WILLIAM, SENIOR. Yeoman. East Bradford.
9/1/1777. Codicil 11/22/1777. Oct. 2, 1778.
To son William a part of my land in East Bradford paying out of the same £700 as follows - To son Saml. £300. To son Nathan £300 and to son Saml. for use of Elias £100. To son Nathaniel remainder of lands in East Bradford. To 3 daughters Mary, Martha and Hannah household goods. To granddaughters Hannah and Rebecca daughters to son Wm. £5 each. To Margaret wife of son Samuel large cooking glass. tp Peninah wife of son Nathan £30. To Elias son of Mary Bradley (late Mary Wolf) £100 when of age. Remainder to Saml.
Executors: Son Samuel and son-in-law John Hunt.
Wit: Joseph Peirce, Ann Peirce, Jose. Peirce, Jr.

DAVIS, DANIEL. East Bradford.
Dec. 28, 1771. Oct. 10, 1778.
To son John Davis £50 and wearing apparel. To daughter Ann Davis £100 and household goods. To daughter Hannah wife of Seth Eavenson £50. To the 4 children of son James deceased £25. To Lydia, Mary and Ann Davis at 18 and James at 21. To grandson Aaron son of son James £5 at 21. Letters to John Fred.
Executors: Friends John Hall of Concord and Wm. Hunt.
Wit: Thomas Taylor, Francis Williams, Isaac Calvert.

BAKER, NEHEMIAH. Edgmont.
4/13/1778. Oct. 21, 1778.

Provides for wife Lydia. To daughter Mary Reece £5. To son Joseph
£5. To daughter Hannah Baker £5. To daughter Lydia Richardson
£10. To son Nathan the north end of my plantation now in his
possession containing about 40 acres, also £5. To daughter Phebe
Baker £5. To son Nehemiah my plantation in Edgmont and Thornbury
where I now dwell, also stock. To grandson Nehemiah Richardson £5,
grandson Nehemiah Baker £5, grandson Nehemiah Reece £5. To
grandson Aaron son of Nathan Baker £5 when they arrive at 21.
Executors: Sons Joseph and Nehemiah.
Wit: Daniel Broomall, Thomas Evans.

POWELL, PATIENCE. Widow. Marple.
Apr. 10, 1776. Oct. 24, 1778.
To daughter Elizabeth wife of Jos. Toyly £15. To daughter Mary
Powell £35. To daughter Sarah wife of Daniel McAffee £35. To
daughter Hannah Bonsall widow £15. To daughter Jane wife of Saml.
Gracy £35. To daughter Susanna wife of Lewis Griffith £35. To son
Thomas £35. To son Joseph £15. To son George £35. To daughter
Patience wife of Geo. Hayworth £35. To granddaughter Prudence
Powell £10.
Executors: Sons Joseph and George and daughter Mary Powell.
Letters to Joseph, George renouncing.
Wit: Jona. Heacock, Seth Pancoast, Jr., Jacob Beery.

PEARSON, HANNAH. Widow of Thos. Darby.
Jan 5, 1775. Codicil Dec. 19, 1777. Oct. 28, 1778
To son James all my lots of ground in Philadelphia. To son John
the northeast half of piece of land in Darby paying to my Executors
what it may be appraised at. To son Thomas the remaining 1/2 of
same paying as above. To daughter Hannah wife of Jacob Serrill
piece of land in Darby paying as before mentioned. To daughters
Ann, Sarah, Susanna, Mary, Hannah and Elizabeth all household
furniture and wearing apparel.
Executors: Son John and sons-in-law Hugh Lloyd and Jacob Serrill.
Letters to Pearson and Serrill.
Codicil gives to son Thomas (he having now arrived at 21) certain
ground rents from lots in Darby.
Wit: Wm. Parker, John Sellers, Nathl. Sellers.
Wit to Codicil: Richd. Humphreys, Geo. Pearson.

PAINTER, PHILIP. Darby.
Apr. 20, 1777. May 26, 1777.
Provides for wife Mary. To children John, Lewis, Jacob, George,
William, Philip, Frederick, Mary, Elizabeth, Catherina and Barbara
£15 each. Remainder to wife Mary.
Executors: Wife and brother-in-law Wm. Lowman of Passyunk.
Wit: Philip Clime, Isaac Pearson.

MA CUE, SAMUEL. Willistown.
Jan 15, 1777. May 29, 1777.
Provides for "Anchant and beloved wife Ann." To son Anthony £10.
To daughter Mary Farrow £10. To daughter Hannah Butler £15. To
daughter Ann Jodgon £10. To son Thomas 5 shillings. To daughter
Alice Macue my plantation and all remainder of personal estate, but
if she should die without heirs, the said plantation is to be sold

by my kinsmen Anthony Wayne and Rich. Richison, proceeds divided 1/3 to daughter Hannah Butler and the other 2 parts to my son Anthony and daughters Mary and Ann, share and share alike. Orders a tombstone on his grave. No record of probate.
Executors: Daughter Alice and friend Richard Richison.
Wit: Richard Morris, Samuel Bell.

THOMAS, MARY. Widow. "On the Five Hundred Tract"
July 1, 1778. Nov. 6, 1778.
To daughter Sarah household goods. To daughter Rachel Thomas rent of part of plantation for 7 years and household goods, also £50 and £100 to daughter Sarah. Mentions sons Nathan and Isaac who inherit the land from their father at 21.
Executors: Friends Joshua Evans and John Williams, Jr.
Wit: Joseph Barton, Hugh Quay.

SMITH, JOHN. East Whiteland.
June 15, 1778. Nov. 6, 1778.
Provides for wife Elizabeth. To son Philip all my lands on death of wife. To son John all my lands adj. land of Thos. Roberts, Theophilus Rees and Jas. Thomas at 21. To daughters Margaret, Ann and Cathrine household goods and to Catherine £100 at 21. To sons Thomas and Adam £100 each at 21. Mentions daughter Elizabeth wife of Peter Keine and son-in-law Christopher Coon. Letters to Philip Smith, the other not appearing.
Executors: Son Philip and Christopher Coon.
Wit: Abednego Jones, David Jones, Fos. Bowen.

MILLESON, JONATHAN. Goshen.
9/17/1778. Nov. 7, 1778.
Provides for wife Charity. To oldest son John 5 shillings. To daughter Hannah Milleson £10 at 21. To daughter Ann Milleson £10 at 21. To son Johanthan 1/2 of plantation when son Jesse is 21. To daughter Mary Milleson £10 at 21. To son Jesse the remaining 1/2 of plantation at 21. To daughter Phebe Milleson £10 at 21. Letters to Charity.
Executors: Wife Charity and friend Geo. Ashbridge.
Wit: John Polis Seal, Seth Evenson, James Gibbons.

HARRIS, JANE. East Whiteland.
Sept. 23, 1778. Nov. 9, 1778.
to cousin Sarah McClure all my estate when she is 18 with rev. to brother Thomas Harris, who is to be Executor.
Wit: Richd. Richison, Thomas Cummings.

WEBBER, JACOB. Darby.
Sept. 13, 1773. Nov. 14, 1778.
To cousin Ann wife of Aaron Oakford, Fuller, £20 and to their children Isaac, Elizabeth and Hannah £100. To cousin Grace wife of Wm. Evans of Evesham, Burlington Co., N.J. £100. To wife Ann the interest and profits of my whole estate during life, legacies to be paid after her death. To Darby Meeting of Friends £20. To cousin Benj. Webber Oakford son of Aaron and Ann all remainder of estate real and personal.

Executors: Wife Ann, David Gibson and Josiah Bunting. Letters to Ann and Gibson.
Wit: John Grimes, Danl. Humphrey, John Pearson.

INDEX

-A-
ABRAHAM, James, 39
Noah, 39
ACOR, Henry, 43
ACORE, Anthony, 110
  Jacob, 110
  Mary, 110
ADAM, 103
  Hugh, 20
  Jean, 20
  Margaret, 20
ADAMS, Frank, 20
  Hans, 14
  James, 20, 85
  John, 43
  Jonathan, 20
  Rebecca, 111
  Samuel, 20
  William, 111
AILES,
  Elizabeth, 98
  Stephen, 48
ALCOTT, Mary, 52
  Thomas, 52
ALEXANDER,
  Elizabeth, 24, 115
  Francis, 25, 53, 100, 116
  James, 85, 115
  Jane, 116
  Jean, 72
  Jennet, 100
  John, 64
  John McNit, 72
  Margaret, 47
  Samuel, 24
  Susanna, 8
  William, 47
  William Bean, 72
ALFORD, Alice, 37
  Elizabeth, 37
ALL, Robert, 87
ALLEBACH, Louisa, 101
ALLEN, Amy, 48
  Ann, 48
  Benjamin, 48
  Hannah, 48
  John, 48

Joseph, 48
Lydia, 2
Samuel, 48
William, 7, 48, 84, 85
ALLISON,
  Francis, 69, 87
  Hugh, 72
  Mary, 69
  Rev., 69
  Robert, 23
ANDERSON, Agnes, 7
  Gilbert, 54
  Henry, 7
  James, 7, 14, 37, 69, 92, 95, 97, 100
  John, 7, 14, 85
  Margaret, 69
  Mary, 85
  Samuel, 7
  William, 96, 97
ANDREWS, John, 114
ARBUCKEL, Anna, 114
  Eleanor, 114
  Esther, 114
  James, 113
  John, 114
  Mary, 114
ARCHER, John, 104
ARMAR, Samuel, 110
ARMENT, John, 90
ARMSTRONG,
  Ephraim, 23
  John, 23
  Joseph, 23
  Margaret, 23
  Thomas, 54, 88
  William, 22
ARNDOFF,
  Elizabeth, 111
  John, 111
  Lewis, 111
  Margaret, 111
  Mary, 111
  Philip, 111
  Susanna, 111
ARTHUR, Jane, 53, 111

William, 53
ARTHURS, Joseph, 97
  Mary, 97
ASGIL, William, 11
ASH, Caleb, 115
  Joshua, 115
ASHBRIDGE,
  Aaron, 99
  Daniel, 63
  David, 99
  George, 17, 19, 20, 35, 63, 70, 99, 101, 121
  Hannah, 63
  Jane, 63, 99
  John, 35, 99
  Jonathan, 35, 92
  Joseph, 77, 99
  Joshua, 63, 99
  Mary, 63
  Phebe, 63
  Priscilla, 99
  Sarah, 35, 99
  Susanna, 63
  William, 63
ASHE, Samuel, 109
ASKEW, John, 50
  Lazarus, 48
  Sarah, 86
ASTIN, George, 57
  Hannah, 57
  Owen, 57
  Rachel, 57
ASTON, Abraham, 82
  Esther, 82
  Margaret, 34
  William, 34
ATHERTON,
  Henry, 37, 66
  Jane, 50
  William, 50
AXLINE, Adam, 16
  Catharine, 16
  Christopher, 16

-B-
BABB, Mary, 68
  Peter, 68
  Sampson, 68

123

INDEX

Samson, 116
Sarah, 8
Susanna, 68
Thomas, 68
BAGGS, Thomas, 109
BAILEF, Sarah, 64
BAILIFF, Daniel, 41
Sarah, 41
BAILLEY,
Elizabeth, 39
Jean, 39
BAILY, Ann, 94
Betty, 94
Caleb, 79
Charles, 94
Cottrell, 94
Evan, 61
Isaac, 94
Joel, 15, 66, 94
Joshua, 94
Josiah, 99
Mary, 94
Phebe, 94
Thomas, 61
BAINBRIDGE,
Absalom, 107
Edmund, 107
Elizabeth, 107
John, 107
Kezia, 107
BAKER, Aaron, 4, 94, 120
Alice, 59
Christian, 102
Hannah, 32, 73, 120
John, 73
Joseph, 116, 120
Lydia, 75, 116, 120
Margery, 103
Martha, 102
Nathan, 75, 84, 120
Nehemiah, 21, 75, 84, 116, 119, 120
Peter, 32
Phebe, 120
Rachel, 94
Richard, 15, 23, 94, 103
Robert, 103
William, 103

BALDWIN, Hannah, 67
John, 38, 73
Joshua, 38, 52, 57
Robert, 67
Sarah, 52, 73
BALLA,
Alexander, 38
Elizabeth, 114
Hannah, 38, 114
BANE, William, 20
BARBER, James, 107
BARCLAY,
Eleanor, 34
James, 85
John, 34
BARKEFILE,
Thomas, 104
BARKER, Richard, 31
BARKLY, Hannah, 17
BARNARD,
Barbara, 118
Jeremiah, 10
Richard, 10, 28
Susanna, 72
Thomas, 39
BARNET,
Elizabeth, 6
Martha, 6
Sarah, 77
Thomas, 77
BARNS, Isaac, 77
William, 77
BARR, Andrew, 100, 113
James, 100
Jane, 100
Janet, 113
John, 100
Mary, 100
Moses, 100
Robert, 100
Samuel, 100
Sarah, 100
William, 100
BARRETT,
Arthur, 103
Thomas, 103
BARTHOLOMEW,
Benjamin, 103
John, 117
Margaret, 103
Thomas, 103
BARTON, James, 78

Joseph, 121
Thomas, 25
BARTRAM, Eliza, 50
Elizabeth, 45, 50
James, 45
John, 45, 50
BASON, John, 40
BATTIN, John, 63
BAXTER, James, 84
Mary, 84
BAYLIFFE,
Edward, 33
Thomas, 33
BEAKES, Lydia, 66
BEALE, John, 106
Mary, 42
William, 42, 59, 106
BEALS, John, 91
BEAN, Abigail, 72
Jean, 72
William, 72
BEANE,
Catharine, 66
BEAR, Andrew, 1
Jean, 1
BEARAT, James, 8
Mary, 8
William, 8
BEARD, John, 13
BEATON, John, 106
BEATTY, Agnes, 88
David, 88
Elizabeth, 88
Esther, 88
Rachel, 88
Robert, 88
BEAUMONT, John, 105
BECKHOLT,
Borick, 31
BECKS, Stephen, 38
BEERBOWER,
Kiny., 106
BEERY, Jacob, 89, 95, 120
BELL, Anne, 107
David, 74
Edward, 8, 45, 74
Elizabeth, 8, 93
Humphrey, 18, 64, 107
James, 93
Jane, 93

INDEX

Jean, 70
John, 18
Joseph, 70
Margaret, 74, 107
Mary, 8, 74
Peter, 107
Robert, 113
Samuel, 74, 121
William, 8, 18, 73, 74
BENARD,
Abraham, 119
Catherine, 119
Elizabeth, 118, 119
George, 119
Hannah, 119
Jacob, 119
John, 119
Mary, 118
Paul, 118
Rebecca, 118
BENNETT,
Christian, 38
Hannah, 62
James, 32, 38, 62, 78, 87, 89
John, 62, 104
Margaret, 38
Mary, 38
Ruth, 104
Sarah, 62
Titus, 29, 62, 89
William, 29, 62
BENSON, Ann, 118
Benjamin, 118
Hannah, 105
James, 105, 118
Jane, 61
Jonathan, 118
Rachel, 118
BENTLEY,
Banner, 91, 117
Caleb, 118
Eleanor, 91
Eli, 117
Elizabeth, 16
Ellis, 117
George, 118
Jane, 118
Jeffrey, 91, 117
John, 16
Jonathan, 91

Joseph, 91, 117, 118
Mary, 91, 117, 118
BERAT, William, 106
BERTBOUR,
Phineas, 112
BERWICK, Ann, 25
BEST, John, 16
BETTAY, John, 108
BETTEY, Samuel, 42
BETTLE,
Edward, 45, 92
BEVAN, Agnes, 116
Ann, 116
David, 116
Davis, 35
BIERBOWER,
Casper, 14
BILHA, 17
BILLERBY, Isaac, 89
John, 55, 89
BINES, Robert, 28
BISHOP, Ann, 38
Elizabeth, 68
Esther, 23
Joseph, 8
Margaret, 50
Samuel, 80
Sarah, 80
Thomas, 3, 44, 45, 46, 50, 59
BLACK, Ann, 102
Anne, 45
Benjamin, 72
Charles, 28
Hannah, 10
John, 54, 88
Joseph, 45
Margaret, 45
Mary, 45, 102
Newton, 10
Samuel, 45
Sarah, 10
William, 10, 45
BLACKBURN, Ephraim, 76
James, 76
Jean, 77
John, 16, 76
Mary, 76, 77
Nathaniel, 77
Rebecca, 91
Robert, 76

Samuel, 76
BLANDFORD,
Thomas, 52
BLELOCK, James, 47
William, 47
BODLEY, William, 106
BOGGS, John, 102
Joseph, 102
Margaret, 102
Robert, 39
BOLSEL, Philip, 24
BOND, Ann, 44, 100
Benjamin, 43
Hannah, 44
Joseph, 44, 100
Mary, 44
Paul, 44
Samuel, 52, 99
BONSAL, Edward, 41
BONSALL,
Abraham, 59
Benjamin, 27, 32
David, 27
Edward, 41
Enoch, 27
Hannah, 27, 41, 89, 120
Isaac, 27
Jesse, 22, 62, 84, 109
Jonathan, 27
Joseph, 27
Joshua, 27
Ruth, 109
Sarah, 27
BOON, Andrew, 93
Barbara, 93
Bridget, 93
Hans, 13, 93
Joseph, 93
BOONE, Barbara, 104
Diana, 104
William, 104
BOOTH, Charles, 96
Jeremiah, 65
BOUGH, Jacob, 103
BOUND, John, 5
BOURNE, Thomas, 93
BOWEN, Ann, 16
Daniel, 118
Ezekiel, 16
Fos., 121

INDEX

Hester, 39
Jane, 105
John, 26, 105
Jonathan, 39
Joseph, 39
Levi, 16, 40
Linard, 39
Mary, 16, 39
Owen, 39
Stephen, 39
Thomas, 39
BOWING, Rees, 57
William, 57
BOYCE, Mary, 95
Robert, 95
BOYD, Adam, 15, 22
Andrew, 22, 70
Catherine, 116
Elizabeth, 22
Francis, 7
Hannah, 6, 7, 22, 59
James, 6, 7, 14, 23, 59
Jane, 6, 7
Jean, 59
John, 6, 7, 17, 22, 59, 111, 113
Mary, 6, 7, 22, 59
Samuel, 22, 75
Thomas, 22, 112, 116
William, 6, 7, 59, 111
BOYER, Ann, 106
Catherine, 106
Elizabeth, 106
Hannah, 106
Juliana Terasia, 106
Margaret Elizabeth, 106
Mary, 106
Michael, 106
Michal Magdelene, 106
Philip, 106
Rebecca, 106
Sarah, 106
Susanna, 106
BOYES, Mary, 1
Robert, 1
BOYLAND, John, 59

BOYLE, Ann, 60
Dorinton, 60
Mary, 60
Robert, 60
Samuel, 60
Thomas, 91
BRADLEY, Elias, 119
Mary, 119
BRANNEN, Benjamin, 22, 23, 69
Grace, 22
John, 22
Margaret, 23
Mary, 23
BRATTEN, Robert, 37
BRICE, Letitia, 90, 98
BRIGGS, William, 115
BRINTON, Christian, 38
David, 29
Edward, 64
Esther, 49
George, 38, 49, 81
John, 97, 98
Rebecca, 97, 98
BRODELY, Edward, 77
BROMALL, Daniel, 21
BROOKS, Ebenezer, 90
John, 23
Martha, 77
Thomas, 77
BROOM, Daniel, 104
John, 18
BROOMALL, Daniel, 66, 120
David, 66
BROOMHALL, Ann, 99
BROWER, Daniel, 110
Henry, 110
John, 110
Magdalena, 101
BROWN, Abigail, 32
Catherine, 32
Daniel, 13, 48
David, 8, 103
Elisha, 33
Elizabeth, 32
Esther, 32, 111
George, 33
Hannah, 13

Isaac, 6, 32, 33
Jacob, 54
Jane, 91
Jeremiah, 6, 32, 33
John, 31, 73
Joseph, 13, 48
Joshua, 2, 6, 33
Mabel, 48
Mary, 6, 32, 33
Matthew, 100
Nathaniel, 13
Neill, 42
Rebecca, 117
Robert, 14, 26, 31, 34, 68, 91
Samuel, 33, 34
Sarah, 32
Solomon, 13
Stephen, 32
Susanna, 13
Thomas, 51
William, 27
BRYAN, Barbara, 93, 104
John, 44, 93, 104, 116
BUCHANAN, Agnes, 41
Andrew, 35
Ann, 33
Elizabeth, 33
George, 33
Gilbert, 41
Janet, 41
Margaret, 41
Martha, 33
Mary, 41
Sarah, 41
Walter, 33, 41
William, 33
BUCHANNON, Gilbert, 35
BUCKWALTER, Daniel, 101
David, 101
Esther, 101
Hannah, 101
Jacob, 101
John, 101
BUFFINGTON, Elizabeth, 82, 89
Frances, 25
Jacob, 82

Jane, 82
John, 75, 82, 89
Jonathan, 40
Joseph, 58, 118
Joshua, 82
Mary, 82, 89
Phebe, 82
Richard, 25, 82
Robert, 25, 82
Ruth, 30
Thomas, 30
BULL, Henry, 66
John Gronow, 96
Mary, 96
BULLAR, Jane, 6
John, 6
Richard, 6
BULLOCK, Francis, 34
John, 35
BUNTIN, Margaret, 14
BUNTING, Josiah, 122
BURGESS, Ann, 12
Elizabeth, 12
Gervase, 12
John, 12
BURKE, Rowland, 40
BURNET, John, 38
BURNETT, John, 31, 79
William, 31
BURNS, Jane, 102
BUSSARD, Frederick, 101
Susanna, 101
BUTCHER, Hannah, 8
Mary, 8
Zachary, 8
BUTLER, Hannah, 120, 121
Noble, 44, 52
Thomas, 49
BUTTERFIELD, John, 33
BUYERS, Elizabeth, 3
John, 3
Margaret, 3
Robert, 3
BYERS, David, 1, 5
Elizabeth, 5

Florence, 5
John, 5
Joseph, 5
Margaret, 1, 3, 5
Mary, 5
Samuel, 3, 5
William, 3, 5

-C-
CAHOON, John, 6
Phillis, 6
CAIEN, Robert, 90
CAIN, John, 96
CALDWELL, Agnes, 83
Alexander, 7
David, 60
Elizabeth, 55
George, 55
Joanna Frances, 55
John, 7, 55
Joseph, 42
Margaret, 3
Martha, 7, 55
Mary, 7, 55, 83
Robert, 7, 83
Sarah, 7
William, 7
CALHOON, James, 39
Mary, 39, 69
CALVER, Daniel, 62
CALVERT, Daniel, 3, 21
Hannah, 82
Isaac, 119
Jane, 98
CAMARAN, Rebecca, 71
CAMBELL, Mary, 79
CAMPBELL,
Alexander, 75
Benjamin, 60
Catherine, 97
Charles, 74
Daniel, 23
Elizabeth, 75
Janet, 75
John, 39, 60, 74, 75
Josiah, 53
Margaret, 60
Mary, 60
Samuel, 60
Thomas, 60

William, 60
CANBY, Ann, 41, 64
Edith, 42
Thomas, 41
CANN, Catherine, 30
John, 30
CARLETON, Dinah, 44
Hannah, 44
Lydia, 44
Mark, 44
Martha, 44
Samuel, 44
Sarah, 44
Thomas, 44, 52
CARLILE, John
Mease, 67
Mary, 67
William, 67
CARMICHAEL, John, 15, 33, 115
Mr., 109
CARPENTER, John, 60
Samuel, 103
CARRIE, Mary, 110
CARRUTHERS,
William, 117
CARSON, Agnes, 1
Francis, 1
Hannah, 1
Mary, 1, 91
Rebecca, 1
Samuel, 1
Sarah, 1
Walter, 1
William, 1
CARTER, Abraham, 110
Edward, 110
George, 30, 75
Hannah, 37, 63
Isaac, 22
John, 37, 63
Lydia, 22
Phebe, 91
CATHER, David, 7
CEASER, 82
CERNS, John, 12
CHALFANT, Ann, 86
Elizabeth, 16
John, 86
Martha, 6
Robert, 6, 12
Thomas, 6

INDEX

CHAMBERLIN, Ann, 42, 78
　Elizabeth, 46, 78
　Hannah, 78
　Isaac, 46
　John, 29, 46, 55
　Joseph, 46, 54
　Martha, 44
　Mary, 46
　Robert, 42, 71, 78
　Susanna, 55
　William, 46
CHAMPION, John, 30
　Ruth, 30
CHANDLER, Ann, 88
　Elizabeth, 12, 30
　Isaac, 30
　Mary, 30
　Rebecca, 48
　Samuel, 78
　William, 48
CHAPMAN, Alice, 81
　Ann, 81
　George, 85
　John, 81
　Mary, 81
　Phebe, 81
CHARLTON,
　Elizabeth, 42
　Henry, 42
　Isabella Amy, 42
　Thomas, 42
CHERRIE, Aaron, 102
CHERRY, Isaac, 102
　James, 31
　Samuel, 96
CHEYNEY, Ann, 50
　Deborah, 46
　John, 5, 46, 50
　Joseph, 50
　Mary, 64
　Richard, 50, 51, 64
　Thomas, 46, 50, 51, 52
CHIDDICK, William, 95
CHRISTIE, Peter, 106
CHRISTMAN, George, 112
CHRISTY, Sarah, 110
CHURCHMAN, George, 2, 6
　Hannah, 103
　John, 6
　William, 58
CLARK, Ann, 25
　David, 25
　Elizabeth, 37
　Florence, 5
　Jane, 5
　John, 5, 23, 24, 25, 37, 60
　Joseph, 25
　Mary, 24, 37
　Samuel, 60
　Sarah, 60
　Thomas, 25
　William, 37, 54, 60
CLAYPOOLE, James, 62
CLAYTON, Adam, 45
　Ann, 40
　Hannah, 40, 45
　John, 40
　Joshua, 40
　Sarah, 40
　Susanna, 40
　Susannah, 40
　Temperance, 89
　Thomas, 31, 71
　William, 40
CLELAND, Benjamin, 42
　Mary, 42
　Samuel, 42
　Sarah, 42
CLENDENNIN, Phebe, 11
　Robert, 11
CLEVER, Joshua, 80
CLIME, Philip, 120
CLINGAN, William, 61
CLINGING, Margaret, 17
CLOTHIER, Eleanor, 51
CLOUD, Abner, 79
　Ann, 79
　Betty, 79
　Esther, 81
　Hannah, 79
　Jason, 92
　Jeremiah, 78, 79, 81
　Joseph, 38
　Mordecai, 38, 79
　Priscilla, 38
　William, 72, 79, 93
CLOYD, David, 43
　Elizabeth, 43
　James, 43, 47
　Jane, 43
　Margaret, 43
　Mary, 43
　Rebecca, 43
　Sarah, 43
COATES, Aaron, 56
　Hannah, 99
　Isaac, 77
　Jonathan, 101, 108, 112
　Moses, 77, 99, 108
COATS, Elizabeth, 85
　Hannah, 85
　Moses, 85
　Sarah, 44
　Susanna, 44
COBOURN, David, 32
　Joseph, 103
　Mary, 32
　Robert, 66
　William, 103
COCHRAN, Andrew, 26, 103
　David, 17, 26
　George, 17
　Isbel, 17
　Jacob, 26
　James, 17, 26
　Jane, 17
　John, 7, 17, 26
　Josiah, 26
　Mary, 26
　Robert, 17
　Stephen, 17
　William, 26
COCKRAN, Stephen, 68
COLE, Agnes, 24
COLHOON, Adam, 109
　Elizabeth, 109
　Jenet, 109
　John, 109

Robert, 109
COLLET, Margaret, 8
COLLIER, John, 87
　Mary, 36
　Richard, 36
COLLINS, Ann, 15
　Charity, 15
　Elisha, 15
　Jane, 64
　Mary, 15
COLVEN, Robert, 82
CONOWAY, Hannah, 37
　John, 37
CONWAY, John, 5
COOK, Hannah, 78
　Joseph, 34
　Samuel, 78
COOKE, Sarah, 99
COON, Christopher, 121
COOPE, Caleb, 63
　Hannah, 63
　John, 62, 63
　Joseph, 63
　Joshua, 63
　Mary, 63
　Nathan, 63
　Samuel, 6, 62
COOPER, Adam, 46
　Alexander, 46
　Andrew, 67
　Betty, 67
　Calvin, 48
　Finval, 46
　Hugh, 46
　James, 14, 46, 67, 114
　Jane, 67
　John, 14, 46, 67
　Margaret, 14
　Margret Jane, 46
　Mary, 46, 67
　Robert, 14, 48, 107
　Sebbelah, 81
　Susanna, 77
　Thomas, 46, 67
　William, 14, 30, 48, 82, 114
COPE, Ann, 89
　Joseph, 89
COPELAND, George, 68

COPPOCK, Abner, 104
　John, 104
　Sibella, 92
CORKER, daniel, 110
CORNOG, Daniel, 17, 107
CORNTWAIT, John, 8
CORREY, ---, 6
　David, 109
　George, 7
　Robert, 7
CORRY, Jane, 1
　Moses, 1
　Samuel, 1
CORSE, Thomas, 85
CORSGRAVE, Mary, 42
COULSON, Joseph, 42
　Thomas, 57
COWAN, Ann, 108
　Elizabeth, 108
　George, 108
　Henry, 108
　Hugh, 80
　James, 108
　Jean, 61, 108
　John, 108
　Joseph, 105, 108
　Margaret, 108
　Mary, 80, 108
　Robert, 15, 105
　Sarah, 108
　Thomas, 61, 105, 108
　William, 108
COWPLAND, Ann, 21
　Caleb, 116
　David, 116
　Isabel, 116
　Joshua, 21, 103, 116
　Sarah, 116
COX, John, 45
　Joseph, 45, 80
　Lawrence, 68
　Mary, 45
CRABB, Benjamin, 35
　Mary, 35
　Sarah, 35
　Susanna, 35
　William, 35
CRAGE, Elizabeth, 109
　James, 67, 81

CRAIG, George, 27, 31, 55, 71
CRAIGE, Grace, 94
CRAWFORD, Agnes, 32
　James, 18, 19
　Josiah, 49
　Margaret, 87
　Martha, 23
　Rebecca, 18, 19
　William, 25, 108
CREELY, Ann, 5
CRESWELL, George, 87
　Mary, 87
　Samuel, 73
CRISWELL, Elisha, 53
　Joseph, 53
　Robert, 76
CROMWELL, Vincent, 61
CROOKS, Edward, 42, 90
CROSBY, David, 97
　Esther, 57
　John, 58, 97, 99
　Rachel, 97
　Richard, 9, 37
　Samuel, 9, 97
　Thomas, 97
CROSSLEY, Samuel, 71
CROXON, Mary, 63
CROZER, Elizabeth, 69
　Hannah, 36, 118
　James, 69, 88
　John, 118
　Rachel, 69
CULBERTSON,
　Abigail, 15
　Agnes, 35, 88
　Andrew, 15
　Benjamin, 15
　Elizabeth, 15
　James, 15
　Jane, 31
　John, 15, 31
　Marthew, 31
　Mary, 31
　Patrick, 108
　Samuel, 15, 88, 117

INDEX

Sarah, 31
CULIN, Andrew, 116
Daniel, 14, 87, 89, 114
Elizabeth, 114
Isaac, 114
John, 114
Lydia, 116
Margaret, 114
Rachel, 116
Rebecca, 114, 116
Swan, 99, 114, 56
CUMING, Mary, 68
William, 68
CUMMINGS, Thomas, 121
CUNNINGHAM, Arthur, 81
Jane, 4
John, 4, 33
CURLE, James, 57
Jenet, 57
John, 19, 57, 87
Margery, 57
Mary, 57
Sarah, 57
CURREY, George, 6
William, 45
CURRIE, Sarah, 116
William, 62, 103
CURRY, Robert, 76
CUTHBERT, Allen, 66
John, 66
Thomas, 66
CYPHER, Michael, 30

-D-
DAHARTY, Lidy, 49
DALE, Samuel, 53
DARLINGTON,
Abraham, 17, 32, 97, 98
Deborah, 17, 97
Elizabeth, 17, 97
Hannah, 97
John, 17, 98, 118
Joseph, 110, 113
Mary, 98
Rachel, 97
Robert, 110
Thomas, 98
DAVID, Evan, 110
John, 37

Moses, 50
DAVIDSON,
Alexander, 51
Janet, 13
William, 108
DAVIES, Amos, 104
Benjamin, 31, 91
Ellis, 73
Hezekiah, 47
Walter, 70
Zepheniah, 43
DAVINSON, Sarah, 7
DAVIS, Aaron, 119
Ann, 34, 44, 56, 119
Anne, 59
Asa, 12, 83
Barbara, 106
Beninah, 69
Benjamin, 34, 59, 61
Caleb, 88
Catharine, 78
Catherine, 85
Daniel, 48, 119
David, 29, 75, 76, 95, 96, 117
Eleanor, 95
Elizabeth, 12, 69, 70, 79, 83, 96, 111, 113
George, 85
Griffith, 11, 111
Hannah, 12, 56, 59, 63, 65, 83, 95, 106, 118
Isaac, 9, 12, 83, 85, 110, 113
Israel, 69
Jacob, 69
James, 9, 12, 34, 48, 59, 69, 73, 83, 119
Jane, 95
Jenet, 70
Jerman, 96
Jesse, 12, 83
John, 34, 37, 56, 59, 70, 75, 76, 95, 111, 113, 117, 119
Joseph, 43, 69, 79
Joshua, 69

Leah, 69
Lettice, 95
Lewis, 2, 9, 12, 34, 45, 50, 56, 59, 65, 69, 83, 101
Lydia, 73, 119
Marek, 96
Margaret, 95
Mary, 34, 37, 48, 56, 75, 117, 119
Methuselah, 69
Miles, 96
Nathan, 34
Nehemiah, 78
Philip, 96
Rachel, 69
Rebecca, 34, 56
Rees, 59
Sampson, 3
Samuel, 39, 72, 79, 117
Sarah, 34, 56, 96
Sidney, 79
Thomas, 29, 75, 78, 95
William, 2, 9, 12, 44, 83, 101
DAWES, Edward, 36
DAWSON, Abraham, 22
Ann, 22, 53
David, 25, 53
Elizabeth, 53
Fortunata, 22
Fortune, 25
Isaac, 22, 25
Jacob, 25
Jean, 53
Margaret, 22, 25, 53, 108
Mary, 22, 25, 53
Rachel, 53
Richard, 22
Sarah, 25
Thomas, 22, 25, 53
William, 53
DAY, Catharine, 86
George, 86
James, 63
John, 85, 86
Joseph, 86
Lydia, 86
Rebecca, 86

Sarah, 8
DEAN, William, 29
DEE, Mary, 111
Richard, 111
DEEM, Henry, 106
DEERY, George, 112, 115
DELANY, Eleanor, 70
DELRUMPLE, Mary, 31
Thomas, 31
DEMPSEY, Cornelius, 79
DENNEN, William, 23
DENNY, Samuel, 97
William, 100
DERBROW, Hugh, 19
DERRICK, Zachariah, 102
DEVOR, Elizabeth, 79
James, 79
DICK, 47
DICKEY, John, 114
Mary, 103
DICKINSON, Mary, 3
DICKS, Abigail, 88
Roger, 78, 92
Sarah, 88
DILLOR, John, 63
DILWORTH, Caleb, 29
Charles, 12, 29, 64
George, 29
Hannah, 29
James, 12, 29
Joseph, 29, 116
Letitia, 29
Lydia, 29
Mary, 29, 64, 88
Richard, 29, 30
Sarah, 29
Susanna, 30
William, 29
DINAH, 7, 57
DINGEE,
Christopher, 13
Jacob, 13, 103
DIX, Ann, 38
Peter, 91
DIXON, Elizabeth, 48
DIZART, William, 90
DOGHERTY, James, 9

DONAHEY, Martha, 93
William, 93
DONAL, Margaret, 55
DONALDSON, William, 36
DOTSON, Ann, 64
Elenor, 64
DOUGHERTY, Charles, 76
Dennis, 17
Edward, 17, 77
James, 13
John, 13
Margaret, 13
Martha, 13
Patrick, 102
Samuel, 13
DOUGLAS, Sarah, 58
DOUGLASS, James, 72
DOWDLE, John, 34
DOWNING, Eleanor, 2
Jane, 52
John, 52
Joseph, 52
Richard, 49, 52, 57
Thomas, 52
William, 2, 52
DRENNAN, David, 97
DREW, David, 7
DREWITT, John, 28
Mary, 28
DUCKE, John, 114
DUFFIELD,
Catherine, 107
Edward, 107
Elizabeth, 107
DUNCAN, Mary, 72
DUNGING, Esther, 72
William, 72
DUNLEY, William, 97
DUNN, George, 101
James, 79, 80
John, 80
Rebecca, 79
DUNWOODIES, Andrew, 95
James, 95
Janet, 95
William, 95
DUNWOODY, William, 49
DURROUGH, John, 67

DUTTON, Ann, 22
David, 88
Elizabeth, 65, 104
Francis, 50
Hannah, 65, 86
Isaac, 73
Jacob, 65
James, 65
John, 13
Jonathan, 86
Joseph, 65
Lydia, 88
Mary, 65
Rachel, 13
Richard, 65
Susanna, 65
Thomas, 86
DYBRIMPLE, Mary, 59
DYSANT, James, 19

-E-
EACHUS, Daniel, 79
Hannah, 19
Phineas, 19
Robert, 79
Sarah, 19
EASTON, Margaret, 50
EAVENSON,
Elizabeth, 1, 44
George, 46, 66
Nathaniel, 1
EBERHARD,
Christian, 107
EBERHART, Benjamin, 113
Christian, 112
Elizabeth, 113
James, 113
Mary, 113
Samuel, 113
Sarah, 113
Sophia, 113
ECKHOFF, David, 81
ECKOFF, Ann, 72
David, 71, 72
Joseph, 72
Michael, 72
Phillis, 72
William, 72
EDDY, Joseph, 37
Mary, 37
William, 37

INDEX

EDENS, William, 85
EDGE, Ann, 22
  Jacob, 80
  Mary, 22
EDMESTON, David, 55
  Hannah, 55
  Margaret, 55
  Samuel, 55
  Sarah, 55
EDMISTON, Abraham, 27
  David, 27, 114
  Elizabeth, 27
  James, 27
  Jean, 27
  Mary, 27
  Moses, 27
  Rachel, 27
  William, 27
EDWARDS, Ann, 86
  Caleb, 99
  Hannah, 94
  John, 99
  Joseph, 59, 94
  Joshua, 99
  Moses, 99
  Nathan, 99
  Reese, 94
  Thomas, 99
  William, 18, 78
EFFINGER, Mealchi, 48
ELDER, James, 81
ELDRIDGE, Jonathan, 86
  Joseph, 38
  Sarah, 86
ELLIOT, Ann, 51
  Esther, 88
  John, 51, 88
  Thomas, 27
ELLIOTT, Agnes, 26
  Amy, 74
  Anne, 87
  Benjamin, 11, 74
  Christopher, 11, 23, 74
  Elizabeth, 11, 37
  Enoch, 11
  Jean, 26, 27
  John, 11, 27, 74
  Margaret, 5
  Martha, 11
  Mary, 11, 26
  Peter, 11, 23
  Robert, 11
  Ruth, 11
  Samuel, 26, 27
  Thomas, 26, 27
  William, 12, 26, 37
ELLIS, Ann, 78
  David, 89
  Edward, 26
  Hannah, 21, 22
  Jesse, 56
  Rowland, 17
ELTON, John, 113
  Robert, 113
  Thomas, 113
EMMITT, Abraham, 8
EMPSON, Mary, 64
ENGLAND, David, 48
  Sarah, 98
  William, 67
ENGLE, Abigail, 9, 115
  Edward, 115
  Elias, 115
  Frederick, 9, 38, 115
  Isaac, 115
  John, 115
  Joseph, 38, 115
  Mary, 38, 115
ENTERKIN, George, 10
  James, 10
  Jane, 10
  Mary, 10
  Rachel, 10
  Samuel, 10
ERNEST, Jacob, 37
ERWIN, John, 84
EVAN, Mary, 61
  Thomas, 40
  William, 64
EVANS, Alexander, 32
  Ann, 16, 21, 64
  Anna, 21
  Anne, 49
  Cadwallader, 3, 21, 98
  David, 48, 64, 110
  Dorothy, 62
  Elenor, 59
  Elizabeth, 59, 66
  Evan, 53, 59, 83
  Grace, 121
  Griffith, 59
  Hannah, 21, 32, 59
  Issacher, 96
  James, 4, 5, 6, 7, 8, 59, 64
  Jane, 64
  Joel, 52, 103
  John, 5, 48, 64, 71, 83
  Jonathan, 9, 16, 48, 69, 107
  Joseph, 114
  Joshua, 34, 35, 39, 62, 66, 69, 71, 96, 103, 121
  Lydia, 59
  Margaret, 59
  Mary, 16, 48, 64, 94
  Pennell, 21
  Rebecca, 59
  Robert, 21, 59
  Rose, 59
  Rowland, 103, 109
  Sarah, 21, 69
  Thomas, 21, 53, 56, 118, 120
  William, 16, 18, 64, 121
EVENSON, Seth, 121
EVENWINE, Alvertus, 5
  John, 5
EVES, John, 11, 31
EWING, James, 23, 97
  Patrick, 13
  Samuel, 77, 83
  William, 42, 97
EYRE, Ann, 50, 71
  Isaac, 16, 50, 51
  John, 16, 22, 50, 66, 92
  Lewis, 50
  Mary, 50
  Rebecca, 22, 92
  Robert, 50, 71
  William, 50

-F-

FAGAN, Ann, 108
  John, 108
FAIRLAMB, John, 3, 5, 33
  Mary, 55
FARROW, Mary, 120
FAWKES, Richard, 51
  William, 51
FEAGAN, Charles, 6
  Sarah, 6
FELL, Edward, 54
  William, 2, 48, 54, 69
FERGUSON, Mary, 13
FERRELL, Lewis, 66
FERRIOR, Agnes, 32
FIKE, Ann, 47
  Barbara, 47
  Cathrin, 47
  Christian, 47
  Jacob, 47
  John, 47
  Margaret, 47
  Mary, 47
FILSON, Agnes, 101
  Ann, 101
  Davison, 87, 101
  Elenor, 101
  Elizabeth, 101
  Jane, 5
  Jean, 101
  John, 5, 101
  Joseph, 101
  Moses, 101
  Robert, 101, 105
  William, 5, 101
FINLEY, Agnes, 73
  James, 72
  Michael, 73
  Robert, 7
FINLY, Thomas, 83
FINNEY, Ann, 13
  Dorothea, 13
  John, 13
  Mary, 13
  Robert, 13, 68
  Thomas, 13
  Walter, 70
FISHER, Ann, 94
  Christian, 18
  Elizabeth, 94
  Hannah, 78

Magdalen, 18
  Martha, 78
  Robert, 78
  Samuel, 81
  Thomas, 78
  William, 78
FITZSIMONS, George, 104
  Margaret, 45
FITZSUMMONS, John, 45
FLEMING, Abigail, 108
  Alexander, 7, 8, 77, 90, 104
  Alice, 8
  Ann, 7
  Archibald, 68, 73
  David, 7, 54, 88
  Henry, 7, 8, 77
  James, 7, 8, 51, 54, 68, 90
  Jean, 54
  John, 7, 8, 25, 26, 34, 47, 53, 54, 77, 105, 108
  Joseph, 7, 8
  Margaret, 7
  Robert, 54
  Susanna, 7
  William, 7, 8
FLETCHER,
  Elizabeth, 36
  John, 36
  William, 36
FLING, Abigail, 10
  David, 10
FLOWER, John, 47
  Mary, 89
  Richard, 79
FLOYD, Samuel, 70
FOLKERTH,
  Christopher, 106, 112
FOOSE, Nicholas, 47
FORD, Abraham, 87
  Ann, 2, 41
  Benjamin, 2, 34
  Jane, 2
  Margaret, 2
  Philip, 2, 20
  William, 2
FORDHAM, Joseph, 84

Lydia, 84, 109
  Sarah, 109
FORGESON, Mary, 104
  William, 104
FORREST, Matthew, 10
FORRESTER,
  Elizabeth, 38
  Margaret, 86
  Ralph, 49
FORSYTH, Andrew, 84
FOULKE, Eneas, 87
FOX, Hannah, 17
  James, 17
  John, 17
FRAIZER, John, 48
FRAME, Jane, 6
  Nathan, 6, 40
  Ruth, 6, 40
FRANCIS, John, 16
FRAZER, Persifer, 102
  Persifor, 52, 66
FRED, John, 119
FREDERICK,
  Christiana, 14, 20
  Elizabeth, 14, 20
  George, 14, 20
  John, 14, 20
  Lawrence, 14
  Luke, 13, 14, 20
FREEMAN, Daniel, 74
  Hannah, 74
  Nathan, 74
  Samuel, 74
FRIER, James, 1
  Jean, 1
  Robert, 1
FRITZ, Jacob, 20
FRYER, George, 52, 82
  Jean, 73
FUERY, Elizabeth, 111
  Joseph, 111
FULLERTON, Ann, 25
  Humphrey, 25
  Robert, 104
  Thomas, 25
FULTON, James, 54
  John, 54
  Samuel, 42

INDEX

William, 54
FULTORM, John, 6
FUSS, Valentine, 37
FUTHEY, Samuel, 53

-G-
GALBREATH, Ann, 69
  John, 13, 69
  Sarah, 69
GALT, James, 72
  Margaret, 35
  Mary, 72
GARDNER, Francis, 85
  John, 18, 19
  Joseph, 17
  Mary, 18
  Rachel, 18
  Rebecca, 18
  Samuel, 18
  Sarah, 18
GARRET, Anne, 26
  Elisha, 26
  Hannah, 26
GARRETT, Aaron, 103
  Abraham, 69
  Abram, 38
  Ann, 100
  Benjamin, 26, 100
  David, 94
  Elisha, 100
  Esther, 26
  George, 94
  Hannah, 26, 44, 100
  James, 38, 100
  John, 26
  Jonathan, 38
  Joseph, 38, 99
  Josiah, 67, 103
  Lawrence, 56
  Lydia, 94
  Mary, 101
  Nathan, 59, 69
  Peter, 94
  Rebecca, 56
  Reece, 94
  Thomas, 67, 69
  William, 10, 26, 63, 69, 71, 92, 101, 111, 115, 118
GARTON, Hannah, 50

GARTRIL, George, 84
  John, 85
GARVER, Henry, 51
  Peter, 51
GASKILL, Samuel, 94
GENNET, Elizabeth, 115
GEST, Daniel, 75
  Enoch, 40
  Hannah, 75, 88
  James, 25
  Jane, 75, 88
  John, 104
  Joseph, 25, 40, 75, 88
  Lydia, 40
  Mary, 75
  Phebe, 40, 75
  Ruth, 75, 88
  Sarah, 40
  William, 87
GIBBONS, Hannah, 15
  James, 55, 61, 121
  Joseph, 11, 51, 64, 88
  Margery, 64
  Susanna, 63
  William, 63, 117
GIBBS, Cathrin, 84
  Elizabeth, 25
  Gilbert, 84, 108, 113
  Hugh, 84
  Isabella, 84
  James, 84
  Margaret, 84
  Mary, 25
  Thomas, 25
  William, 84
GIBSON, Alexander, 72, 90
  David, 65, 122
  Hannah, 4
  Isaac, 90
  Isabel, 116
  James, 90
  John, 90, 116
  Mary, 65
  Samuel, 90
  Thomas, 4, 12, 23
GIDER, Adam, 74
GILKEY, Jonathan, 15

Leah, 15
  Margaret, 15
  Mary, 15
  Samuel, 15
  Walter, 15
  William, 15
GILL, William, 108
GILLELAND, Agnes, 119
  Elizabeth, 119
  James, 119
  Thomas, 119
GILLESPIE, John, 44
  William, 44
GILLILAND, William, 118
GILPIN, Betty, 71
  George, 71
  Gideon, 71
  Isaac, 71
  Samuel, 52
  Sarah, 71
  Thomas, 71
  Vincent, 71
GIVANS, Robert, 17
GIVEN, John, 59
  William, 59
GIVENS, James, 58
  Jean, 58
  John, 58
  Jonathan Thomas, 58
  Lucie, 58
  Robert, 58
  Sarah Mary, 58
  William, 58
GLADLEY, Mary, 89
GLASGOW, James, 13
  John, 85
  Samuel, 58
  Sarah, 7
  William, 13
GLASSFORD,
  Elizabeth, 18
  Henry, 18
GLEAVE, Elizabeth, 41
  James, 41
  Mary, 41
  Rebecca, 41
GLEN, Jean, 39
  John, 39
  Mary, 39

INDEX

GLENDINING,
  William, 15
GLENN, James, 103
  John, 35
  Margaret, 103
GLOVER, William, 24
GOBBLE, Elizabeth,
  101
GODFREY, Hannah, 10
GOFF, Richard, 31
GOLDEN, William, 28
GOODWIN, Ann, 46,
  86
  Isaac, 86
  John, 86
  Richard, 86
  Thomas, 86
GORDON, William,
  104
GORMAN, Hannah, 27
  Mary, 27
GRACY, Jane, 89,
  120
  Samuel, 89, 120
GRAHAM, Abigail, 78
  Abraham, 92
  Charles, 24
  Eleanor, 92
  Elizabeth, 92
  H. H., 2, 45, 116
  Hannah, 92
  Henry H., 27
  Henry Hale, 86
  James, 92
  Jarett, 92
  John, 92, 104
  Margaret, 92
  Martha, 95
  Michael, 92
  Phebe, 24
  Robert, 7
  Susanna, 92
  William, 106, 109
  Zedekiah Wyatt, 78
GRAME, John, 31
  Mary, 31
GRANT, Abigail, 105
  James, 105
  Mary, 105
  William, 101, 105
GRANTHAM,
  Catherine, 18
  Charles, 18, 82

  George, 18, 82
  Jacob, 18
  John, 18
  Lydia, 18, 82
  Margaret, 18
  William, 18, 82
GRAVES, Jacob, 38
GRAY, Joseph, 14,
  26
  Mary, 1
GREEN, Abel, 3, 54,
  72
  Daniel, 4, 78
  Edward, 51, 52
  George, 52
  Job, 72
  John, 72
  Joseph, 52
  Margaret, 52
  Mary, 78
  Rachel, 52
  Rebecca, 52
  Robert, 6
  Sarah, 52, 62
  Thomas, 52, 62
GREENFIELD, James,
  48
GREGG, Benjamin,
  40, 66, 75
  Enoch, 40
  Hannah, 40, 66
  Isaac, 40, 49
  Joseph, 40
  Michael, 11, 40,
  49
  Ruth, 2
  Sarah, 75
  Solomon, 40
GREGORY, Margaret,
  26
GREGSON, George, 98
  Hannah, 98
GRIBB, Mary, 55
GRIBBLE, John, 98
GRIFFITH, Abel, 26
  Asenath, 53
  Dan, 104
  David, 69
  Eb., 69
  Ezekiel, 101
  Hannah, 28, 32
  Hugh, 96
  Jane, 24

  John, 2, 14, 15,
  18, 38, 69, 81,
  114
  Lewis, 89, 120
  Mary, 2, 49, 81
  Samuel, 81
  Sarah, 106
  Susanna, 89, 120
  William, 32, 53,
  71, 81
GRIFFITHS, John, 62
GRIMES, John, 122
GRONOW, Isabella,
  96
  John, 29, 96
  Lewis, 29, 35, 79,
  96
  Sarah, 96
GROSS, George, 112
GRUB, Abraham, 114
  David, 114
GRUBB, Adam, 61, 92
  Ann, 39
  Charity, 23
  Curtis, 45
  Emanuel, 42, 72
  Hannah, 23, 39
  Henry, 45
  Isaac, 23, 89
  John, 23
  Lydia, 23, 103
  Martha, 39
  Mary, 23, 39, 44,
  89, 92
  Peter, 45
  Prudence, 23
  Rachel, 23
  Rebecca, 23
  Samuel, 23, 89
  Sarah, 23
GUBBY, Mary, 32
GUEST, James, 56
GUIRY, Hannah, 58
GURNEY, Catharine,
  58
GUTHER, Ann, 71
  James, 71
GUTHERY, James, 71
  Sarah, 71
GUY, Isabella, 10
  Samuel, 10

-H-

HADDEN, John, 112
  Mary, 112
HADLEY, John, 25
  Nathaniel, 25
  Patience, 6
  Peter, 25
  Phebe, 25
  Simon, 25
HAFAN, Peter, 51
HAGANS, Elizabeth, 60
  Hugh, 60
HAGIN, John, 113
HAINES, Catherine, 19
  Ellis, 19
  Hannah, 41
  Isaac, 10, 19, 36
  Jane, 38
  Job, 46, 57
  Joshua, 41, 84
  Josiah, 19
  Rudolph, 118
  Sarah, 19
  William, 46, 57
HAIR, Hillen, 111
  James, 9, 10, 19, 109
  Lydia, 9
HALCOMBE, Jacob, 22
HALL, Andrew, 32
  Elizabeth, 32, 67
  Hannah, 32
  Henry, 58
  Jane, 67
  John, 32, 119
  Joseph, 32, 106
  Lurenda, 117
  Margaret, 32
  Mary, 32, 67, 106
  Parry, 106
  Rowland, 106
  Ruth, 106
  Samuel, 67
  Sarah, 65, 67
  Steward, 32
  Susanna, 67
  Thomas, 67
  Walter, 32
  William, 32
HAMBLETON, John, 35
HAMILL, Robert, 112

HAMILTON, Agnes, 113
  Hugh, 73
  James, 113
  Janet, 113
  John, 113
HAMPHILL, James, 55
HAMPTON, Benjamin, 13
  Rachel, 13
  Sarah, 73
  Simon, 73
  Thomas, 73
  Walter, 73
HANBEST, Elizabeth, 11
  Martha, 11
  Peter, 11
HANCOCK, John, 31
  Joseph, 110
  Love, 110
HANLEY, Eleanor, 27
  John, 27, 45
HANLIN, John, 11
HANNA, Abigail, 24
  Esther, 24
  James, 35, 83
  Jane, 35, 83
  John, 24, 35
  Robert, 35
  William, 21, 24, 35
HANNINS, John, 18
  Rachel, 18
HANNUM, James, 64
  Jane, 64
  John, 4, 40, 44, 55, 63, 64
  Margery, 64
  Mary, 64
  William, 64
HANSBEST, Peter, 11
HANSON, Jonathan, 12
  Margaret, 12
HARBISON, David, 35
  James, 34, 35
  Mary, 34
HARDING, John, 15
  Mary, 15
  William, 101
HARLAN, Ann, 30, 79
  Betty, 30

  David, 19
  Ebenezer, 30
  Elizabeth, 88
  Hannah, 30, 44
  Henry, 30, 79
  Israel, 94
  James, 79, 101
  Joseph, 23, 30
  Lydia, 94
  Ruth, 89
  Sarah, 44
  Solomon, 30, 79
  Susanna, 30, 44, 79
  Thomas, 94
  William, 4
HARPER, Samuel, 88
HARRIFORD, Hannah, 53
  Joseph, 53
  William, 53
HARRIS, Elizabeth, 85
  Hannah, 50, 58
  James, 85
  Jane, 50, 121
  John, 62
  Martha, 85
  Nathan, 84
  Richard, 50
  Thomas, 121
  William, 85
HARRY, David, 101
  Esther, 81
  Jesse, 65
  Rachel, 104
  Thomas, 104
HART, Mary, 7
HARTSHORN, Jonathan, 13, 58
HARTT, John, 77
  Mary, 77
  Thomas, 77
HARVARD, Samuel, 35
HARVEY, Isaac, 40
  Job, 21
  Martha, 114
  Samuel, 114
  William, 30
HASTINGS, David, 53
  James, 39
  Joseph, 53
  Margery, 53

INDEX 137

Mary, 53
HATTEN, Sarah, 18
HAVARD, John, 35
HAVILAND, Arthur, 13
HAWK, John, 104
Sarah, 104
HAWLEY, William, 10
HAY, Andrew, 37
Elizabeth, 37
HAYCOCK, Hannah, 55
Jonathan, 55
Margaret, 86
Nathan, 86
HAYES, Ann, 62, 94
Betty, 104
David, 12, 94
Hannah, 61, 104
Henry, 62, 90
Jane, 90
Joseph, 12
Mordecai, 25
Rachel, 61
Ruth, 61
Sarah, 61
Stephen, 104
HAYNES, Deborah, 61
Ellis, 61
Evan, 61
Hannah, 61, 64
Jane, 61
Jonathan, 61
Nathan, 61
Rachel, 61
Sarah, 61
HAYS, Hannah, 18
Rachel, 18
HAYWORTH, George, 89, 120
Patience, 89, 120
HEACOCK, James, 16
John, 41
Jonathan, 120
Jone, 73
Joseph, 73
HEALD, Elizabeth, 66
Jacob, 52
Rachel, 52
Ruth, 55
Samuel, 44, 52, 55
Sarah, 52
HEANY, James, 13

HECK, Jonas, 74
HEGOR, 47
HEIMBERGER, Thomas, 112
HEISER, Philip, 24
HEMP, Hezekiah, 65
HEMPHILL,
  Alexander, 17
  Ann, 102
  Elizabeth, 102
  James, 17, 45, 105
  Joseph, 17, 55
  Thomas, 102
  Wills, 102
HENDERSON, Agnes, 113
  Archibald, 13
  Benjamin, 100
  Daniel, 23, 33, 100
  David, 100
  Edward, 87
  Isabella, 33
  James, 100
  John, 73, 81, 87, 100
  Joseph, 23, 33, 100
  Margaret, 87
  Mary, 81, 100
  Matthew, 23
  Samuel, 100, 113
  William, 100
HENDRICKSEN, Isaac, 82
  Israel, 6
  John, 6
  Matthias, 115
  Susanna, 6
HENDRICKSON, Isaac, 82, 104
  John, 115
HENNEN, James, 49
HENRY, Agnes, 61
  Catharine, 61
  Ebenezer, 61
  James, 46, 61, 67, 76
  Jean, 61
  Margaret, 61
  Mary, 61
  Robert, 107
  Samuel, 33, 61

William, 61
HENVIS, Elizabeth, 74
  Martha, 74
  Robert, 74
HETHERINTON, Henry, 44
  John, 44
HETHERLIN, Jacob, 114
  Orsila, 114
HETHERY, Henry, 80
HIBBERD, Jane, 55
  John, 3, 34, 36, 83
  Phinehas, 3
  Samuel, 3
  Sarah, 63
HICKMAN, Ann, 39
  Francis, 39, 101
  John, 5
HIETT, Phebe, 64
HIGH, Daniel, 30
HILL, Ann, 19
  James, 38
  John, 38
  Peter, 38
  Samuel, 19
  William, 38
HINDMAN, John, 97
HINDS, Elizabeth, 98
  James, 98
  John, 98
  Mary, 98
HINES, Sarah, 43
HINKIN, Henry, 110
  Margaret, 110
HINKSON, John, 82
  Thomas, 82
HIPPLE, Anna, 60
  Catherine, 60
  Christiana, 60
  Elizabeth, 60
  Frederick, 60
  Henry, 60
  Jacob, 59, 60
  John, 60, 112
  Lawrence, 60
  Mary, 60, 112
  Maryliz, 60
  Ommi, 60
HOBSON, Francis, 1,

95
Isabel, 95
John, 1, 95
Joseph, 1, 42
Martha, 1, 95
Mary, 95
HOCKLEY, James, 83
HODGETS, Townsend, 66
HODGSON, Abel, 1
Elizabeth, 90
HOGAN, John, 27
HOLAHAN, John, 104
Phebe, 104
HOLIDAY, Patience, 78
HOLLAND, Nathaniel, 39, 51
HOLLINGSWORTH, Jehu, 91
HOLMAN, Adam, 107
Conrad, 108
Elizabeth, 107
Eve, 107
Henry, 107, 108
John, 107, 108
Martin, 107
Mary, 107
Michael, 107, 108
Peter, 101
HOLMES, Jane, 83
John, 83
Susanna, 106
William, 60
HOLSTON, Martha, 75
HOOFF, Peter, 67
HOOPES, Aaron, 20
Amos, 8
Benjamin, 93
Betty, 93
Daniel, 48
David, 8
Elizabeth, 8
Ezekiel, 8
Hannah, 8, 31
Isaiah, 8
Jane, 92
John, 8, 15
Joseph, 35, 68
Joshua, 31, 68, 93, 102
Margaret, 8
Stephen, 8

Thomas, 8, 19
HOOPS, Isaac, 55
Mary, 55
HOPE, Adam, 49, 105
Agnes, 105
Amos, 30
Anne, 30
Elizabeth, 30
Gennet, 105
Hannah, 84, 105
John, 30
Mary, 30, 105
Richard, 53, 105
Robert, 84, 105
Sarah, 105
Thomas, 30, 77, 105
William, 77
HOPKINS, Ezekiel, 19
Mary, 19
Matthew, 19
Ruth, 19
Sarah, 19
William, 19
HORNE, Edward, 59
Elizabeth, 59
John, 59
Mary, 102
William, 59
HORSFALL, Thomas, 12
HOSKINS, Esther, 66
John, 66
Joseph, 66
Mary, 66
Stephen, 66
HOUNSTOW, Catherine, 112
Jacob, 112
HOUSEKEEPER, Philip, 29
HOWEL, Ruth, 41
HOWELL, Abigail, 16
Anne, 16
Deborah, 16
Eliza, 45
Elizabeth, 41
Ezekiel, 62
Isaac, 16
Jacob, 16
John, 5, 16
Joseph, 16

Joshua, 16
Katherine, 16
Margaret, 5
Mary, 5
Owen, 62
Richard, 117
Robert, 5
Samuel, 16
Sarah, 16, 45, 50
Thomas, 5, 46, 51
HUBBARD, Mary, 57
HUBBERT, Mary, 79
HUDGSON, Alvery, 115
HUDSON, William, 63
HUETT, Edward, 57
HUEY, Eleanor, 10
Gennet, 10
James, 10
Jane, 10
Mary, 10
William, 10
HUGH, Campbell, 60
Margaret, 60
HUGHES, Alexander, 70
Elisha, 9, 50
James, 70
Mary, 25, 50
HUGHS, Edward, 83
HUMPHREY, Daniel, 78, 122
Hannah, 78
HUMPHREYS, Charles, 107
Daniel, 67
Edward, 99, 119
Jacob, 99, 107
John, 74
Josa., 39
Rebecca, 107
Richard, 74, 120
Samuel, 56
Sarah, 99
HUNT, Ann, 19
Elizabeth, 65
Hannah, 41
John, 17, 41, 65, 119
Joseph, 17, 41, 61
Rebecca, 41
William, 17, 41, 119

HUNTER, Andrew, 81
Ann, 81
David, 13, 96
Elizabeth, 80, 81
James, 69, 79, 109
Sarah, 69
Thomas, 63, 80, 81
William, 81
HURFORD, Caleb, 75
Elizabeth, 75
Hannah, 75
Isaac, 75
John, 75
Joseph, 75
Nicholas, 75
Samuel, 75
Sarah, 75
HUTCHISON, Agnes, 6
David, 6
James, 5
Joseph, 5
Robert, 6
Samuel, 6
HUTTON, Benjamin, 77, 87
Nehemiah, 1
Thomas, 1, 77
William, 90
HYETT, Phebe, 41

-I-
INGLIS, Jane, 67
Thomas, 67
IRWIN, Archibald, 51, 109
George, 35, 51
Gideon, 60
Isabel, 51
Isabella, 51
John, 60
Margaret, 51
Mary, 51
Rebecca, 51
Robert, 51
William, 95
ISINMINGER, Margaret, 36
IVES, Rachel, 64
Thomas, 64
William, 64

-J-
JACK, 17

Elizabeth, 115
JACKSON, Charles, 20
David, 20, 84
Ephraim, 62
Gennett, 112
Isaac, 19, 30, 96
Jacob, 35
Jane, 12, 20, 66
John, 53
John Mather, 20
Josiah, 62
Mary, 20
Paul, 12, 20, 66
Samuel, 112
William, 19
JACOB, 17
JACOBS, Isaac, 52
John, 21, 35, 38, 43, 47, 68, 99, 105
JAMES, 111
Ann, 62
Caleb, 39
Elizabeth, 35
Esther, 64, 114
George, 103
Hannah, 35, 55, 56, 99
Isaac, 55, 62
Jacob, 55
Jesse, 35
John, 68
Joseph, 30, 35, 56, 68, 99, 114
Mankin, 30
Margaret, 62
Mary, 39, 62, 114
Micajah, 103
Mordecai, 103
Philip, 30
Rachel, 99
Richard, 30
Samuel, 35, 99
Sarah, 62, 99
Susanna, 103
Thomas, 44, 64
William, 35, 95
JAMESON, Rose, 7
JANNEY, Levis, 110
JEFFERIS, Abraham, 118
Agnes, 118

Betty, 118
Elias, 119
Elizabeth, 89
Emmor, 75, 89
Hannah, 97, 118, 119
James, 88
Jane, 118
Job, 118
Lydia, 88, 118
Margaret, 119
Martha, 119
Mary, 119
Nathan, 119
Nathaniel, 118, 119
Peninah, 119
Rachel, 118
Rebecca, 118, 119
Samuel, 119
William, 97, 98, 118, 119
JENKIN, Amos, 44
Ann, 44
Anna, 31
Benjamin, 42, 43
Catherine, 43
David, 31, 42, 43, 44, 59
Elizabeth, 42
Evan, 43
Jehu, 44
Jeremiah, 44
John, 43, 44
Margaret, 44
Mary, 44
JENKINS, David, 4
Hannah, 59
Thomas, 59
William, 9
JERMAN, Lewis, 63
Mary, 63
JOB, Archibald, 68, 76
JODGON, Ann, 120
JOE, 115
JOHN, Abel, 118
Ann, 118
Dames, 53
Daniel, 2
David, 10, 14, 15, 18, 37, 50, 60, 64, 85

Elizabeth, 8
Evan, 44
Griffith, 48, 68, 118
James, 2, 10, 95, 111
Jehu, 53, 118
Joshua, 118
Lettice, 95
Margaret, 2, 10, 44
Reuben, 53, 118
Robert, 118
Samuel, 2
Sarah, 50
Thomas, 50
JOHNSON, Abraham, 32
Benjamin, 33
Catharine, 42
Cloas, 110
David, 23, 33, 119
Elizabeth, 119
Hannah, 22, 33, 34
Henry, 47
Hugh, 113
James, 33, 38
John, 42, 119
Magdalen, 99
Martha, 18, 32, 119
Mary, 119
Phebe, 91
Rachel, 33, 34
Samuel, 119
Sarah, 34
Susanna, 119
Tacy, 117
Thomas, 33, 65, 78, 91
William, 7, 119
JOHNSTON, Alice, 10
David, 36, 41
Elizabeth, 41
Francis, 41
Henry, 36
Humphrey, 23
James, 36, 68
Jane, 36, 51
John, 36
Joseph, 36
Margaret, 35, 36
Mary, 23

Rachel, 41
Samuel, 36
Susanna, 68
Uphray, 41
William, 10, 36, 51
JONES, Abednego, 39, 121
Ann, 61
Benjamin, 87, 88
Betty, 88
Cadwallader, 31, 56, 83, 118
Charles, 16
David, 83, 121
Deborah, 46
Edward, 76, 88, 89
Evan, 61, 118
Ezra, 63, 70
Griffith, 15
Hannah, 3, 88
Isaiah, 63, 70
Israel, 63
James, 59, 61
Jane, 63, 70
Jesse, 61, 63
John, 3, 15, 52, 61, 63, 64, 88, 108
John Israel, 70
Joseph, 17, 32
Lewis, 86
Lydia, 88
Mary, 63, 70, 89, 96, 116
Nehemiah, 46
Priscilla, 63, 70
Rebecca, 46
Rees, 46
Richard, 46, 61
Robert, 46
Samuel, 89
Sarah, 16, 52, 61, 88, 108
Thomas, 3
William, 3, 109, 116, 118
JORDAN, Elizabeth, 60
Hugh, 87
John, 16
Rachel, 16
JOSEPH, Hannah, 56

JUNKIN, David, 72
JUSTASON, John, 20
JUSTICE, Mary, 116
JUSTIS, John, 36

-K-
KEELEY, Elizabeth, 112
Henry, 112
John, 112
Matthias, 112
Sebastian, 112
KEELY, Matthias, 111
KEIM, George, 106
KEIMER, Thomas, 55
KEINE, Elizabeth, 121
Peter, 121
KELLAM, Benjamin, 31
KELLEY, margaret, 111
Patrick, 58
William, 111
KELLY, John, 103
KELSO, Mable, 51
Martha, 51
KENAN, Mary, 111
KENDAL, Mary, 41
KENNEDY, Ann, 75
Archibald, 97
David, 73
Dinah, 117
Dorety, 97
Elizabeth, 91, 97
George, 91
Isabella, 97
James, 26
Jane, 97
John, 73, 97, 115
Joseph, 73
Margaret, 73
Mary, 97, 106, 115
Montgomery, 73, 115
Nelly, 97
Rachel, 25
Rebecca, 91
Samuel, 34, 73, 115
Sarah, 115
Thomas, 84, 97

INDEX

Thomas Ruston, 115
William, 68, 91, 97, 106
KENNEY, James, 40
KENNY, James, 63, 94, 102
KER, Robert, 8
Thomas, 8
KERANS, Hannah, 77
John, 77
KERLIN, Ann, 38
James, 38
John, 38
Joseph, 38
Leah, 38
Mary, 38
Peter, 38
William, 34
KERR, David, 21
Elizabeth, 21
James, 21
Jean, 80
Joseph, 21
Margaret, 21, 25
Martha, 21
Thomas, 80
William, 42
KETS, Michael, 82
KEY, Allen, 66
William, 66
KEYS, Barbara, 54
James, 54
Jennet, 54
John, 54
Margaret, 54
Mary, 54
Sarah, 54
William, 54
KIGHTLEY,
Elizabeth, 41
James, 41
KIMES, Peter, 106
KINCEDE, Margaret, 24
KING, Edward, 98
Elizabeth, 98
Isabel, 60
Michael, 2, 14
KINKEAD, Charles, 49, 108
David, 49
James, 49
John, 49, 68, 118,
119
Mary, 49
Robert, 54
Samuel, 49
KIRK, Abner, 9, 71
Elisha, 9
Ezekiel, 9
Isaac, 69, 71
Jacob, 9
Jesse, 69, 71
John, 58, 103
Joseph, 9, 69
Mary, 9, 48, 69
Nathaniel, 9
Samuel, 69, 71
Sarah, 69
Susanna, 71
Timothy 9, 50, 54, 86
William, 9
KIRKPATRICK,
Andrew, 8
David, 17
Hannah, 59
Hugh, 17, 59
James, 8
John, 17, 59, 112
Lettice Charlton, 59
Thomas, 49
William, 17, 59
KIZER, Adam, 106
KNIGHT, William, 54
KNOWER, Barbara, 30
Catherine, 30
Christopher, 30
Elizabeth, 30
John, 30
Margaret, 30
KNOWLES, Hannah, 118
James, 118
John, 18, 103, 118
KNOX, Andrew, 52
KYLE, John, 112
Joseph, 112
William, 112
KYSINGER, Barbara, 101

-L-

LAFFERTY, Sarah, 24
LAMBORN, Francis, 94
John, 44, 94
Josiah, 94
Naomi, 65
Robert, 49, 93, 94
Sarah, 94
Thomas, 94
William, 81, 94
LAMPLAY, Elizabeth, 41
LAMPLUGH,
Elizabeth, 73
Jacob, 84
Samuel, 73
William, 84, 92
LANE, John, 13
LANGLEY, Ruth, 55
LARKIN, Jane, 4, 73
Joseph, 104
LATSHAW, Catherine, 101
LAVERTY, Mary, 2
LAW, James, 1, 42, 67
Thomas, 54
LAWRANCE, William, 9
LAWRENCE, Amy, 56
Daniel, 83
Ellen, 61
Hannah, 61
Henry, 3, 11, 37, 61
Isaac, 1
Joseph, 61
Margaret, 61
Mary, 61
Mordecai, 61
Richard, 1
Samuel, 61
Tacy, 56
Thomas, 61
William, 56, 99
LAWSON, John, 38
LEA, James, 51
LEACH, Joseph, 111
LEAMY, Jacob, 26
LEAP, Ann, 101
LEAS, George, 40
LEECH, William, 110
LEMERT, Lewis, 48
LEMON, Elizabeth, 40

Phebe, 40
LENDERMAN, John, 11
LEONARD, Joseph, 91
LEPER, Andrew, 42
  Elizabeth, 42
  James, 42
LESTER, Peter, 101
LEVIS, Isaac, 79
  John, 34, 56
  Martha, 39
  Thomas, 34, 69, 79
  William, 39
LEVISTON, William, 106
LEWIS, Abigail, 50
  Abner, 61, 115
  Abraham, 20, 27, 28, 97, 107
  Alex, 97
  Ann, 97
  Anthony, 20, 27, 28
  Azariah, 91
  Betty, 29
  Curtis, 57
  David, 61
  Ellis, 19
  Enoch, 17, 50, 100
  Enos, 61
  Esther, 28
  Evan, 59
  Hannah, 61
  Harvey, 111
  Henry, 61
  Isaac, 38, 44, 55, 57, 102
  Jacob, 50
  Jane, 61
  Joel, 50
  John, 16, 45, 57, 62, 82, 111, 113
  Joshua, 100
  Josiah, 68
  Levi, 80
  Lewis, 57, 61, 80
  Lydia, 50
  Margaret, 80, 106, 111, 115
  Martha, 57
  Mary, 19, 28, 44, 57, 61, 111
  Nathan, 50, 80
  Obed, 57

Phinehas, 57
  Rachel, 50, 57, 61
  Samuel, 6, 27, 108, 111
  Sarah, 94
  Thomas, 44, 50, 71
  William, 72, 114
LIDENUS, John
  Abraman, 36
LIGGETT, James, 97
LIGHTFOOT, Samuel, 36, 48
  Susanna, 36
  Thomas, 32
  William, 36
LINDLEY, James, 85
  Jonathan, 34, 35, 85
  William, 34
LINDSAY, James, 38, 97
  John, 97
  Joseph, 97
  Margaret, 97
  Martha, 33
  Robert, 97
  Samuel, 97
  Thomas, 97
  William, 97
LINDSEY, Alexander, 61
  Andrew, 61
  Jane, 61
  Jeremiah, 61
  William, 61
LINEDIGER, Nicholas, 4
LINFIELD, Margaret, 34
LINN, Andrew, 86
  Charles, 51, 86, 99
  Eleanor, 99
  Esther, 86
  Hannah, 86
  Hugh, 3, 23, 41, 86
  Jean, 86
  John, 86
  Margaret, 86
  Martha, 86
  Mary, 86
  Sarah, 86

LINVILL, Edward, 13
LITTLE, Roger, 37
LITTLER, Ann, 63, 80
  Cathrine, 80
  Elizabeth, 80
  Rachel, 80
  Thomas, 63, 80
  William, 80
LIVESTON, John, 106
LLEWELLIN, Martha, 106
LLEWELYN, David, 106
  Hannah, 106
  Martha, 106
LLEWLIN, Eleanor, 70
LLOYD, Elizabeth, 58, 84
  Enoch, 84
  Erasmus, 8, 58
  Hugh, 65, 114, 120
  Humphrey, 68, 96
  Isaac, 11, 65, 109
  John, 58, 96
  Levi, 71
  Lydia, 58
  Margret, 58
  Nicholas, 58
  Sarah, 84
  Thomas, 58
LOBB, Abraham, 36
  Benjamin, 11, 25
  Diana, 36
  Dinah, 36
  Isaac, 25, 36
LOCKEY, George, 6
LOCKLAND, Mary, 32
LOGAN, Jane, 104
  Mary, 104
  William, 97
LONG, Alexander, 109
  David, 2, 109
  Dorcas, 109
  Janet, 109
  John, 109, 115
  Joseph, 109
  Martha, 115
  Mary, 109
  William, 15, 115

LONGACRE, David, 101
Israel, 116
LORA, Mathias, 31
LORD, Hannah, 69
LOUGHRIDGE, John, 13
LOVE, Elizabeth, 33
Janet, 88
Thomas, 88
LOWMAN, William, 120
LOWNES, Alice, 10, 11, 69
Benanuel, 10, 69
Eleanor, 27
George, 69
Hugh, 69
James, 11
John, 27, 116
Joseph, 69
Mary, 69
Sarah, 69
LOWRDEY, Andrew, 54
LOYD, Hannah, 43
Thomas, 43
LUCAS, Thomas, 58
LUKENS, James, 45
LUNN, Catharine, 28
Thomas, 28
LUSK, James, 10
Robert, 92
LYNCH, Philip, 2, 113
Sarah, 2
LYNN, James, 57
LYON, Cathrin, 83

-M-
MC LOGHLIN, Philip, 1
MCAFFEE, Daniel, 120
MACAFFEE, David, 89
MCAFFEE, Sarah, 89, 120
MCANTIER, Andrew, 93
MACARTY, Miles, 104
MCBETH, Ann, 7
MCCADDEN, Ann, 68
Elizabeth, 23, 68
Henry, 23, 47, 68

Hugh, 68
Rebecca, 68
Robert, 68
MCCADDON, Henry, 46
Margaret, 46
MCCALL, Abigail, 111
Benjamin, 111
MCCALLA, James, 91
MCCALLISTER, Daniel, 79
MCCALMONT, Mary, 70
MCCARAHER, Alexander, 115
MCCARRAUGHER, Alex, 106
MCCARTER, Abraham, 1
Elizabeth, 1
MCCARTY, Jamima, 59
Jemima, 31
Miles, 61
Patrick, 31
MCCAUSLAND, Ann, 69
MCCAY, Galbreath, 69
John, 69
William, 69
MCCLAIN, William, 24
MCCLANNAUGHAN, Elinor, 77
MCCLASKEY, James, 67
Patience, 87
MCCLAY, James, 31
Margaret, 31, 59
MCCLEAN, Alexander, 24
Esther, 118
John, 28
William, 24
MCCLEES, James, 26
MCCLELAN, James, 33
William, 23
MCCLISTER, Alex, 104
MCCLURE, James, 100
Jane, 107
Rachel, 88
Samuel, 88
Sarah, 121
MCCOLOUGH, Mary, 69

MCCONNAUGHY, James, 103
Robert, 103
MCCONNELL, Joseph, 46
Mary, 17
MCCOOL, Elizabeth, 35
MCCORKEL, James, 54
MCCORMICK, James, 110
Sarah, 110
MCCOULOUGH, Agnes, 95
MCCOY, Andrew, 46
Mary, 46
MCCRACKEN, Catharine, 64
John, 64
Joshua, 64
Sarah, 64
Thomas, 64
William, 64
MCCUE, Alice, 58
MCCULLOUGH, John, 88
MCDOWELL, Alexander, 28
Ann, 28
Catharine, 28
Cathrine, 28
James, 67
Jane, 28
John, 28, 108
Joshua, 28, 39
Phebe, 28
Sarah, 28, 39
William, 28
MCEACHREN, James, 106
MCELHATTEN, Alexander, 57
MCELHENY, Robert, 82
MCEWEN, Martha, 57
MCFAGGON, William, 34
MCFALL, Ann, 106
Hannah, 106
John, 106
Mary, 106
Patrick, 106
MCFARLAN, mary, 5

INDEX

William, 24
MCFARLAND,
  Elizabeth, 21
  George, 21
  John, 21, 113
MCFARSON, John, 4
  Stephen, 1
MCFATRICH, William, 32
MCFETTRIDGE,
  Daniel, 30
  Matthew, 30
MCGEE, Hannah, 74
MCGLISTER, John, 9
  William, 9
MCGOUN, John, 10, 35
MCGUGAN, Robert, 73
MCHARG, John, 47
MCHARY, George, 47
MCILWAIN, Andrew, 115
MCKEAD, John, 10
MCKEAN, Thomas, 72
MCKEE, Andrew, 82
  Isaac, 90
  John, 10, 90
  Joseph, 10
  Robert, 10
  Sarah, 90
MACKELDUFF, Samuel, 109
MCKENA, Thomas, 72
MCKENNY, Mary, 52
MACKEY, Agnes, 83
  David, 73, 87, 96, 108
MCKEY, William, 87
MCKIM, John, 31
MCKINLEY,
  Elizabath, 113
  Joseph, 113
MACKLY, David, 108
MCKNIGHT, Martha, 53
  William, 22
MCLAUGHLIN, James, 41
  Janet, 67
  John, 41
  William, 41
MCLEAN, Agnes, 39
  Daniel, 39
  Isabella, 39
  James, 39
  Jean, 39
  John, 39
  Margaret, 39
  Mary, 39
  Patrick, 39
MCLENE, Daniel, 39
MCLUCE, Thomas, 53
MCLURE, Benjamin, 107
  Esther, 107
  James, 107
  John, 107
  Joseph, 107
  Mary, 107
  Rachel, 107
MCMATH, Mable, 51
MCMICHEN, Abigail, 105
  James, 1
  John, 105
  Margret, 1
  William, 1
MCMICKIN, John, 31
MCMILLAN, Agnes, 114
  Ephraim, 114
  James, 55, 114
  Jane, 114
  John, 33, 114
  Joseph, 114
  Martha, 114
  Mary, 114
  Rachel, 114
  Robert, 114
MCMILLON, John, 77
MCMONIGAL,
  Alexander, 92
  Jane, 92
MCMORDIE, Janet, 22
MCNEAL, Archibald, 4
  Samuel, 19, 76, 112
  William, 74
MCNEELY, Mary, 107
  Thomas, 107
MCPHERSON, Agnes, 105
  Alexander, 47, 105
  Cathrin, 47
  Jane, 47
  John, 47
  Robert, 47, 105
  Thomas, 105
  William, 19
MACUE, Alice, 121, 120
  Ann, 120, 121
  Anthony, 120, 121
  Mary, 121
  Samuel, 120
  Thomas, 120
MCVEY, Mary, 74
MCWHORTER,
  Elizabeth, 32
  William, 32
MADISON, Thomas, 57
MALIN, Elizabeth, 19
  Gideon, 41
  Mary, 19
MALLIS, Mary, 25
  William, 25
MALPUS, Mary, 53
MARIS, Aaron, 10
  Ann, 78
  Elizabeth, 45, 50, 78
  Harvey, 111
  Isaac, 45, 50
  James, 7, 11, 37, 61
  Jane, 63, 102
  Jesse, 3, 63, 73, 102, 117
  John, 10, 111, 116
  Jonathan, 78
  Margaret, 111, 116
  Mary, 50, 111
  Rebecca, 3, 78
  Richard, 78
  Samuel, 111
  Tacey, 78
MARLING, Margery, 32
MARSH, William, 8
MARSHALL, Abraham, 15, 30
  Abram, 15
  Benjamin, 39
  Humphrey, 15, 61, 77
  Humy., 63
  Isaac, 15

INDEX

James, 15, 30, 43, 60, 75, 82, 87, 88
Johanna, 18
John, 4, 15, 18, 39
Joseph, 34
Joshua, 24
Margaret, 18
Mary, 15, 18
Rachel, 99
Samuel, 15
Sarah, 18, 43
Susanna, 18, 65
Thomas, 115
MARSTELLER, Frederick, 84
MARTEN, Ann, 84
MARTIN, Abraham, 43
Alexander, 61
Anna, 101
Catharine, 61
David, 14
Dinah, 14
Eleanor, 14, 15
George, 12, 43, 98
Hannah, 93
James, 47, 108
Jane, 37
Joel, 15, 101
John, 37, 89
Joseph, 43, 74, 87
Lydia, 43
Margaret, 108, 109
Martha, 43
Mary, 19, 69, 89, 98
Matthias, 14
Rachel, 108
Roger, 37
Ruth, 43
Samuel, 15, 89
Sarah, 43, 47, 108
Thomas, 2, 43
MASHMAN, Esther, 46
James, 46
John, 46
Joseph, 46
Margaret, 46
Phebe, 46
MASON, Benjamin, 82
George, 49, 82, 83
Grace, 83

James, 83
Jane, 83
John, 83
Joseph, 82
Margaret, 81
Mary, 81, 82
Mathew, 82
Rachel, 83
William, 51, 81
MASSEY, Isaac, 32
James, 62
Jane, 86
Levi, 29, 32
Phebe, 32
Thomas, 74
MATHER, Elizabeth, 20
Francis, 20
James, 20
Jane, 20
John, 20
Joseph, 20, 84
Mary, 20
Ruth, 20
Sarah, 20
Thomas, 20
MATHERS, John, 29
Peter, 62
Sarah, 62
MATLACK, Amos, 49
Esther, 49
Hannah, 68
Isaiah, 49, 68
Jemima, 49
Jonathan, 49, 110
Joseph, 49
Nathan, 49, 80, 96
Ruth, 49
MATNALL, Elizabeth, 43
Joseph, 43
Mary, 43
Sarah, 43
MATSON, Aaron, 100
Enoch, 100
John, 100
Levi, 100
Margaret, 38, 100
Mary, 100
Morris, 38, 100
Moses, 100
Nehemiah, 100
Peter, 114

Phebe, 100
Rachel, 100
Sarah, 100
William, 100
MATTSON, Margaret, 3
MAXFIELD, Ann, 76
Elizabeth, 76
Isabel, 76
Jane, 76
Janet, 76
John, 47
Margaret, 47, 76
Mary, 76
Rebecca, 76
Robert, 76
Samuel, 76
William, 76
MAXWELL, Isabel, 42
James, 13, 42, 58, 83
Jane, 35
John, 79
William, 39
MEANES, Catrine, 17
Edward, 17
MEARS, John, 8
Samuel, 23
MEASE, James, 67
Janet, 67
John, 67
Matthew, 67
Thomas, 67
MECHEM, Jane, 86
John, 86
MECK, Elenor, 83
MECKE, Alexander, 113
MEEK, Elizabeth, 2
William, 68
MEINA, 56
MELCHIOR, John, 29
MELCHIOZ, William, 119
MELIN, Elizabeth, 40, 62
Jacob, 40
Mary, 40
Randle, 50
William, 40
MENDENHALL, Benjamin, 88
Isaac, 75

INDEX

Jesse, 88
Mary, 29
Moses, 23
Robert, 39
Samuel, 24
Sarah, 94
MENOCH, John, 81
MENOUGH, John, 60
MENTZ, Barbary, 112
  Christopher, 112
MERCER, Thomas, 15,
  38, 41, 46
MEREDITH,
  Elizabeth, 80
  Jane, 96, 118
  Jesse, 96
  John, 79
  Mary, 79, 96
  Susanna, 96
METEER, Thomas, 53
MILES, Ann, 102
  George, 34
  James, 102
  John, 102
  Mary, 102
  Sarah, 102
MILHOUS, Ann, 91
  Deborah, 91
  Dinah, 91
  Elizabeth, 91
  Enos, 91
  Hannah, 91
  James, 84, 91
  Jesse, 91
  John, 91
  Lydia, 91
  Margaret, 91
  Mary, 91
  Mercy, 91
  Paschall, 91
  Phebe, 91
  Robert, 91
  Ruth, 91
  Samuel, 91
  Sarah, 91
  Susanna, 91
  Thomas, 91
  William, 91
MILHOUSE, James, 35
  John, 35
  Robert, 35
  Sarah, 35
  Thomas, 35

William, 107
MILLARD, Joseph,
  106
MILLER, Agnes, 76
  Ann, 19, 47, 77,
    96
  Brice, 33
  Dorothy, 44
  Francis, 76, 95
  George, 4, 5, 41,
    44, 50, 67, 72,
    92
  Hannah, 12, 77,
    87, 95, 110
  Henry, 44
  Hugh, 76
  Isaac, 87
  Isabel, 33
  Jacob, 95
  James, 12, 27, 77
  Jane, 95
  Jean, 33
  Jesse, 98
  John, 19, 22, 25,
    33, 47, 54, 74
  John Adam, 84
  Joseph, 62, 77, 95
  Lydia, 12, 95
  Margaret, 12
  Martha, 56, 95
  Mary, 12, 19, 48,
    62, 77, 110
  Peter, 43, 115
  Phebe, 4
  Rebecca, 33, 95
  Robert, 33, 49
  Ruth, 12
  Samuel, 10, 12,
    35, 48, 95
  Sarah, 44, 77
  Warrick, 77, 91
  William, 12, 19,
    33, 35, 59, 77,
    87, 93, 96
MILLESON, Ann, 121
  Charity, 121
  Hannah, 121
  Jesse, 121
  John, 121
  Jonathan, 121
  Mary, 121
  Phebe, 121
MILLHOUSE, Bates,

36
  Sarah, 36
  William, 36, 72
MILLISON, John, 27
MILLS, John, 38
  Mary, 44
MILLSOM, Thomas, 95
MILSOM, John, 41
  Thomas, 65
MILSON, John, 44
MINOR, Agnes, 70
  Jean, 70
  John, 70
  Mary, 70
  Susanna, 70
  Thomas, 6, 70
MINSHALL, Aaron, 66
  Agnes, 73
  John, 5, 44, 68
  Sarah, 68
  Thomas, 16, 73, 75
MITCHELL,
  Alexander, 66
  James, 109
  John, 24
  Sarah, 105
MONTGOMERY,
  Annable, 93
  Elizabeth, 35
  Jane, 93
  Margaret, 90
  Mary, 25, 90
  Moses, 11, 93
  Robert, 108
  William, 7, 70,
    85, 90
MOODE, Emey, 48
  Hannah, 48
  Ruth, 48
  William, 48, 101
MOORE, Amos, 26
  Andrew, 79
  Ann, 2
  Benjamin, 109
  Charles, 10
  Daniel, 2, 48
  David, 20
  Elizabeth, 2, 10,
    12, 26, 83
  Emmor, 109
  Francis, 79, 80
  George, 79
  Hannah, 109

Howard, 79, 80
Israel, 11
James, 21, 34, 68
Jane, 2, 3
Job, 1
John, 2, 110
Joseph, 60, 94,
  109
Margaret, 10, 68
Martha, 87
Mary, 6, 21, 48,
  87, 95
Mordecai, 83
Moses, 2, 6, 21
Nathaniel, 15, 109
Philip, 10, 89
Rachel, 10
Robert, 3, 79
Sarah, 2, 4, 73
Thomas, 109
William, 2, 3, 10,
  14, 49, 79, 100
MOORHEAD, Andrew,
  82
MORETS, Jacob, 106
MORGAN, Jane, 108
  John, 81, 101
  Margaret, 106
MORRIS, Aaron, 100
  Ann, 42
  Ester, 42
  Hannah, 16, 95
  James, 70, 71
  Jane, 16, 95
  John, 16, 37, 71,
    95, 117
  Jonathan, 21, 77
  Joseph, 42
  Levi, 100
  Margaret, 42, 70
  Mark, 70
  Mary, 16, 70, 75
  Mordecai, 94, 108
  Phebe, 16, 95
  Richard, 121
  Robert, 16, 95
  Samuel, 84
  Sarah, 70
  Thomas, 42
MORRISON, Agnes, 4,
  90, 98
  Alexander, 1
  Elizabeth, 4, 90,

98
Ephraim, 1, 26
Esther, 4
Hugh, 1
James, 1, 4, 90
Jane, 4
Janet, 81
Jean, 1
John, 4, 13, 90
Joseph, 1, 4, 90
Mary, 4, 90
Nathaniel, 4, 90
Neill, 26
Priscilla, 4, 90
Robert, 4, 90
Sarah, 98
Thomas, 90
MORTON, Aaron, 115,
  116
  Ann, 115, 116
  Elizabeth, 115,
    116
  Israel, 13, 26
  James, 51
  John, 2, 14, 18,
    20, 36, 56, 57,
    64, 78, 82, 87,
    90, 93, 115, 116
  Jonas, 115
  Lydia, 115, 116
  Mark, 26
  Mary, 115
  Rebecca, 26
  Robert, 51
  Samuel, 30
  Sarah, 115
  Sketchley, 67, 82,
    115, 116
  Sketchy, 104
  Skitchley, 116
  Thomas, 30, 51
  Tobias, 26
MOSS, James, 34
MOULDER, Mary, 60
  Robert, 60
  William, 35
MUCKLEDUFF, Samuel,
  8
MULLER, Mary, 5
  Patrick, 5
MULLOY, Patrick, 77
MURPHY, James, 11
MURRAY, John, 46

MURRIN, Hugh, 41
MURRY, Jacob, 30
MUSGRAVE, Hannah,
  99
MUSGROVE, Abraham,
  85

-N-
NEAL, James, 107
  John, 84
  Rachel, 107
NEELEY, William, 68
NETHERMARK,
  Christian, 13
  Luke, 14, 20
  Margaret, 20
  Mathias, 14
  Sarah, 14
NETHERY, John, 89
NETSILLIS, Arthur,
  36
  Mary, 36
  Mathias, 36
  Rachel, 36
NEWBERRY, Andrew,
  90
NEWBROUGH, Joshua,
  99
NEWLIN, Abigail, 3
  Anne, 16
  Cyrus, 3
  Esther, 3
  John, 3, 93
  Joseph, 98
  Nathan, 13
  Nathaniel, 3, 4,
    16, 73, 93, 98
  Nicholas, 16, 90
  Rebecca, 3
  Susanna, 13
  Thomas, 3, 56
  Tobitha, 3
NICE, Hannah, 107
NICHOLS, Amos, 98
  Elizabeth, 98
  Emey, 98
  Hannah, 98
  James, 98
  Jonathan, 98
  Mary, 98
  William, 98
NICKLIN, Joseph, 64
NICKOLS, Ann, 11

INDEX

Charity, 11
Hannah, 11
Jacob, 11
James, 11
John, 11
Samuel, 11
Thomas, 11
NIDERMARK, Luke, 36
NISBET, Elizabeth, 17
NISBITT, Joseph, 17
NIVIN, Isabel, 90
Martha, 90
William, 90
NOBLE, James, 97
William, 1
NOLLART, Elizabeth, 36, 37
George, 36, 42
NORTH, George, 45
Joshua, 31
Richard, 31
Susanna, 31
NOWLES, John, 57
NUPHRIN, Veronica, 4
NUZUM, Hannah, 9

-O-
O DAVILLEN, Hugh, 82
OAKFORD, Aaron, 74, 121
Ann, 121
Benjamin Webber, 121
Elizabeth, 121
Hannah, 121
Isaac, 121
OBURN, Henry, 30
OCHILTREE, James, 33, 64
O'FARRAN, Michael, 1
OGDEN, Aaron, 102
Abigail, 102
David, 40
Hannah, 102
John, 102
Martha, 102
Stephen, 5, 102
OGLEBE, James Harris, 85

John, 85
O'HEER,
Neil, 11
OLDHAM, Rachel, 8
OLIVER, Alexander, 63, 105
Andrew, 105
Elizabeth, 102, 105
James, 105
Jane, 105
John, 40
Mary, 40
Nathaniel, 105
Samuel, 55, 105
O'NEILL,
Constantine, 76
ORR, James, 11
John, 6
OSBORN, Samuel, 25
OSBORNE, Peter, 17
Samuel, 98
OTLEY, Anne, 4
James, 4
OWEN, Abigail, 56
David, 56, 110
Edward, 4, 56
Elizabeth, 110
Hannah, 50
John, 56
William, 56, 102
OWENS, John, 1

-P-
PACKER, James, 2, 91, 118
PAINTER, Ann, 78
Barbara, 120
Catherina, 120
Elizabeth, 78, 120
Frederick, 120
George, 120
Jacob, 120
John, 120
Lewis, 120
Mary, 120
Philip, 120
Samuel, 78
William, 120
PAKER, Ann, 53
PALMER, John, 3, 38, 44, 90
Joseph, 116

Margaret, 2
Martha, 44
Mary, 22
Moses, 38, 44
PANCOAST, Seth, 16, 45, 50, 120
PANNOL, Elizabeth, 89
Evan, 89
PARK, Arthur, 105
Gennet, 105
Joseph, 53
Rachel, 25, 53
Rebecca, 25
Thomas, 25, 105
PARKE, Ann, 68
Deborah, 6
Jonathan, 6
Robert, 68
PARKER, Elisha, 81
George, 91
Margaret, 81
Sarah, 35, 91
Sebellah, 81
Thompson, 35
William, 34, 56, 65, 120
PARKS, Richard, 13
Samuel, 13
PARRY, Hannah, 21, 32, 106
John, 40, 106
Rowland, 21, 32
PARVIN, Benjamin, 48
PASCHALL, Henry, 96, 118
John, 96
Stephen, 27
PASSMORE, Abraham, 12
Elizabeth, 12
George, 4, 43
John, 43, 101
Joseph, 12
Lydia, 12
Phebe, 12
Susanna, 8
PATTEN, David, 83
Thomas, 17
William, 17
PATTERSON,
Alexander, 98

INDEX 149

Jane, 24
John, 24
PATTON, David, 83
Thomas, 83
William, 17, 83
PAUL, John, 112
Mary, 112
PAWLING, John, 109
PEARSOL, Alice, 117
PEARSOLL, Alice, 117
  Bathsheba, 117
  Elizabeth, 117
  Hannah, 117
  John, 117
  Mary, 117
  Mordecai, 117
  Peter, 117
  Sarah, 117
  Zacheus, 117
PEARSON, Ann, 120
  Elizabeth, 120
  George, 120
  Hannah, 120
  Isaac, 27, 34, 45, 50, 65, 109, 111, 120
  James, 120
  John, 120, 122
  Joseph, 27, 62
  Mary, 120
  Powell, 112
  Sarah, 120
  Susanna, 120
  Thomas, 120
PEASLEY, Margaret, 72
PEDRICK, Adam, 78
  Ann, 78
  John, 45, 64, 78, 92
  Rachel, 78
  Thomas, 35, 66
PEIRCE, Ann, 99, 119
  Cal., 5
  Caleb, 24, 81, 99
  Cromwell, 107
  Edward, 107
  Frances, 107
  George, 38, 100, 107
  Hannah, 95, 99

Henry, 33
Isaac, 99
John, 33, 95
Joseph, 3, 21, 99, 119
Joshua, 30, 99
Lydia, 99
Mary, 33, 38, 95
Rachel, 95, 99
Sarah, 95
William, 33, 95
PEIRSOLL, Ann, 68
  Bathsheba, 42
  Jeremiah, 42
PENCOAST, Seth, 3
PENNEBACKER, Jacob, 109
PENNELL, Abigail, 55
  Edith, 5, 22
  Elizabeth, 22
  Evan, 48
  Hannah, 48
  Hayes, 48
  Isaac, 65
  James, 5, 49
  Jemima, 5, 49
  Jonathan, 5
  Joseph, 21, 55
  Joshua, 48, 92
  Lydia, 55
  Mary, 5, 21
  Nathan, 5
  Rebecca, 5, 22
  Robert, 5
  Ruth, 5, 22
  Thomas, 5, 55
  Timothy, 5
  William, 5, 22
PENNOCK, Alice, 59, 77
  Caleb, 43
  Elenor, 65
  Elizabeth, 43
  John, 62, 65, 77
  Joseph, 43, 77
  Joshua, 43
  Levis, 43, 77
  Mary, 77
  Moses, 59
  Nathaniel, 43, 77
  Samuel, 43, 77
  Sarah, 43, 77

Susanna, 77
William, 43, 77
PEOPLES, Agnes, 87
  Alexander, 87
  Martha, 87
  Robert, 87
  Sarah, 87
  William, 87
PERGRIN, John, 76
  Nicholas, 76
PERKINS, Charles, 33
  Hannah, 95
PERRIE, Martha, 106
PERRY, John, 114
  Rachel, 114
PERVERS, Anthony, 104
PETERS, Margaret
  Elizabeth, 36
  Rees, 4
  William, 38
PETERSON, Sophia, 80
PETTERSON,
  Elizabeth, 100
  James, 17
PHILIPS, Rebecca, 2
  Stephen, 2
PHILLIP, Evan, 62
  John, 62
  Joseph, 31, 83
  Josiah, 83
  Thomas, 62
PHILLIPS, Ann, 13, 115
  Anne, 9
  Daniel, 44
  David, 44
  Elizabeth, 9, 13, 102
  Griffith, 9, 13, 102, 115
  Sarah, 9, 13
  Stephen, 44, 81
  Thomas, 8, 9, 13, 62
PHILLPS, Ann, 9
  Rebecca, 9
  Sarah, 9
PHIPPS, Aaron, 57
  Anne, 57
  Benjamin, 57

INDEX

Caleb, 55, 57
George, 2
Hannah, 53, 57
Jonathan, 57
Joseph, 31, 53, 55, 57
Joshua, 57
Margaret, 31
Mary, 57
Nathan, 53
Rachel, 57
Samuel, 53
Sarah, 53
PICKEN, John, 97
PICKERD, Daniel, 76
PIERCE, Caleb, 93
David, 93
George, 93
Jesse, 93
John, 71
Joseph, 12, 15, 29, 30, 42, 62, 71, 93
Joshua, 93
Robert, 93
Thomas, 93
PIERSE, Joseph, 88
PILKINGTON, Edward, 49
Margaret, 49
Rebecca, 39
Vincent, 39
PIM, Hannah, 57
Thomas, 85
PIMM, Thomas, 5, 7
PINKERTON, William, 75
PLANE, Daniel, 59
PLATT, Samuel, 28
POAK, James, 27
William, 27
PORTER, David, 31
Elenor, 85
Elizabeth, 85
Isabald, 85
James, 85
John, 108
Margaret, 42, 108
Mary, 14, 108
Nancy, 31
Nathaniel, 85
Patrick, 84, 108
Rebecca, 85

Samuel, 31
Sarah, 117
Thomas, 108
Violet, 85
William, 85
POWELL, Benjamin, 37, 96
Benjamn, 34
David, 16
Elizabeth, 16, 120
George, 89, 120
Hannah, 120
James, 37
Jane, 120
John, 37
Joseph, 89, 112, 120
Mary, 37, 89, 120
Patience, 89, 120
Prudence, 120
Samuel, 37, 96
Sarah, 120
Susanna, 34, 37, 120
Thomas, 89, 120
William, 94
POWER, John, 22
PRATT, Abraham, 92, 98
Alice, 98
Ann, 98
David, 92, 98
Jane, 98
Joseph, 92, 98
Mary, 92, 98
Priscilla, 92
Rose, 98
Sarah, 92, 98
Thomas, 92
PRICE, Ann, 71
E., 77
Elisha, 27, 57, 71
Elizabeth, 71
Hannah, 71
John, 71
Martha Davis, 116
Samuel, 71
Sarah, 71, 116
William, 116
PRIMUS, 11
PROCTOR, Elijah, 72
Job, 72
Joshua, 72, 62

Margaret, 72
Sarah, 72
PROUDFOOT, Mr., 109
PUGG, 57
PUGH, Anna, 31
David, 21, 31, 59, 102
Hannah, 21
Hizziah, 59
James, 31
Jemima, 31, 59
Jonathan, 21
Kezia, 31
Margaret, 31
Mary, 21, 31
Patience, 93
Samuel, 21
Sarah, 21
William, 93
PUNTLE, James, 90
PUSEY, Ann, 19
Betty, 65
Elenor, 65
Enoch, 65
Jane, 65
John, 65, 75, 79
Joshua, 19, 65, 75, 79, 99
Lewis, 75, 79
Mary, 19, 65
William, 19, 65
PYLE, Abigail, 49
Abraham, 98
Elizabeth, 49, 97
Isaac, 3, 97, 99
James, 49
Jane, 3
John, 40, 49, 84, 87
Joseph, 65
Judith, 84
Levi, 52
Lidy, 49
Mary, 49
Moses, 98
Olive, 49
Rebecca, 73
Sarah, 49
William, 37, 49

-Q-
QUAINTANCE, Susanna, 62

INDEX

William, 109
QUANDRIL, Deborah, 57
John, 57
QUAY, Hugh, 121
QUEAF, Susanna, 85
QUICKLESS, Hugh, 110
QUIN, William, 37
QUINN, John, 72
Samuel, 97

-R-

RALSTON, ---, 80
Elizabeth, 45
James, 45, 119
John, 45, 80, 119
Joseph, 92
Robert, 37, 45, 80
RAMSAY, David, 75
John, 39
RAMSEY, Edward, 9
John, 68
Mary, 42
Samuel, 75
William, 42
RANKIN, Margaret, 4
RATEW, Mary, 100
RAWLES, Francis, 63
RAY, Margaret, 113
Thomas, 72
REA, George, 4
Joseph, 4, 79, 100
REATH, William, 30
REDD, Adam, 23
REDMOND, Margaret, 61
REECE, Ann, 79
Caleb, 117
Daniel, 47
David, 94, 117
Francis, 117
Hannah, 84, 117
John, 117
Joseph, 117
Lewis, 94
Lydia, 84, 117
Mary, 120
Nehemiah, 84, 117, 120
Sarah, 47
Thomas, 117
William, 84, 117

REED, Andrew, 96, 97
Charles, 106
Hugh, 52, 85
Isabel, 97
James, 28, 57, 111
John, 52, 57, 97
Joseph, 57
Lattice, 97
Margaret, 28, 97
Mary, 96
William, 97
REES, Jane, 61, 64
John, 61
Theophilus, 121
REESE, Caleb, 102
Hannah, 102
Mary, 84
Rachel, 16
William, 84
REGAN, Frances, 63
James, 63
John, 63, 113
Michael, 63
William, 63, 113
REGESTER, James, 75
William, 72
REGISTER, John, 75
Rebecca, 75
RETTEW, Rebecca, 46
William, 46
REYNOLDS, Benjamin, 103
David, 4
Francis, 13
Henry, 32
Jacob, 86
John, 4
Mary, 32
Rebecca, 86
Samuel, 13, 46
Sarah, 103
RHOADS, Elizabeth, 3, 63
Isaac, 3, 51, 86
James, 3, 39, 45, 50
John, 3
Joseph, 1, 3, 51, 86, 102
Mary, 3
Rachel, 102
RHODES, Michael, 14

RICE, Simon, 82
RICHARD, Jacob, 55
RICHARDS, Benjamin, 116
Isaac, 72
Jacob, 73
Jane, 72
John, 41
Jonathan, 3
Lydia, 3
Mary, 88
Phebe, 32
Susanna, 102
William, 72
RICHARDSON, Francis, 20
Lydia, 120
Nehemiah, 120
RICHESON, Richard, 39
RICHEY, Alexander, 45
Andrew, 46
Francis, 110
George, 45, 46
Jean, 110
John, 45, 46, 110
Mary, 46
Robert, 31
Susanna, 46
William, 46, 110
RICHISON, Richard, 43, 47, 58, 121
RICHMAN, George, 108
Jean, 108
RICHMOND, George, 108
RICKENBERGER, Adam, 47
RIDGWAY, Job, 9
RIGBY, Hannah, 13
James, 13
RILEY, John, 64
Mary, 50
Richard, 35, 51, 71
RING, Benjamin, 4, 6, 12
Betty, 101
Elizabeth, 4
Hannah, 4
Nathaniel, 4, 6,

12, 71
Rachel, 99
Susanna, 12
ROADS, Henry, 43
John, 43
Mary, 43
Peter, 43
ROAN, Ann, 17
Michael, 42
ROATS, Catharine, 111
Christina, 111
Elizabeth, 111
Hannah, 111
Jacob, 112
Margaret, 112
Martin, 111
Mary, 111
ROBB, Agnes, 39
Daniel, 39
George, 39
Jean, 39
Sarah, 39
Susanna, 7
ROBERTS, Abel, 74
Jane, 52
John, 52
Jonathan, 53
Nathan, 53
Thomas, 121
ROBERTSON, Matthew, 14
ROBESON, Rachel, 107
ROBINS, Hannah, 107
ROBINSON, Abraham, 15
Annable, 93
David, 93
Eleanor, 40
James, 102
Jemima, 23
John, 30, 32, 81, 102, 116
Joseph, 93
Margaret, 14
Mary, 30, 102
Phebe, 81
Robert, 21, 40
Thomas, 23
William, 102
RODGERS, John, 107
ROE, Annable, 93

Jane, 92
William, 92
ROGERS, Alexander, 22
Catherine, 54
David, 28, 86
Elizabeth, 54
Hannah, 86
Rachel, 54
Robert, 35, 112
Samuel, 54
Thomas, 54
William, 54
ROMAN, Isaac, 26
Jacob, 115
Joseph, 81
Mary, 26
Ruth, 81
ROOKE, Catherine, 107
ROSBROUGH, John, 26
ROSEBROUGH, John, 27
ROSS, John, 45, 58, 59, 68, 76, 88
Jonathan, 86
Joseph, 60
Stephen, 86
William, 19
ROUTH, Francis, 22
John, 22
ROWAN, Agnes, 44
David, 44
Dorcas, 44
Elizabeth, 53
James, 44, 53, 84
Jane, 44
John, 33
Mary, 44
Mary Ann, 44
Michael, 44
Moses, 10
Samuel, 44
Sarah, 44
William, 84
ROWEN, James, 10
ROWLAND, Ann, 83
Hugh, 83
James, 52
Jane, 52
John, 34, 83
William, 83
RUDULPH, John, 22

Mary, 22
RUMFORD, Jonathan, 36
RUP, John, 51
RUSHTON, Robert, 17
RUSSEL, Samuel, 65
RUSSELL, Dinah, 92
Edward, 20, 92
Elizabeth, 92
Jemima, 92
Joseph, 92
Mary, 92
Thomas, 73, 98
William, 73, 92
RUTHERFORD, Sarah, 87
William, 87

-S-
SALKELD, Ann, 104
Elizabeth, 104
Isaac, 104
John, 104
Joseph, 104
Sarah, 104
SALMON, Robert, 28
SAMPLE, Agnes, 90
Margaret, 90
SANDERSON, Richard, 31
SANDS, Patrick, 11
Sarah, 11
SARAH, 17
SAYLOR, Cronomus, 111
Mary, 111
SCANLAN, Luke, 53
SCARLETT, Nathaniel, 75
SCHOFIELD, Edith, 3
Samuel, 3
SCHOLFIELD, Thomas, 19, 20, 110
SCOTT, Abraham, 34
Andrew, 34
Elisa, 72
Elizabeth, 92
James, 42, 54, 76, 81, 91, 109
John, 32, 34, 39, 76, 81, 92, 104, 105, 109, 111
Margaret, 76

Mary, 23
Moses, 95, 109
Patrick, 105
Philip, 76
Rebecca, 76
Samuel, 55, 76, 85
Sarah, 91
Thomas, 104, 105, 109
William, 109
SEAL, Abraham, 32
Benjamin, 32
Caleb, 32, 87
John Polis, 121
Joseph, 32
Joshua, 32
Rachel, 31, 32, 97, 98
Thomas, 32
William, 3, 31, 32, 87, 97
SELLERS, Elizabeth, 65
John, 18, 65, 120
Joseph, 65
Mary, 65
Nathan, 18, 77
Nathaniel, 61, 120
Samuel, 65
SEMPLE, Ann, 108
John, 108
Nathaniel W., 108
SERRILL, Hannah, 120
Jacob, 120
SEVERD, Michael, 30
SEWAL, Arthur, 35
John, 35
SHARAR, Conrod, 60
SHARP, George, 11, 40, 49, 84
John, 22
Margaret, 72
Mary, 72
Rachel, 19, 72
Samuel, 48
Thomas, 11, 19, 72
William, 72
SHARPLESS, Abigail, 92
Ann, 88
Benjamin, 54
Daniel, 46, 55, 91, 92
Elizabeth, 88
Hannah, 88
Isaac, 89
Jacob, 41, 88
James, 59, 88
Jane, 88
Jesse, 88
John, 9, 22, 29, 88
Joseph, 23, 88
Joshua, 88
Lydia, 88
Martha, 88
Mary, 23
Nathan, 88, 89
Nathaniel, 88
Rebecca, 88, 92
Samuel, 46
Sarah, 91
Thomas, 91, 92
SHARRAR, Conrad, 74
SHAW, Edward, 44
John, 12
Mary, 66
Samuel, 12, 55
SHEERER, Mary, 37
William, 21, 37
SHELTON, Owen, 59
SHERADON, Abraham, 102
Henry, 102
Priscilla, 102
SHEUTON, Hannah, 18
SHEWARD, Ruth, 49
Thomas, 49
SHEWMAN, Elizabeth, 115
Peter, 115
SHIELDS, James, 22
Mary, 6, 22
Patrick, 105
Robert, 22
SHIPLEY, William, 36
SHIPPEN, Joseph, 107
SHIRARDIN, Abraham, 74
Catharin, 74
Elizabeth, 74
Henery, 74
Jacob, 74
Johaneta, 74
Magdalen, 74
Margaret, 74
Mary, 74
Otillia, 74
Paul, 74
Susanna, 74
Yustin, 74
SHIRLEY, Agnes, 24
Thomas, 24
SHMISER, Cathrin, 32
SHOWALTER, John, 47
SHUGGART,
  Catherine, 49
  Zachariah, 49
SHUMAN, Peter, 112
SHUNK, Conrod, 43
SHUSTER, Catherine, 106
Jacob, 106
Philip Jacob, 106
Sievela, 106
SIDWELL, Abraham, 84
Charity, 84
Hugh, 84
SILL, Ann, 75
George, 75
James, 40, 75
Joseph, 75
Michael, 75
Richard, 45, 75
SIMMONS, Samuel, 94
Thomas, 103
SIMON, Thomas, 95
SIMPSON, David, 110
James, 110
Jannet, 110
Jeremiah, 110
Margaret, 110
SIMRAL, Alexander, 47
John, 49
SIMRALL, James, 47
SINGLETON,
  Elizabeth, 28
  John, 28
  Thomas, 28
SITER, Adam, 68
SKEEN, John, 38
SKETCHLEY, mary, 116

SKYLES, Harman, 113
SLACK, John, 98
  Mary, 98
SLAUGHTER,
  Charlotte, 101
  Jacob, 29
  Mary, 29
  Philip, 29
SLOAN, George, 112
  Mary, 112
SMEDLEY, Ambrose,
  4, 73
  Ann, 68
  Caleb, 4, 73
  Francis, 68
  George, 4, 68, 81,
    84
  Hannah, 58, 81
  James, 4
  John, 24, 68
  Joshua, 4, 73, 81
  Mary, 4, 73
  Sarah, 68
  Thomas, 4, 35, 50,
    68, 73
  William, 4, 73
SMITH, Adam, 121
  Agnes, 22
  Ann, 121
  Catherine, 121
  Cathrine, 121
  David, 42
  Dorothy, 2
  Elizabeth, 92, 121
  Frances, 89
  Hannah, 14, 34,
    56, 100, 116
  Hugh, 76
  Jacob, 118
  James, 14, 79, 100
  Jane, 79
  John, 2, 14, 52,
    60, 71, 73, 76,
    81, 83, 100, 109,
    116, 121
  Joseph, 14, 31,
    40, 89
  Joshua, 38, 41
  Lydia, 41, 66
  Margaret, 40, 56,
    81, 121
  Martha, 81
  Philip, 121
  Rebecca, 100, 118
  Richard, 79
  Robert, 19, 46,
    76, 79, 100, 103,
    116
  Sampson, 22
  Samuel, 77
  Sarah, 100
  Thomas, 2, 56,
    110, 115, 121
  Tristram, 66
  William, 14, 100,
    103, 117
SNEWLIN, Nicholas,
  73
SNOW, John, 25
SPARKLE, Elizabeth,
  67
SPEAKMAN, Ebenezer,
  60
  Micajah, 16
SPEAR, Robert, 75
SPEARY, James, 83
SPENCE, Andrew, 109
SPIKEMAN, Ann, 77
  Joshua, 77
SQUIBB, Nathaniel,
  73
STALKER, thomas, 57
STANTON, John, 93
STARR, Alexander,
  19
  Elizabeth, 99
  Hannah, 61
  Isaac, 99
  Jane, 99
  Jeremiah, 84
  Moses, 84
  Rachel, 61
  Sarah, 61
  Thomas, 99
STARRETT, Anne, 49
  James, 49
  John, 49
STEDMAN, Richard, 2
STEEL, Andrew, 71
  James, 76
  John, 74
  Joseph, 90
  Peter, 27
STEIGER, Hannah,
  111
  Jacob, 111
  Peter, 111
STERN, George, 61
  Paul, 61
STEUART, Eleanor,
  113
  George, 113
  Robert, 113
  William, 113
STEVESTON, Mary, 55
STEWARD, Jesse, 115
  Martha, 115
  William, 112
STEWART, Alexander,
  5, 112
  Andrew, 112
  Archibald, 5
  David, 5, 34
  Hugh, 32
  James, 112
  Jane, 34
  John, 34, 71, 76
  Martha, 112
  Robert, 34
  Sarah, 34
  Walter, 112
  William, 112
STOCKMAN, Isabell,
  114
  James, 114
STONE, Elizabeth,
  36
STONES, James, 32
  Sarah, 32
STRAWBRIDGE,
  Thomas, 42
STRICKLAND, Hugh,
  42, 63, 110
STRINGER,
  Elizabeth, 95
  Joseph, 95
STRODE, Caleb, 21
  George, 75
  Richard, 21, 118
STUARD, Phebe, 40
STUART, Faithfull,
  15
  John, 46
STUBBS, Sarah, 93
STULL, John, 6
SULLAN, John, 31
SULLIVAN, Dennis,
  31
  Mary, 31

INDEX

SUPER, Philip, 107
SUSANNA, Barbara, 14
SWAFFER, Ann, 78
  Elizabeth, 78
  Joseph, 78
  Richard, 78
  William, 9, 66, 67, 78, 92
SWAYNE, Edward, 56, 98
  Elizabeth, 98
  Francis, 56, 98
  Isaac, 56
  Jesse, 56, 98
  Jonathan, 56, 98
  Martha, 98
  Rachel, 56
  Robert, 56, 98
  Sarah, 56, 98
  Susanna, 56
  Thomas, 29
  William, 56, 98
SWITZER, Jacob, 114
SYRUS, 7

-T-

TAGGART, James, 74
  Jane, 74
  John, 74
TALBOT, Hannah, 5
  Joseph, 35, 54
  mary, 5
TANNER, James, 27
TATE, Alexander, 18
  Margaret, 22
TATNALL, Elizabeth, 43
TATNEL, Edward, 94
TAYLOR, Abiah, 68, 102
  Ann, 89, 104
  Anne, 36
  Benjamin, 36, 89, 91
  Christiana, 14
  Deborah, 58, 97
  Elisha, 28, 117
  Elizabeth, 36, 57, 62, 89
  Enoch, 102
  Esther, 58
  Frederica, 57

George, 2
Hannah, 36, 89
Isaac, 16, 24, 36, 52, 58, 89
Israel, 117
Jacob, 24, 64
James, 24, 60
Jane, 16
Jeremiah, 36
Jesse, 104
John, 2, 30, 35, 57, 58
Joseph, 2, 36, 57, 89, 91
Lydia, 57
Mary, 58, 117
Nathan, 59
Peter, 41, 74
Rebecca, 14, 90
Robert, 95, 117
Samuel, 58, 66, 97
Sarah, 2, 36, 89, 117
Stephen, 66
Susannah, 24
Thomas, 2, 10, 17, 24, 36, 41, 117, 119
William, 91
TELFORD, Joseph, 23
  Mary, 23
TEMPLE, Benjamin, 87
  Hannah, 87, 88
  Jane, 99
  John, 91
  Joseph, 75, 89
  Thomas, 32, 62, 87, 88, 89, 91
  William, 87
TEMPLETON, John, 27, 37
TENNENT, Jane, 69
TENYEAR, Joseph, 80
  Rebecca, 80
THATCHER, Ann, 41
  Edith, 41, 42
  Hannah, 41
  John, 12
  Jonathan, 41, 64
  Mary, 42, 64, 89
  Richard, 89
  Samuel, 41, 64

Sarah, 41
Stephen, 41, 64
Thomas, 42, 64, 78
William, 41, 64
THEMPLE, Thomas, 89
THOMAS, Abraham, 118
  Ann, 18, 47
  Anne, 107
  Azariah, 68
  Benjamin, 47, 76, 101, 111
  Catharine, 107
  Catherine, 18
  David, 8, 68, 96, 97, 107, 111, 113
  Ester, 80
  George, 61
  Hannah, 61
  Hazael, 97
  Isaac, 53, 85, 121
  Jacob, 53
  James, 85, 121
  Jehu, 83
  John, 18, 83, 107, 113
  Jonathan, 107
  Joseph, 21, 53, 86, 117
  Martha, 69
  Mary, 43, 47, 85, 86, 107, 117, 121
  Michael, 80
  Morris, 1, 10, 26, 28
  Nathan, 85, 121
  Oliver, 37
  Rachel, 85, 121
  Rebecca, 47, 83
  Richard, 53, 56, 61, 70, 73, 99
  Samuel, 117
  Sarah, 37, 85, 121
  Tamer, 21
  Theophilus, 17
  Thomas, 80, 85
  William, 47
THOMPSON, Charles, 18
  Daniel, 66
  Esther, 2
  Grace, 51
  Hannah, 2

INDEX

Henry, 49
Isaac, 18
James, 25, 84, 91
Jane, 28
John, 104, 109
Joseph, 25
Margaret, 2, 18
Martha, 8, 51
Mary, 51
Moses, 51
Nancy, 28
Nathan, 2, 18
Phebe, 48
Robert, 48
Thomas, 18, 28
Veronica, 51
William, 93
THOMSON, Charles, 20, 66
Elizabeth, 34
Hugh, 28
John, 34
Joshua, 34
Margaret, 39
Matthew, 39
Rebecca, 37
Robert, 112
Ruth, 20, 66
Thomas, 51
THORNBURY, Richard, 41
Sarah, 40
THORNTON,
Elizabeth, 32
Hannah, 74
Robert, 74
Samuel, 74
THORPE, Thomas, 89
TODD, Hannah, 54
Hugh, 54
James, 54, 90
Jane, 90
Jennet, 54
John, 54, 90
Margaret, 54, 90
Mary, 54
William, 90
TODE, John, 113
TOLBERT, Hannah, 21
TOM, 14, 115
TORREL, Frances, 70
Francis, 70
John, 70

TORTON, Letitia, 56
Margaret, 56
Rebecca, 56
TOTHRE, Catherine, 36
Philip, 36
TOWNSEND, John, 98
TOYLY, Elizabeth, 120
Joseph, 120
TRAPNALL, John, 13
TREGO, Alice, 117
Ann, 20, 41, 66
Bathsheba, 68
Benjamin, 20
Elizabeth, 20
Joseph, 19, 20, 117
Margaret, 19
Mary, 20
William, 19, 117
TREVILLA, James, 68
TREVILLER, Mary, 35
TREVILLO, Alice, 83
Price, 83
TRIMBLE, Abigail, 58
Abraham, 58
Alice, 58
Daniel, 56
Henry, 28, 58
James, 30, 39
John, 55
Lewis, 28, 58, 59
Lydia, 55
Mary, 28, 58
Phebe, 55
Rachel, 55
Rebecca, 6
Samuel, 33, 56
Thomas, 55
William, 55, 56, 61
TROUTTEN, Lydia, 79
TRUMAN, Thomas, 49
TURNER, Abraham, 76
Charles, 29
Daniel, 76
Elizabeth, 76
George, 11, 89
Isaac, 76
James, 87
John, 76

Mary, 76, 87
Matthew, 33
Moses, 87
Rebecca, 76
Robert, 76, 87
Ruth, 76
Sarah, 76, 87

-U-

UNDERWOOD, James, 89
Jeremiah, 79
UPDEGRAFF, Ann, 79
John, 79
URIAN, Andrew, 66, 67, 93
Benjamin, 66
Israel, 67
USHER, Mary, 109

-V-

VALENTINE, Robert, 52
VANCE, Caleb, 35
Joseph, 20
VANEMAN, Isaac, 15
Margaret, 18
VANHOLD, Valentine, 58
VANLEER, Branson, 1
VAUGHAN, Amelia, 56, 101
Edward, 106
Isaac, 56, 101
John, 101
Prudence, 107
Thomas, 101, 106
VEHAN, John, 56
Thomas, 56
VERNON, Aaron, 9, 80
Abigail, 9
Abraham, 80, 81
Ann, 38, 82
Edward, 9, 30, 80
Elias, 9
Elizabeth, 38, 82
Esther, 82
Frederick, 82
Gideon, 9
John, 80, 82
Jonathan, 38, 82

INDEX

Joseph, 9
Lydia, 82
Margaret, 80, 81, 100
Mary, 9, 33, 82
Mordecai, 82
Moses, 9
Nathan, 9, 30, 91
Nathaniel, 82
Rose, 8
Samuel, 38
Sarah, 80
Thomas, 82
William, 38
VIRT, Aartin, 97
Fray, 97

-W-
WADDEL, Elizabeth, 106
James, 106
WAGGONER, Barbara, 82, 113
Catharine, 113
John, 82, 113
WAGONER, Mary, 101
WAIT, Moses, 30
WALDREN, Sarah, 24
WALKER, Ann, 20
Benjamin, 118, 119
David, 14
Elizabeth, 118
Hannah, 118
Isaac, 118
Isabel, 118
James, 60
Jane, 118
Jerman, 34
John, 14, 80, 118
Joseph, 34
Lydia, 34
Mary, 34, 118
Nathaniel, 118
Rebecca, 118
Ruth, 118
Sarah, 34
Thomas J., 34
Thomas Jerman, 34
William, 42
WALL, John, 25
Phebe, 25
William, 80
WALLACE, Gayen, 106

George, 100
John, 111
Robert, 113
Thomas, 111
WALLAS, Nathaniel, 1
WALLICE, Robert, 106
WALN, Mary, 48
Samuel, 17
WALTER, James, 107
John, 90
Thomas, 17
William, 44
WALTERS, James, 82
Lydia, 82
WARD, Elizabeth, 48
Philip, 48
Thomas, 48
WARNER, Elizabeth, 28
Mary, 66
WASON, Matthew, 64
Rachel, 64
WATKIN, Aaron, 45
WATKINS, Aaron, 80
Ann, 80, 98
Benjamin, 80
Enoch, 107
Jacob, 80
Jane, 80
Margaret, 80
Mary, 18, 107
Robert, 80, 107
Theophilus, 107
Thomas, 98
William, 80
WATT, David, 110
WAUGH, John, 90
WAY, Amos, 104
Ann, 104
Hannah, 39, 81, 104
Jacob, 103, 104
James, 104
John, 39, 104
Joseph, 103, 104
Joshua, 52
Mary, 103
Sarah, 104
WAYNE, Anthony, 96, 121
Elizabeth, 67, 96

Humphrey, 63
Isaac, 96
Michael, 67
Sarah, 52
WEAVER, Isaac, 92
Valentine, 20
WEBB, Christiana, 65
Cordilla, 88
Daniel, 65
Eli, 65
Elizabeth, 91
Ezekiel, 65, 90
Isaac, 65
Jane, 90
Orpha, 65
Rebecca, 65, 90, 91
Ruth, 65
Sarah, 2, 65, 91
Stepehn, 65
Stephen, 65, 87, 90, 91
Thomas, 65
William, 65, 90, 91
WEBBER, Ann, 121, 122
Jacob, 11, 27, 121
WEBSTER, Ann, 2
John, 25, 94
William, 2
WEISS, Lewis, 62
WELCH, Elizabeth, 74
Hannah, 58, 59
John, 58
Thomas, 74
WELDON, John, 56
Sarah, 56
WELLS, Edward, 119
Jonathan, 47, 119
Peter, 119
WELSH, Ann, 52
Rachel, 52
WESLER, John, 114
Margaret, 114
WEST, Thomas, 111
William, 18, 69, 97
WHARRY, Ann, 48
David, 48
James, 48

Mary, 48
WHELEN, Israel, 59, 91
WHIGAM, John, 14
WHIPPLE, Joseph, 38
WHISTLER, Barbara, 14
  Casper, 14
  John Wolf, 14
  Lenora, 14
  Michael, 14
  Sophia, 14
WHITACRE, Dinah, 57
WHITE, Abigail, 74, 101
  Edward, 88
  Elizabeth, 68
  Isaac, 88
  James, 88
  Jean, 47
  John, 86, 87, 88
  Joseph, 101
  Margaret, 46, 88
  Mathew, 47
  Matthew, 68
  Rachel, 113
  Rebecca, 88
  Robert, 46, 54, 68
  Samuel, 88
  Sarah, 38, 88
  Thomas, 23, 46, 68, 88, 91, 113
WHITEHILL, Jean, 15
  John, 15
  Margaret, 15
  Robert, 25
WHITESIDE, Hannah, 93
  William, 93
WHITESIDES, Hannah, 12
  William, 12
WHITTAKER, Susanna, 41
WHRAY, Elizabeth, 53
  James, 53
  John, 53
WICKERSHAM, Abel, 72, 79, 81
  Ann, 79
  Anna, 81
  Betty, 65

Caleb, 65
  James, 72, 79, 81, 104
  John, 45
  Peter, 24
  Sampson, 72, 79
  Thomas, 40
  William, 24, 65
WILCOX, James, 26
  Mark, 26, 55
  Purdence, 26
WILDAY, Edward, 110
  Elizabeth, 110
  John, 110
  Obadiah, 110
  Phebe, 110
  Sarah, 110
  Thomas, 110
WILEY, David, 1, 34
  Mary, 34
WILKEN, John, 105
  William, 105
WILLEY, John, 26
  William, 26
WILLIAM, 82
  John, 103
WILLIAMS,
  Alexander, 29, 107
  Amos, 94
  Ann, 94, 108
  David, 28, 70
  Edward, 61
  Eleanor, 94
  Elizabeth, 24
  Esther, 107
  Francis, 119
  Hannah, 94
  Hugh, 29
  Isaac, 2
  James, 49
  Jane, 117
  Jesse, 86
  John, 28, 34, 94, 103, 121
  Joseph, 25, 49, 50, 56, 77, 94
  Joshua, 94
  Lettice, 28
  Lewis, 44
  Lydia, 19
  Margaret, 28
  Mary, 94, 103

Minshall, 94
  Miriam, 44
  Robert, 29, 38, 108
  Samuel, 24, 84
  Walter, 62
  William, 117
WILLIAMSON, Hannah, 50
  Jane, 34
  John, 34
  Thomas, 46
  William, 24
WILLIS, Joel, 2
  William, 79
WILLS, Ann, 102
  Thomas, 17, 55
WILLSON, Abigail, 24
  Anne, 26
  Caleb, 24
  Charles, 24
  Elijah, 24
  Elizabeth, 24
  Francis, 109
  Henry, 26
  Isabel, 73
  James, 26, 54, 60, 90
  John, 90
  Margaret, 90
  Martha, 90
  Mary, 24, 29, 68, 90
  Phebe, 24
  Robert, 4, 24
  Sarah, 90
  Thomas, 24, 29, 32
WILSON, Alexander, 7
  Ann, 29, 51
  Anne, 26
  Charles, 98
  Elizabeth, 7, 29
  James, 7, 51
  Jane, 26, 29
  Jean, 7, 51
  John, 7, 29
  Joseph, 17
  Lettice, 26
  Mable, 51
  Mary, 7, 29, 51
  Robert, 7, 53

Ruth, 66
Samuel, 26
Sarah, 7, 29
Thomas, 26, 29, 98
WILY, Jane, 48
WITHROW, James, 80
Robert, 51, 80, 84
Samuel, 51, 80, 81
William, 51, 80
WOLF, Mary, 119
WOMSLEY, Jonathan, 24
WOOD, All, 62
Ann, 62
Catharine, 86
Elizabeth, 51
George, 62, 74
Hannah, 62
Harriet, 62
Henry, 62
Isaac, 51
James, 115
Jane, 62
Jona., 74
Jonathan, 62, 74
Joseph, 86
Margaret, 62, 88
Mary, 62
Nathan, 41
Sarah, 62, 118
Thomas, 29, 88
William, 88
WOODBURN, John, 16
WOODROW, Lydia, 98
Simeon, 98
WOODS, Lawrence, 11
WOODWARD, Abraham, 29
Amos, 21
Ann, 25, 111
Caleb, 24
Edward, 115
Eli, 24, 25
Elizabeth, 83
Enoch, 49
Hannah, 25, 29, 30
James, 29, 30, 43
John, 21, 28, 29
Joseph, 43
Lydia, 24, 25
Mary, 29, 115
Nayl., 24
Phebe, 25

Richard, 25
Robert, 87
Sarah, 25, 28
T., 12, 24, 83
Thomas, 78, 98, 104
William, 15, 29, 30
WOOLLEY, Ann, 16
Jane, 16
John, 16
Sarah, 16
WORRALL, Abel, 67
Abigail, 41, 53, 54
Ann, 22
Benjamin, 9, 87
Edward, 67
Elijah, 87
Elisha, 9, 45, 50, 51
Elizabeth, 54
Esther, 9, 67
Jacob, 87
John, 53, 67
Jonathan, 9, 87
Joseph, 10, 87
Joshua, 9
Lydia, 38
Martha, 67
Mary, 41, 54, 87
Peter, 9, 53
Phebe, 9
Rachel, 54
Samuel, 87
Sarah, 54
Seth, 87
Thomas, 9, 67
William, 9, 37, 87, 89
WORTH, Samuel, 82, 94

-Y-
YARNALL, Aaron, 103
Abigail, 3
Abner, 24
Abraham, 24
Amos, 95, 103
Ann, 35, 54
Benjamin, 3
Caleb, 86, 117
David, 24, 32

Dows, 32
Elizabeth, 24, 99, 117
Enoch, 32, 84, 103, 117
Esther, 24
Ezekiel, 24
Francis, 117
Hannah, 48, 98, 117
Isaac, 3, 19, 86, 117
Jacob, 21
James, 3, 103
Jane, 24, 117
John, 3, 86
Joseph, 103, 117
Joshua, 86
Mary, 3, 24, 86, 117
Mordecai, 54
Moses, 32
Nathan, 24, 54, 86, 90, 92
Philip, 24
Rachel, 24
Rebecca, 32
Samuel, 24, 103
Sarah, 4
Uriah, 24
YEARSLEY, Ann, 41
Hannah, 41
Isaac, 41, 66
Jacob, 66
John, 41
Lydia, 41
Mary, 41
Nathan, 41, 66
Patience, 41
Phebe, 66
Robert, 41
Sarah, 41
Thomas, 38, 41, 66
YODER, Jacob, 18
YOUNG, Elizabeth, 74
Francis, 36
Hugh, 74
Jane, 67
Susanna, 25

-Z-
ZINK, Jacob, 87

Mary, 87
Michael, 87
ZUCK, Rudulph, 78
 Veronica, 78
ZUG, John, 47

Other books by F. Edward Wright:

Abstracts of Bucks County, Pennsylvania Wills, 1685-1785

Abstracts of Cumberland County, Pennsylvania Wills, 1750-1785

Abstracts of Cumberland County, Pennsylvania Wills, 1785-1825

Abstracts of Philadelphia County Wills, 1726-1747

Abstracts of Philadelphia County Wills, 1748-1763

Abstracts of Philadelphia County Wills, 1763-1784

Abstracts of Philadelphia County Wills, 1777-1790

Abstracts of Philadelphia County Wills, 1790-1802

Abstracts of Philadelphia County Wills, 1802-1809

Abstracts of Philadelphia County Wills, 1810-1815

Abstracts of Philadelphia County Wills, 1815-1819

Abstracts of Philadelphia County Wills, 1820-1825

Abstracts of Philadelphia County, Pennsylvania Wills, 1682-1726

Abstracts of South Central Pennsylvania Newspapers, Volume 1, 1785-1790

Abstracts of South Central Pennsylvania Newspapers, Volume 3, 1796-1800

Abstracts of the Newspapers of Georgetown and the Federal City, 1789-99

Abstracts of York County, Pennsylvania Wills, 1749-1819

Bucks County, Pennsylvania Church Records of the 17th and 18th Centuries Volume 2: Quaker Records: Falls and Middletown Monthly Meetings
Anna Miller Watring and F. Edward Wright

Caroline County, Maryland Marriages, Births and Deaths, 1850-1880

Citizens of the Eastern Shore of Maryland, 1659-1750

Cumberland County, Pennsylvania Church Records of the 18th Century

Delaware Newspaper Abstracts, Volume 1: 1786-1795

Early Charles County, Maryland Settlers, 1658-1745
Marlene Strawser Bates and F. Edward Wright

Early Church Records of Alexandria City and Fairfax County, Virginia
F. Edward Wright and Wesley E. Pippenger

Early Church Records of New Castle County, Delaware, Volume 1, 1701-1800

Frederick County Militia in the War of 1812
Sallie A. Mallick and F. Edward Wright

Inhabitants of Baltimore County, 1692-1763

Land Records of Sussex County, Delaware, 1769-1782

Land Records of Sussex County, Delaware, 1782-1789
Elaine Hastings Mason and F. Edward Wright

Marriage Licenses of Washington, District of Columbia, 1811-1830

Marriages and Deaths from the Newspapers of Allegany and Washington Counties, Maryland, 1820-1830

Marriages and Deaths from The York Recorder, 1821-1830

Marriages and Deaths in the Newspapers of Frederick and Montgomery Counties, Maryland, 1820-1830

Marriages and Deaths in the Newspapers of Lancaster County, Pennsylvania, 1821-1830
Marriages and Deaths in the Newspapers of Lancaster County, Pennsylvania, 1831-1840
Marriages and Deaths of Cumberland County, [Pennsylvania], 1821-1830
Maryland Calendar of Wills Volume 9: 1744-1749
Maryland Calendar of Wills Volume 10: 1748-1753
Maryland Calendar of Wills Volume 11: 1753-1760
Maryland Calendar of Wills Volume 12: 1759-1764
Maryland Calendar of Wills Volume 13: 1764-1767
Maryland Calendar of Wills Volume 14: 1767-1772
Maryland Calendar of Wills Volume 15: 1772-1774
Maryland Calendar of Wills Volume 16: 1774-1777
Maryland Eastern Shore Newspaper Abstracts, Volume 1: 1790-1805
Maryland Eastern Shore Newspaper Abstracts, Volume 2: 1806-1812
Maryland Eastern Shore Newspaper Abstracts, Volume 3: 1813-1818
Maryland Eastern Shore Newspaper Abstracts, Volume 4: 1819-1824
Maryland Eastern Shore Newspaper Abstracts, Volume 5: Northern Counties, 1825-1829
F. Edward Wright and Irma Harper
Maryland Eastern Shore Newspaper Abstracts, Volume 6: Southern Counties, 1825-1829
Maryland Eastern Shore Newspaper Abstracts, Volume 7: Northern Counties, 1830-1834
Irma Harper and F. Edward Wright
Maryland Eastern Shore Newspaper Abstracts, Volume 8: Southern Counties, 1830-1834
Maryland Militia in the Revolutionary War
S. Eugene Clements and F. Edward Wright
Newspaper Abstracts of Allegany and Washington Counties, 1811-1815
Newspaper Abstracts of Cecil and Harford Counties, [Maryland], 1822-1830
Newspaper Abstracts of Frederick County, [Maryland], 1816-1819
Newspaper Abstracts of Frederick County, 1811-1815
Sketches of Maryland Eastern Shoremen
Tax List of Chester County, Pennsylvania 1768
Tax List of York County, Pennsylvania 1779
Washington County Church Records of the 18th Century, 1768-1800
Western Maryland Newspaper Abstracts, Volume 1: 1786-1798
Western Maryland Newspaper Abstracts, Volume 2: 1799-1805
Western Maryland Newspaper Abstracts, Volume 3: 1806-1810
Wills of Chester County, Pennsylvania, 1766-1778

www.ingramcontent.com/pod-product-compliance
Lightning Source LLC
Chambersburg PA
CBHW060657100426
42734CB00047B/2030